Baedeker

Vienna

Contents

The Principal Places of Tourist Interest at a Glance

Preface

This Pocket Guide to Vienna is one of the new generation of Baedeker city guides.

Baedeker pocket guides, illustrated throughout in colour, are designed to meet the needs of the modern traveller. They are quick and easy to consult, with the principal sights described in alphabetical order and practical details about opening times, how to get there, etc., shown in the margin.

Each guide is divided into three parts. The first part gives a general account of the city, its history, population, culture and so on; in the second part the principal sights are described; and the third part contains a variety of practical information designed to help visitors to find their way about and make the most of their stay.

The new guides are abundantly illustrated and contain numbers of newly drawn plans. At the back of the book is a large city map, and each entry in the main part of the guide gives the co-ordinates of the square on the map in which the particular feature can be located. Users of this guide, therefore, will have no difficulty in finding what they want to see.

How to use this book

Following the tradition established by Karl Baedeker in 1844, sights of particular interest are distinguished by either one ★ or two ★★ stars.

To make it easier to locate the various sights listed in the "A to Z" section of the Guide, their co-ordinates on the large map of Vienna are shown in red at the head of each entry.

Only a selection of hotels, restaurants and shops can be given: no reflection is implied, therefore, on establishments not included.

The symbol   on a town plan indicates the local tourist office from which further information can be obtained. The post-horn symbol indicates a post office.

In a time of rapid change it is difficult to ensure that all the information given is entirely accurate and up to date, and the possibility of error can never be completely eliminated. Although the publishers can accept no responsibility for inaccuracies and omissions, they are always grateful for corrections and suggestions for improvement.

Facts and Figures

Arms of the
City of Vienna

General

Vienna is both the capital of the Republic of Austria and one of neutral Austria's nine provinces. It is the seat of the Austrian President, the Federal Government, the supreme administrative governmental bodies and of local government for the province of Vienna.

Capital

Despite its peripheral location in present-day Austria, it is very much the political, economic, intellectual and cultural hub of the Republic.

Located in northern Austria, the city is encircled by the province of Lower Austria and, at an altitude of 558ft (170m), it lies on latitude 48°14′N and longitude 16°21′E.

Situation

Most of the city extends along the right bank of the Danube and it is bordered in the W by the Vienna Woods.

Vienna is situated at the junction of the oceanic and continental climatic regions; the winter temperatures, on average −1.4°C, hardly ever fall below −5°C and the summer temperatures are rarely in excess of 30°C, averaging at 20°C. Rain showers are frequent, especially in the summer, but not persistent. There is an almost constant light breeze which has been called the "Wiener Wind".

Climate

Vienna, like most large cities, has its share of environmental problems. A five-year scheme to improve water purity was started in the mid-1980s at an estimated cost of 224 million schillings, linking more suburban districts to the public water system. The municipal utilities have been converted to use natural gas and oil to reduce sulphur emission and improve the air quality. Waste incineration plants have been equipped with filters to reduce levels of toxic emissions. These measures are to be extended to other sectors by the city's environment department, concentrating on pollution caused by vehicle exhaust fumes, domestic heating and industry.

Ecology

The projects undertaken for this programme are designed to benefit the environment and quality of life in the city. The leisure area created on Danube Island has already proved a great success. On a similar scale, the woods and meadowland to the N and S of the city are to be developed and new woodland areas created. During the next ten years 500 acres/200ha of woodland will be established in the Favoriten, Simmering, Floridsdorf, Donaustadt and Liesing districts. In 1987, as part of this project, Viennese school children began planting a wood in

The Green
Programme

◄ *Burgtheater*

the 22nd district to commemorate the 65,000 Jewish citizens of Vienna who died in the holocaust. The wood will be indicated by a memorial stone. The recreational area at Wienerberg-Ost in the Favoriten district is almost complete.

Four new parks were created in 1987 alone, in the 10th, 14th, 16th and 19th districts. Residents, local committees and district councils have all been involved in the redevelopment of existing parks such as Schönborn Park and the Denzel-Gründen. Other projects to enlist the support of residents include a scheme to encourage firms to buy protective supports for trees in exchange for free advertising space; a competition, "Vienna in Bloom", with generous prizes, and advice and grants from the city's department of gardens and parks.

Cleaning the Danube

The Danube is heavily polluted and cleaning the Viennese waterways poses one of the greatest environmental problems to the city and provincial authorities alike. In 1985 the Austrian government resolved to clean the Danube and its tributaries. The paper industry is one of the main contributing factors to the level of pollution, filtering only 40% of 1 million tons of waste produced each year.

The cleaning operation is only part of a larger project to restore the landscape along the river. Work has already begun on the Eastern National Park which is to extend from the Lobau to the Czech and Slovak borders. Indigenous plant-life will be reintroduced into the Lobau and arable fields will be returned to meadowland. After attempts to establish beaver colonies on the river banks were successful, the European terrapin and fish otter, once native to this area, will also be reintroduced.

The area cannot be entirely reverted to its natural state and the oil tanker wharf at Lobau will be retained. The construction of an additional wharf at the Albern docks has been prevented, however, by the installation of new cargo handling equipment.

Area and population

With a total area of 160 sq. miles (415km^2) Vienna falls within the middle range of European capitals.

Its population has declined in numbers since the First World War. In 1910 Vienna still had a population of 2·1 million but today it has only 1·5 million inhabitants. However, the city's population has grown again following the opening-up of the borders with the East. Although the death rate (about 23,000 p.a.) is much higher than the birth rate (about 11,000 p.a.) on average 22,000 more people moved to the city each year between 1990 and 1993 than moved out.

The Inner City has been particularly hard hit by depopulation and in 20 years has lost a third of its residents. The province of Vienna has also been affected; at present ranking as the most heavily populated province, it is expected to drop to third place in the next 30 years. The trend is a migration from East and South Austria, which borders mainly on socialist states, to western Austria and the neighbouring economies of Bavaria, Switzerland and North Italy.

City Districts (Stadtbezirke)

The city is divided into 23 Districts: I Innere Stadt (City Centre), II Leopoldstadt, III Landstrasse, IV Wieden, V Margareten, VI Mariahilf, VII Neubau, VIII Josefstadt, IX Alsergrund, X Favoriten, XI Simmering, XII Meidling, XIII Hietzing, XIV Penzing, XV Rudolfsheim-Fünfhaus, XVI Ottakring, XVII Hernals, XVIII Währing, XIX Döbling, XX Brigittenau, XXI Floridsdorf, XXII Donaustadt and XXIII Liesing.

District I, the City Centre, corresponds to the historic city of Vienna. Districts III–IX, developed from outlying villages, were termed "Inner Districts", while districts X–XIX, the former suburbs outside the Gürtel, the outer ring road, are the "Outer Districts". In a broader sense districts II and XX, together with the fringe districts XXI–XXIII, also belong to the Outer Districts. The smallest district (Josefstadt) covers

Vienna

■■■ Provincial boundary

—— District boundary

© Baedeker

Danube

Danube

CITY DISTRICTS

1. Innere Stadt (City Centre)	7. Neubau	13. Hietzing	18. Währing
2. Leopoldstadt	8. Josefstadt	14. Penzing	19. Döbling
3. Landstraße	9. Alsergrund	15. Rudolfsheim-	20. Brigittenau
4. Wieden	10. Favoriten	Fünfhaus	21. Floridsdorf
5. Margareten	11. Simmering	16. Ottakring	22. Donaustadt
6. Mariahilf	12. Meidling	17. Hernals	23. Liesing

an area of ¾ sq. mile (1·8km²) while the largest (Donaustadt) is 40 sq. miles (102km²) in extent. The most thinly populated district is the City Centre with 19,000 inhabitants and the most densely populated is Favoriten with 146,000.

Every district has its own individual character. A part of the 3rd district (Landstrasse) is known as the diplomatic quarter; the 4th (Wieden) and the Inner City as the most fashionable; the 5th (Margareten), 6th (Mariahilf) and 7th (Neubau) represent the growth of the middle classes; trade and industry have been established, factories built and workers' settlements placed next to residential complexes. Vienna's largest shopping street crosses the Mariahilf district; the picturesque but somewhat neglected Spittelberg quarter in the 7th district is being renovated. The quiet 8th district (Josefstadt) retains its traditional role as the civil servants' district; the 9th district (Alsergrund) is Vienna's academic quarter with many clinics, hospitals and sanatoria. The 10th (Favoriten), 11th (Simmering), 12th (Meidling) and 15th (Rudolfsheim-Fünfhaus) districts are home to the blue-collar workers, the lower income bracket and tenement dwellers and is the most densely populated area. The 16th (Ottakring) and 17th (Hernals) stretching to the Vienna Woods are similar to these neighbouring districts; Ottakring is also in the process of renovation. The 18th (Währing) is a popular residential area containing one of Vienna's loveliest parks, the Türkenschanzpark. The park extends through Gersthof and Pötzleinsdorf to the wooded hills bordering the city. The 13th (Hietzing) and the 19th (Döbling) districts contend for the title of Vienna's most beautiful

9

suburb. Elegant villas surround Schönbrunn Palace in Hietzing, where even the municipal buildings have a dignified air. Döbling, by contrast, is a collection of old wine producing villages and country inns which has attracted wealthy residents. Liesing, the 23rd district which borders on Hietzing, is a group of sleepy villages set in rolling hills, to which Rodaun belongs, at one time the home of Hugo von Hofmannsthal.

On the other side of the Danube Canal is the 2nd district (Leopoldstadt) in the past the home of Balkan traders, Turks and Jews from the eastern Mediterranean and Poland. It includes the Prater Park, the trade fair exhibition site, the large sports stadium and the track for trotting races. Many new buildings have sprung up around the canal. Next to this is the 20th district (Brigittenau) with drab tenements and fortress-like municipal buildings. Beyond the Danube is Floridsdorf, the 21st district, a workers' quarter where allotment gardens nestle under factory chimneys. In the neighbouring 22nd district, Donaustadt, a new cityscape has been created called "Transdanubien", dominated by United Nations City and Austria-Center, the Danube Tower and Danube Park.

Renovating the Old City

The age of Vienna's buildings is immediately apparent and statistics prove that Vienna has the greatest proportion of residential properties over 70 years of age than any other city of its size in the world. The latest tally shows that 30 out of 100 dwellings were built between 1881 and 1918. As magnificent as the façades may be, the sanitation facilities of many buildings do not meet modern-day standards, for example 30,300 dwellings have no running water at all, where the "Bassena", the communal tap on the stairway, is still in use. The modernisation of residential properties is one of the most important tasks facing the city authorities in the framework of the renovation

View of the Old Town, with the Stephansdom and Peterskirche

programme. Several projects are being planned and implemented; the Spittelberg district has already undergone successful renovation. The project for the Ottakring district also includes the creation of parks and green spaces.

Both a district and a province, Vienna also plays a dual role in administrative terms. The District Council, consisting of 100 members elected for five years, is at the same time the Provincial Council and the elected Mayor heads both authorities. The Provincial Senate, the effective Government, is composed of the Mayor, two Deputy Mayors and 915 office-holding Councillors.

Administration

In order to decentralise the administration the 23 districts have their own representatives who elect one of their number to act on their behalf. Since 1987 the representatives have been granted greater autonomy: every district has a budget to provide its own maintenance and services to parks and gardens, environmental protection, street and road repairs, civic culture, etc. Residents are being given a greater say in the decisions which affect their immediate environment.

Vienna is the headquarters of a great many international organisations: UNIDO (the United Nations Industrial Development Organisation), IAEA (the International Atomic Energy Agency), the UN High Commission for Refugees, ICEM (International Committee for European Migration) and OPEC (Organisation of Petroleum Exporting Countries). IAEA has 117 and UNIDO has 165 permanent delegations of member countries in the city.

International organisations

The Commission of the European Community has established a representative body in Vienna.

Population and Religion

In the Middle Ages Vienna, with a population of 20,000, was already one of the largest German-speaking cities. The influx into the city was at its height between 1880 and 1910 when the population figures soared from 592,000 to 2 million. The newcomers were mainly from Bohemia, Moravia, Hungary and Galicia and when, at the turn of the century, over 60% were non-German-speaking, Vienna became a gigantic melting-pot for ethnic and religious minorities.

Population

After the Second World War those coming to settle in Vienna were chiefly refugees from Hungary and Czechoslovakia, most of whom have since become Austrian citizens. Between 1963 and 1989 it was mainly Yugoslav and Turkish immigrant workers who sought to settle permanently in Vienna. After the lifting of the Iron Curtain in 1989 many immigrants arrived from the south of Poland, the Czech Republic, Slovakia and Hungary, as well as more from the war-torn areas of the former Yugoslavia.

Of Vienna's 206,000 registered foreigners, most are Yugoslavs, Turks, Germans, Poles, Hungarians, Slovaks, Czechs, Romanians and North Americans. The number of unregistered foreigners is currrently estimated at between 50,000 and 100,000. Among the smaller foreign groups there are many students from Arabic-speaking countries, from Africa and the Far East.

Seventy-four per cent of the Viennese are Roman Catholic, 7·5% Protestant and 0·5 Jewish. In addition there are congregations of the Old Catholic, Greek, Serbian, Russian and Bulgarian Orthodox Churches, and of the Armenian Church, Methodists and Mormons.

Religion

The year 1979 saw the building of an Islamic centre and mosque for the city's Muslims.

Transport

Vienna is situated at the intersection of important N–S and E–W routes, at a point where the Alpine Foreland merges with the Hungarian Plain. In the S, W and NW the encircling hills, with their woods and meadows, penetrate deep into the residential areas while the flat plain extends beyond the city in the E and NE.

A 12½ mile (20km) stretch of the Danube flows through E Vienna, splitting off Districts XXI and XXII from the rest of the city. This ranks as an international waterway and its banks are Federally administered.

The Danube is an important artery for international goods transport and in 1993 accounted for 4·8 million tons on the Austrian stretch of the river. Ships carry agricultural produce, timber, foodstuffs and animal feed, solid fuels and oil products, ores, metal waste and metal products, building materials, fertilisers and chemicals. The Danube is growing in importance as an international waterway: the Cernavoda–Constanta Canal has reduced the route to the Black Sea by some 185 miles/300km and the completion of the Rhine-Main-Danube Canal during the 1990s will establish a navigation link to the major industrial areas of western Europe and to the North Sea, presenting new economic opportunities for Austria.

The Danube, Austria's only navigable river, accounts for over 6% of the country's carriage of export goods.

Port

The port at Vienna had already established the city as an important trade centre in the 10th and 11th c. Nowadays its location is significant as a turntable for international trade and transport between eastern and western Europe and it is the most advanced port in Austria.

The port is situated in the SE corner of the city and is divided into three sections: the grain docks at Albern, general cargo and bulk goods at Freaudenau and the oil docks at Lobau. The trans-shipment of oil at Lobau is 433,000 tons; of iron, paper, oil barrels, building materials, diverse fuels and container cargo is 755,000 tons at Freudenau and 215,000 tons of grain at the Albern docks. In the duty free zone, the turnover of goods stored by foreign firms and transport companies and the handling of cars and goods vehicles amounts to 43,000 tons.

Airport

Schwechat, Vienna's international airport, is by far the largest in Austria and is being made even larger. Situated 10 miles/17km south-east of the city centre, the airport has two runways measuring 3300yd/3000m and 4000yd/3600m respectively, and employs almost 8200 people. It is conveniently linked to the city by fast trains and a motorway. It has increased considerably in importance following the opening up of Eastern Europe. As a result, between 1989 and 1993 the number of passengers carrried increased from 5·1 million to 7·2 million, the number of flights from 77,000 to 117,000 and the freight carried from 67,000 tons to 99,000 tons. 57 airlines use the airport, flying to 100 destinations in all. In order to be able to deal with the 12 million passengers and 120,000 tons of freight envisaged for the year 2000, a large new departure hall came into use in 1993 and for 1996 a second one with twelve passenger gangways is planned; by 1998 the present 30 gates in use should be increased to 41.

Railway stations

European rail services from all points of the compass converge on Vienna, although not all at one central station.

Vienna has three main railway stations:

Westbahnhof (West Station) takes trains coming from W Austria and Western, Central and Northern Europe.

Südbahnhof/Ostbahnhof (South/East Station) handles trains from S Austria, Italy, Slovenia, Croatia, Greece, Bucharest, Budapest, Warsaw and Moscow.

River tours of Vienna

Schwedenplatz

Trains from N Austria, Prague and Berlin arrive at Franz-Josefs-Bahnhof.

Urban rail transport

Commuters in particular are efficiently and speedily catered for by the rail network (117 miles/187km) operated by Austrian Railways within the city, with its 39 stations and 30 halts.

Tramways, S-bahn, Underground, Express railways and municipal buses serve a network of 550 miles/884km. Every year they carry about 630 million passengers.

In autumn 1982 the so-called basic network of the Underground had been completed with four routes, U1, U2, U4 and U6. A new line (U3) was added in 1991; and further extensions are planned.

The "Silver Arrows" of the Underground reach top speeds of 50m.p.h. (80km.p.h.) and run at an average speed (including stops) of 22m.p.h. (35km.p.h.).

The Underground stations are closely supervised at night and are generally considered to be safe.

Roads

The northern, north-eastern and south-eastern areas of the city in particular are served by urban motorways, expressways and by-passes. These areas also have good parking facilities, making it simple to change to the underground if desired.

The W motorway (A1 – Westautobahn) from the W edge of the city leads to Salzburg and Munich, while the S motorway (A2 – Südautobahn) departs in the direction of Styria (Steiermark) Carinthia, Slovenia and Italy. The A21 links the W and S motorways S of the city. The A4 (Östautobahn) leads in an easterly direction S of the Danube to the Hungarian border and in the direction of Bratislava. In 1996 it should be linked with Budapest.

Other major roads (Bundesstrasse) out of Vienna:
Highway 1 – to Linz, Salzburg
2 – to Hollabrunn, Prague
3 – to Krems, Wachau
4 – to Horn, Lower Austria
7 – to Mistelbach, Brünn
8 – to March area, Southern Moravia
9 – to Hainburg, Pressburg
10 – to Bruck/Leitha, in the direction of the Neusiedler See
12 – to Mödling, Baden
14 – to Klosterneuburg
16 – to Eisenstadt, Burgenland
17 – to Semmering, Steiermark
230 – to Laxenburg

Culture

Vienna is one of the world's greatest metropolises from the cultural point of view and in terms of the number of international figures in the artistic world who gather there, particularly musicians. No other city has been the home of so many great composers nor of so many chamber ensembles, orchestras and choirs.

Many works of great value are on show in its more than 100 national and private museums and some 120 galleries while the Brueghel Collection, one of Europe's greatest collection of paintings, is here in Vienna, together with one of the world's most extensive collection of graphics and the largest number of Albrecht Dürer's drawings assembled in one place. The collection of incunabula in the National Library is the third largest in the world.

About 2·9 million visitors a year pass through the city's museums. The prime attraction for sightseers is Schönbrunn Palace (over 1·3

The Albertina – the world's most important collection of graphic art

million visitors), closely followed by the Museum of Fine Arts, the Imperial Apartments in the Hofburg and the Austrian Gallery in the Upper Belvedere.

The University of Vienna, founded in 1365 as Alma Mater Rudolphina, is currently attended by 100,000 students, engaged on studies in all the classic faculties. It enjoys an exemplary reputation in the fields of medicine, psychology, physics and technical studies.

Vienna also has universities for Technical, Veterinary and Agricultural studies and the study of Economics, the latter is attended by as many as 23,500 students.

Universities

The Academy of Fine Art, the Academy of Diplomacy, the College of Applied Arts and the Academy of Music and Dramatic Art are all of international standing.

Artists who have lectured at the Academy include Arik Brauer, Wolfgang Hollegha, Markus Prachensky, Friedensreich Hundertwasser, Anton Lehmden, Josef Mikl and Arnulf Rainer, while at the Academy of Music celebrated musicians, singers and actors are on the teaching staff.

Academies and colleges

The Austrian Academy of Science is located in Vienna. It has 26 institutes and 31 specialist commissions.

It is divided into two classes, that of philosophical and historical sciences and that of mathematical and natural sciences. Each class has 33 members as well as 60 correspondent members from abroad and 40 correspondent members within Austria.

Academy of Science

The foremost of the libraries in Vienna are the Austrian National Library with 10 important leading collections – encompassing 2·5 million volumes – and the University Library with about 2 million volumes. The most extensive specialist collection is that of the Technical University with 800,000 volumes.

Libraries

Vienna's many theatres (see Practical Information – Theatres) can seat about 16,000 in total and their annual audience figures amount to close on 3·3 million.

Theatres, orchestras

The Burgtheater heads the dramatic league. The home of the great classics, it has become a byword among German-speaking peoples for the excellence of the German spoken on its stage.

The Vienna State Opera (Staatsoper) ranks among the three most important opera-houses in the world. It has international opera stars on its permanent staff and can call on the top names among performing artistes and conductors for guest performances. The Vienna Philharmonic gives its concerts in the Staatsoper and the Great Hall of the Musikverein, while the Vienna Symphonic performs in the Konzerthaus. The city has a further six orchestras, 28 chamber music ensembles and 20 choirs.

Music

Over 700,000 a year enjoy the music on offer in Vienna's many concert halls.

The court choir was founded during the reign of Maximilian I in 1498 and for many years the "chapel choir" was financed directly by the Emperor. The choir had its heyday during Vienna's classical period when Mozart, Haydn and Beethoven composed unrivalled Masses; Joseph Haydn was a member of the choir from 1740 to 1749, as was Franz Schubert from 1808 to 1813. There are now four choirs, two spend most of the time touring and one choir sings Mass every Sunday at the chapel of the Hofburg. There are 24 boys in each choir; after their voices have broken they join the Viennensis Choir.

Vienna Boys' Choir

Vienna is a centre of journalism, producing 24 newspapers, including six daily and 18 weekly papers, and 1412 magazines and journals.

The Press

Commerce and Industry

The emergence of Austria as a small republic after the collapse of the Habsburg Empire in 1918, lost Vienna, in its peripheral location, much of its standing as a world power in commercial terms. Today Vienna owes its status as the place where commercially East meets West mainly to good bilateral trading relationships.

International status

Many foreign and multi-national companies and banks are represented in Vienna as Austria's capital, and crucial decisions of far-reaching importance are taken here at the sessions of OPEC, the Organisation of the Petroleum Exporting Countries.

Vienna is the hub of Austria's administration, commerce, industry and money market.

Centre of the Austrian economy

In relation to the size of the province, Vienna has the greatest proportion of workplaces in Austria. There are over 66,000 employers (excluding 1278 agricultural and forestry-related businesses); a quarter of all Austrians work in Vienna. Of the 741,000-strong workforce (including 65,000 immigrant workers), 3400 are engaged in the basic goods sector, 220,300 in industry and commerce and 517,300 in service industries. Some 71,300 are in the direct employ of the city.

For 200 years industry in Vienna has centred on the processing of imported and local raw materials. The sector with the greatest turnover is food and drink, followed by electrical industries, chemicals, mechanical engineering and steel construction, ironware and metal goods, as well as the clothing industry. Currently Viennese industry has a gross annual product valued at over 150 billion schillings.

Industrial tradition

◄ *The Vienna Philharmonic performing in the Musikvereinsgebäde*

Commerce and Industry

The Viennese themselves are also skilled craftsmen when it comes to the production of fashion accessories, lace, petit point, luxury leather goods and gold and silverware. Because rents are high and there is little room for expansion in the city itself many of these small industries have moved to industrial sites on the north, east and western outskirts of the city.

Tourism

In 1993 6,900,000 hotel bookings were registered in Vienna, of which 6,100,000 were foreign visitors. The largest proportion of guests come from Germany, followed by Italian visitors and Austrians.

Famous People

After studying at the Vienna Academy Amerling travelled across half Europe and it was Thomas Lawrence in London and Horace Vernet in Paris who had the decisive impact on his work. The son of a filigree-worker, Amerling became the portrait-painter most sought after by the nobility in his time.

Friedrich von Amerling (1803–87)

Amerling's most famous picture, "Emperor Francis I", hangs in the Marie-Antoinette Room at the Palace of Schönbrunn. Many of his other works are on show in the Historical Museum in the city of Vienna (see entry).

Beethoven, who was born in Bonn, was 22 years old when he came to Vienna where he remained until his death. His misanthropy was notorious. He stood aloof from society and never became a real Viennese although it was here that he found patrons and friends such as Archduke Rudolf and Princes Lichnowsky and Kinsky. Temperamentally never at his ease, he felt impelled frequently to move house. Of the many houses he lived in the most famous is No. 6 Probusgasse. Here he drafted in 1802, as his deafness worsened, his tragic "Heiligenstadt Testament".

Ludwig van Beethoven (1770–1827)

The majority of Beethoven's works were composed in Vienna, all nine symphonies receiving their first performances here. The Ninth (Choral) Symphony was first performed in 1824 at a great concert in the Kärntnertor Theatre.

Brahms settled in Vienna only in 1869 when the Gesellschaft der Musikfreunde invited him to become conductor of their concerts. Brahms's symphonies were originally offered to the public in Vienna, the Second and Third Symphonies receiving their first performances from the Vienna Philharmonic. His greatest success, however, came when his "German Requiem" was performed in the city. Brahms's work is considered to be the culmination of the Viennese Classical tradition in music.

Johannes Brahms (1833–97)

He is buried in the central cemetery.

More a Spaniard than an Austrian, the Emperor Charles introduced strict Spanish Court ceremonial to Vienna. In 1713 he promulgated the Pragmatic Sanction under which his daughter Maria Theresa was allowed to succeed him.

Charles VI (1685–1740)

Buildings erected in Vienna during the reign of Charles VI include the Karlskirche, the Court Library, the Winter Riding School, the Palace of Schönbrunn, Prince Eugene's Belvedere (see entries), numerous palaces for the nobility and several new churches for the religious Orders.

Elisabeth, a Wittelsbach Princess, became Empress when she married Emperor Franz Joseph I in 1854. She also became Queen of Hungary in 1867. The marriage was basically intended to favour German interests in Austria. There were four children, Rudolf, the heir to the throne, and three daughters.

Elisabeth I (1837–98)

Elisabeth I, or Sissi as she was commonly known, was richly talented, artistic, sporting and capricious. Her aversion to strict Court etiquette drove her to spiritual loneliness. After her son, Crown Prince Rudolf, committed suicide in the hunting-lodge at Mayerling, she led a restless life, travelling constantly. In 1898 she was the victim of an attack by the anarchist Luccheni in Geneva.

The magnificent apartments of the Empress in the Hofburg and in the Palace of Schönbrunn are on show (see entry).

Famous People

Ludwig van Beethoven   *Elisabeth I*   *Sigmund Freud*

Johann Bernhard
Fischer von Erlach
(1656–1723)

J. B. Fischer von Erlach was born in Graz. After studies in Rome in the ambit of Bernini he became Imperial Court Building Superintendent. He is rated Austria's greatest Baroque architect.

He discovered a synthesis between Italian exuberance and Viennese charm, between French Early Classicism and Late Ancient style. His façades are not stiff or rigid; they are always dynamic.

Fischer von Erlach's masterpieces in Vienna are the Karlskirche, the Palace of Schönbrunn, the early parts of Prince Eugen's Winterpalais, Trautson and Neupauer Palaces, parts of the Schwarzenbergpalais and the Hofbibliothek which his son completed (see entry).

Francis II (I)
(1768–1835)

With the Emperor Francis II the Holy Roman Empire of the German Nation came to an end. On account of the foundation of the Rhenish Confederation he abdicated as Roman Emperor in 1806 and from 1804 onwards he had assumed the title of Emperor Francis I of Austria.

The first Emperor of Austria participated in a variety of coalitions against France but gained no benefit. Finally Napoleon I moved into Schönbrunn, and in 1810 Francis I found himself obliged, for purely political reasons, to marry his daughter Marie Louise to the Corsican adventurer. The marriage took place in the Augustinerkirche (see entry); Napoleon did not himself attend the ceremony.

Franz Joseph I
(1830–1916)

Franz Joseph I, Austria's penultimate Emperor and at the same time King of Hungary, came to the throne when 18 years old. He reigned for 68 years. In the course of his long reign there were military defeats in 1859 and 1866, the settlement of differences with Hungary, the formation of the Triple Alliance, the annexation of Bosnia and Herzogovina, and the outbreak of the First World War.

Vienna became bigger thanks to the Emperor's plans for enlarging the city, more beautiful when the Ringstrasse was laid out, and more important thanks to his support for the Arts. In his personal affairs the Emperor was dogged by misfortune; his brother Maximilian of Mexico was executed by a firing-squad in 1867, his son Crown Prince Rudolf committed suicide in 1889, Empress Elisabeth was stabbed to death in 1898, and Franz Ferdinand the heir to the throne was assassinated in 1914 in Sarajevo.

Sigmund Freud
(1856–1939)

Sigmund Freud revolutionised the realm of psychology. At a time when the monarchy was collapsing and all was in tumult, he analysed human failure and dreams, developing a method based on response to suppressed traumatic experiences.

The father of psychoanalysis was a professor at the University of Vienna. Taking into account the significance of the unconscious he influenced our understanding of the human mind, of the relationship between mind and body and psychiatry.

Freud's apartment, 19 Berggasse, has become a museum (see Practical Information – Museums).

Franz Grillparzer, Austria's most important playwright, came from an old-established Viennese bourgeois family. He was a civil servant, rising to the rank of Hofrat, going into the "Herrenhaus" (Upper Chamber) in 1871. Although essentially he had his roots in early-nineteenth-century middle-class culture he tried to lead the way towards a new style distinct from Romanticism. He became the classic author in the theatres of Vienna. In 1816 he made his début with "Die Ahnfrau" (The Ancestress) at the Burgtheater. In 1888 the rebuilt theatre opened with his "Esther". In 1955 a performance of his "Konig Ottokars Glück und Ende" (King Ottokar's Prosperity and Demise) was given to mark the opening of the reconstructed theatre.

Franz Grillparzer (1791–1872)

Joseph Haydn, the son of a wheelwright, begun his career at the age of eight as a cathedral chorister in Vienna. He is considered the founder of the symphony and himself wrote more than one hundred works in the new style.

Joseph Haydn (1732–1809)

Even during his lifetime Haydn was recognised and famous. He served first as Musical Director to Prince Esterhazy, later scoring notable successes in Paris (Paris symphonies) and in London (London symphonies). He returned to Vienna in 1797. He was a successful man who composed two more of his finest oratorios in his own house 19 Haydngasse (see entry). "The Creation" was first performed in Vienna in 1798 to be followed by "The Seasons" in 1801.

Lukas von Hildebrandt was the second outstanding architect of the Viennese High Baroque period. He was born in Genoa, settling in Vienna a decade after Fischer von Erlach. Though they were on good terms, great rivalry developed between these two gifted men as they strove to win the favour of patrons.

Johann Lukas von Hildebrandt (1668–1745)

An outward sign of the interplay between these two great talents is evident in various buildings which, reflecting the changing taste of their patrons, are partially by one and partially by the other.

Hildebrandt's masterpieces are his palaces for Prince Eugene, above all the Belvedere (see entry).

Hugo von Hofmannsthal, whose Jewish forebears came from Bohemia and Milan, was a genuine product of cosmopolitan Austria. He became famous as an author, writing plays and libretti for Richard Strauss's operas.

Hugo von Hofmannsthal (1874–1929)

His play "Der Schwierige" (The Bore) belongs to the repertoire of the Viennese theatre. His "Jedermann" (Everyman) is one of the great attractions of Salzburg.

Gustav Klimt belonged to that group of progressive artists who in 1897 broke away from the Künstlerhaus Verein and, as the "Secession", sought new developments.

Gustav Klimt (1862–1918)

As a painter Klimt is considered to be the main representative of the Viennese Jugendstil (Art Nouveau). He also had a major influence on the Wiener Werkstätte (Viennese Workshops). Several of his works of art are in the 19th and 20th c. Austrian Gallery in the Upper Belvedere (see Belvedere-Schlösser). His monumental "Beethoven Frieze" can be seen in the Secession building.

Franz Lehár was the outstanding personality in the second great age of operetta after 1900. Lehár, who was born in Hungary, was active in all centres of the monarchy as a military bandmaster.

Franz Lehár (1870–1948)

"The Merry Widow" received its first performance in Vienna in 1905. It was followed by "The Count of Luxemburg" (1909), "Gypsy Love"

Famous People

Hugo von Hofmannsthal

Gustav Klimt

Joseph Haydn

(1910), "Frasquita" (1922) and "Paganini" (1925). After his 25th work for the stage he decided to write for the theatre in Berlin. He returned to Vienna only for his last two operettas "The World is Beautiful" and "Giuditta".

Maria Theresa (1717–80)

Charles VI's eldest daughter was the first woman to succeed to the throne of the Holy Roman Empire of the German Nation. This woman "with the heart of a king" had to defend her country against France, Prussia, Saxony and Bavaria. Despite three wars which were energetically waged she lost Silesia to Frederick the Great, King of Prussia.

Maria Theresa, who married Francis Stephen of Lorraine, was a thoroughgoing Baroque personality. She had 16 children and with immense energy and a vibrant passion for reform she reorganised the "House of Austria" and filled its empty treasury.

Wolfgang Amadeus Mozart (1756–91)

Wolfgang Amadeus Mozart was born in Salzburg where he became the Archbishop's Musical Director in 1769. He came to Vienna in 1781 and it was here that he wrote his great operas: "Il Seraglio" (Die Entführung aus dem Serail) first performed in 1782, "Marriage of Figaro" in 1786, "Così fan tutte" in 1790 and "The Magic Flute" in 1791. Only "Don Giovanni" and "La clementia di Tito" received their premières in Prague.

Mozart, who was adulated as a child, met with disappointments and successes in Vienna. The disappointments were mainly of a financial nature. Nine weeks after the first performance of "The Magic Flute" Mozart died; he was buried in an unmarked pauper's grave in St Marx's cemetery.

Johann Nestroy (1801–62)

Johann Nestroy, a raffish student, opera-singer, comic improviser and theatre manager, became famous for his farces. He portrayed the lowest social classes brilliantly and fought against the social ills of the time. He was, in many respects, at the opposite end of the scale to Ferdinand Raimund whose imaginary dream world he brought back to reality. His greatest success in Vienna was "Lumpazivagabundus".

Nikolaus Pacassi (1716–90)

Nikolaus Pacassi was Maria Theresa's Court Architect and her favourite. Overwhelmed with commissions he was the busiest architect of his age. Pacassi was responsible for completing the Palace of Schönbrunn, the reconstruction of the Theresianum and Hetzendorf Palace: he built the Gardekirche (see entry) and the Kärntnertor Theatre. Nearly all the major 18th c. public buildings in Vienna were reconstructed, enlarged or restored under his direction.

Wolfgang Amadeus Mozart   *Johann Nestroy*   *Johann Strauss (son)*

Ferdinand Raimund, whose real name was Jakob Raimann, found scope for his dramatic and poetic talents in the Josefstädter Theatre in Vienna. He took the old Viennese fairy-tale and magical play and gave it a poetic form, thus founding a genuine folk drama. After Raimund had been bitten by a dog suspected of rabies he shot himself in a fit of depression.

Ferdinand Raimund (1790–1836)

The repertoire of the Burgtheater today includes some of his plays: "Der Verschwender" (The Spendthrift), "Der Bauer als Millionär" (The Peasant as a Millionaire) and "Alpenkönig und Menschenfeind" (King of the Mountains and Misanthropist).

France refused to let Prince Eugene join the French Army because of his diminutive stature. So he first became an Abbé, entering Austria's service as a soldier only in 1683. He rose to the rank of Field-Marshal, becoming Commander-in-Chief in the war against Turkey in 1697, President of the Court Council of War in 1703 and Viceroy in the Austrian Netherlands in 1714.

Eugene, Prince of Savoy (1663–1736)

Among his triumphs are numbered victories over the Turks at Zenta, Peterwardein and Belgrade as well as successes in the War of the Spanish Succession. Prince Eugene was the Councillor of the Emperors Leopold I, Joseph I and Charles VI, and is considered to be the true creator of Austria's status as a Great Power. The Belvedere Palace provided a fitting surrounding for this great man (see entry).

A protégé of Gustav Klimt, Egon Schiele, a pupil of the Academy, specialised in life studies and drawings. At first an adherent of the Jugendstil, he later developed an entirely personal style and took his place at the head of Viennese Expressionistic avant-garde.

Egon Schiele (1890–1918)

In his short life Schiele produced some 2,000 drawings and watercolours. His most important works are to be found in the Austrian Gallery in the Upper Belvedere (see entry) and in the Museum of the 20th Century (see entry).

Franz Schubert was born in Vienna. He was a composer who was able to express himself in a wide variety of musical forms. Beginning as an assistant to his father who was a schoolmaster, he became "the master of the 'Lieder' ".

Franz Schubert (1797–1828)

His life was short, but as well as suffering from poverty and anxiety he also enjoyed satisfying friendships, with authors such as Bauernfeld and Grillparzer and with the painter Moritz von Schwind. He wrote 600 "Lieder", 8 symphonies, 6 Masses, numerous pieces for piano and for chamber ensemble, overtures, operas, musical comedies and choruses.

The most impressive of his symphonies are "The Unfinished" and "The Great C Major". His song-cycles are in the repertoire of every major Lieder-singer.

Moritz von
Schwind
(1804–71)

Moritz von Schwind, a fresco-painter and pupil of the Viennese Academy, worked for a few years in Vienna but was disappointed by his lack of success. So in 1847 he went to Munich where he taught in the Academy.

Returning in 1863 to Vienna for a few years he painted the frescocycles in the State Opera. This theatre was bombed and gutted by fire in 1945, but the originals of Schwind's scenes from famous operas can still be seen in the foyer and the Loggia. Other frescoes by Schwind are to be found in the dome of the Austrian Gallery in the Upper Belvedere (see Belvedere-Schlösser).

Johann Strauss
(Father) (1804–49)

As composer and conductor, Johann Strauss, together with his contemporary Josef Lanner, created the new form of the Viennese waltz in the second quarter of the 19th c. Strauss was first viola-player in Lanner's Quartet, formed his own dance band in 1825 and developed it into a large orchestra. He made concert tours to Germany, Paris and London. In 1835 he was appointed Musical Director of the Court.

The "Radetzky March" is probably his most popular composition.

Johann Strauss
(Son) (1825–99)

Johann Strauss possessed exceptional charm, temperament and inventiveness. He was only 19 when, against his father's wish, he made his Viennese début with his own orchestra. Five years later he took over his father's famous orchestra and toured half Europe before going on to the USA.

He was called the "Waltz King" because he made the Viennese waltz world-famous. It was only later in life that he turned to operetta. He scored his first major success with "Die Fledermaus" (The Bat) in 1874, followed by "The Gypsy Baron" in 1885 and "Wiener Blut" (Viennese Blood) in 1899.

Strauss composed his waltz "The Blue Danube" at 54 Praterstrasse. It is now the home of the Strauss Museum (see Practical Information – Museums).

Franz von Suppé
(1819–95)

The history of Viennese operetta begins with Franz von Suppé, who was Musical Director at three Viennese theatres. Suppé began by composing comic operas including "Die Schöne Galathee" (Beautiful Galathea). Then, under Jacques Offenbach's influence, he wrote "Fatinitza", the first of his operettas to be performed in Vienna, and "Boccaccio" came just a little later. These are among the finest examples of classical operetta.

History of Vienna

First indications of human settlement.	5000 B.C.
Indo-Germanic settlements on the NW wooded slopes.	2000 B.C.
Celts settle on what is now the site of the "Hoher Markt".	800 B.C.
The Celtic town of Pannonien is occupied by the Romans. "Vedunia" becomes the Roman "Vindobona".	15 B.C.
Vindobona, a fortress with a garrison of 6,000 legionaries, expands, becoming a rectangular walled enclosure on the site of the present "Hoher Markt".	2nd c. A.D.
Vindobona is a city with a population of 20,000.	3rd c.
The Celts destroy the Roman city.	c. 400
Bajouarii found, around present-day Vienna, their first small settlements. The names of these end in -ing; among them are Penzing, Ottakring, Grinzing.	8th c.
Charlemagne founds the Carolingian province.	799
Austria under Babenberg rule.	976–1246
Emperor Conrad II is besieged in Vienna by the Hungarians.	1030
Emperor Henry VI holds a Council at Vienna.	1042
Babenbergs win suzerainty over Vienna.	c. 1135
The Wienerische Kirche (Viennese Church) is erected on the square in front of St Stephen's Cathedral.	1147
Duke Henry II, "Jasomirgott", Duke of Ostarichi, transfers his residence from Regensburg to Vienna. The first palace, Am Hof, is built.	1156
The city becomes larger, and the city wall is reconstructed.	c. 1180–98
Planning of the moat.	c. 1190
The Teutonic Order of Military Knights is summoned to Vienna.	c. 1198–1204
Coins are minted in Vienna.	1190
Consecration of the Schottenkirche (Scots Church).	1200
The Ducal Court moves into a new palace on the site of the present-day Stallburg.	1220
Vienna is granted the status of a city with the right to hold a market.	1221
For the first time Vienna becomes an Imperial Free City, a distinction it forfeits in 1239.	1237
The Babenberg line becomes extinct.	1246

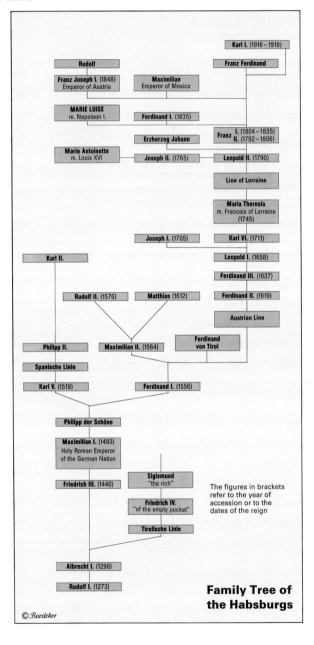

Karl I. (1916 – 1918)

Franz Ferdinand

Rudolf

Franz Joseph I. (1848)
Emperor of Austria

Maximilian
Emperor of Mexico

MARIE LUISE
m. Napoleon I.

Ferdinand I. (1835)

Franz I. (1804 – 1835)
II. (1792 – 1806)

Erzherzog Johann

Marie Antoinette
m. Louis XVI

Joseph II. (1765)

Leopold II. (1790)

Line of Lorraine

Maria Theresia
m. Francois of Lorraine
(1745)

Joseph I. (1705)

Karl VI. (1711)

Karl II.

Leopold I. (1658)

Ferdinand III. (1637)

Rudolf II. (1576)

Matthias (1612)

Ferdinand II. (1619)

Austrian Line

Philipp II.

Maximilian II. (1564)

Ferdinand
von Tirol

Spanische Linie

Karl V. (1519)

Ferdinand I. (1556)

Philipp der Schöne

Maximilian I. (1493)
Holy Roman Emperor
of the German Nation

Friedrich III. (1440)

Sigismund
"the rich"

Friedrich IV.
"of the empty pocket"

Tirolische Linie

The figures in brackets
refer to the year of
accession or to the
dates of the reign

Albrecht I. (1298)

Rudolf I. (1273)

**Family Tree of
the Habsburgs**

© Baedeker

Granting of the status of Imperial Free City.	1247
Rule of the Bohemian King Přemysl Ottokar II.	1251–76
Rudolf of Habsburg is elected King of Germany, taking the title of Rudolf I. He lays claim to Austria as a former Imperial part of the feudal empire. Přemysl Ottokar II refuses to do homage.	1273
Regency of King Rudolf I after the decisive defeat of Ottokar of Bohemia.	1278–82
Founding of the University of Vienna.	1365
Vienna's population grows to 40,000 in the course of this century.	15th c.
The city's privileges confirmed.	1412
Vienna becomes the seat of the Holy Roman Empire of the German Nation.	1438
The Hungarian King Matthias I Corvinus holds sway over Vienna for a short while.	1485–90
Emperor Maximilian I expels the Hungarians from Vienna. Vienna sides with the Reformation.	1493–1519
The double wedding between the children of Vladislav and the grand-children of Maximilian constitutes the foundation of what will become the Danube monarchy.	1515
The failure of a popular uprising is followed by the Bloody Assizes of Wiener Neustadt.	1522
Execution of Caspar Tauber, the first martyr of the Wars of Religion.	1524
The Turkish Siege leads to the erection of a massive circle of permanent defences.	1532–1672
The Jesuits arrive in Vienna and spearhead the Counter-Reformation.	1551
Protestant services are forbidden: Vienna has become a Catholic city once again.	1577
The "monastery offensive": many monasteries and churches are built by Franciscans, Dominicans, Capuchins, Barnabites, Discalced Carmelites and Servites.	c. 1600–38
The Thirty Years' War brings the Bohemians and the Swedes to the gates of Vienna (1645).	1618–48
Vienna is attacked by plague. The dread pestilence claims 30,000 victims in a very short period.	1629
Grand Vizier Kara Mustafa with 200,000 men lays siege to the city which is defended by no more than 20,000 under the leadership of Count Starhemberg. Vienna is delivered from the overwhelming Turkish army by a relieving force under the Polish King Sobieski.	1683
Prince Eugene of Savoy, as Imperial Field-Marshal, gains victories over the Turks and French. This restores Austria to the status of a Great Power, and its capital gains lustre as "Vienna gloriosa".	1683–1736
When Maria Theresa comes to the throne in 1740 160,000 people are resident within its fortifications. The Empress lays the foundations of present-day culture and institutes the system of central government.	1740–80

History of Vienna

1744–49	The Palace of Schönbrunn is built.
1754	First population census: it reveals that Vienna has 175,000 inhabitants.
1780–90	Joseph II develops Vienna as a world city in accord with the concepts of Enlightened Absolutism, leading the capital into the Industrial Era.
1782	Pope Pius VI in Vienna.
1783	Reform of the city's government: appointment of a Chief Magistrate.
1800	Vienna has a population of 231,000.
1804	The French besiege Vienna.
1806	Under pressure from Napoleon, Francis II has to abdicate as Holy Roman Emperor. Henceforth he is simply Emperor of Austria.
1809	Napoleon takes up residence in the Palace of Schönbrunn. The siege of Vienna leads to the financial collapse of the State.
1814–15	The Congress of Vienna, renowned for its glittering festivities, debates under the presidency of Prince Metternich with a view to establishing a new order in Europe (the "Restoration") after Napoleon's defeat.
1830	Danube floods. Vienna's population has swollen to 318,000.
1831–32	Cholera epidemic.
1848	Revolution in March against Prince Metternich's régime. Though the Revolution is put down by Prince zu Windischgrätz it leads to Metternich's retirement and the abdication of Emperor Ferdinand I.
1848–1916	Franz Joseph I is Emperor of Austria.
1857	Plan of the Ringstrasse area (partially opened in 1865) and razing of the fortifications.
1872–73	Building of the New Town Hall.
1890	The suburbs are incorporated in the city (11–19 Districts).
1900	Brigittenau becomes the 20th District.
1918	Collapse of the Dual Monarchy and abdication of the last Austrian Emperor, Charles I. Vienna becomes the Federal capital. Formerly the seat of government of a State with a population of 50 million made up of 12 nationalities it becomes overnight simply the capital of a minor country with a population of 6·6 million. This diminution in size leads to immense political problems within the State. Vienna is surrounded by a belt of hideous modern blocks of flats which were built to relieve the social problems thrown up by this so-called "second foundation era".
1938	Vienna becomes an administrative region within the German Reich. The pan-Germanic interlude costs the lives of 200,000 Viennese inhabitants. Fifty-two air raids and 10 days of fighting in the city itself leave 21,000 houses destroyed and 86,000 dwellings uninhabitable. 120 bridges are blown up and 3,700 gas and water mains are smashed.
1945	The Red Army occupies the city.
1955	Austrian State Treaty. After 10 years of occupation the city, which had been divided up into zones administered by the victorious Allies, celebrates the freedom it gains thanks to the Treaty.

Vienna becomes the seat of the Atomic Energy Authority.	1956
John F. Kennedy, President of the USA and Nikita Kruschev, Chairman of the Soviet Council of Ministers, meet here for the first time on 3 and 4 June 1961.	1961
Vienna becomes the seat of UNIDO.	1967
Construction of an Underground railway begins.	1969
Opening of UNO City. President Carter of the USA meets Leonid Brezhnev, President of the Presidium of the Supreme Soviet of the USSR.	1979
In the parliamentary elections the SPÖ loses its absolute majority. The Federal Chancellor, Bruno Kreisky, resigns; the new Chancellor is Fred Sinowatz (SPÖ). Vienna celebrates the "Turkish Year" (1683–1983), the 300-year existence of the Viennese Coffee House. – U.N. Conference on human rights in Vienna. – Pope John Paul II in Vienna on the occasion of the Austrian Catholic Conference.	1983
The 30th anniversary of the signing of the Austrian State Treaty is marked by a meeting of the Foreign Ministers of the countries which concluded it.	1985
The conference centre "Austria Center Vienna" is opened in April, increasing the conference facilities in the capital by almost 20%.	1987
Death of the former Czarina Zita of Habsburg, aged 96, the last Empress of Austria and Queen of Hungary; she is buried in the Capuchin vault amid great public sympathy (1 April). Opening of the new Underground line U6 (October).	1989
In connection with the centenary of the birth of the painter Egon Schiele, exhibitions of his work are held in Vienna.	1990
The result of a referendum held in May is, surprisingly, a vote against holding the 1995 EXPO in Vienna. The KunstHausWien, built to plans by Hundertwasser, is now to be a museum.	1991
Part of Hofburg is badly damaged by fire. Rebuilding should be completed by the mid-1990s.	1992
Opening of the new Jewish Museum.	1993
Work begins on erecting buildings on the Danube City site which, combined with the adjoining UNO City, will probably become Vienna's second, ultra-modern city centre.	1994

Vienna in Quotations

Fynes Moryson

Wien the metropolitan City of Austria, is a famous fort against the Turkes... It is dangerous to walke the streetes in the night, for the great number of disordered people, which are easily found upon any confines, especially where such an army lieth neere, as that of Hungary, governed by no strict discipline.

An Itinerary, 1617

Lady Mary Wortley Montagu

The streets are very close and so narrow one cannot observe the fine fronts of the Palaces, tho many of them very well deserve observations, being truly magnificent, all built of fine white stone and excessive high. The Town being so much too little for the number of the people that desire to live in it, the Builders seem to have projected to repair that misfortune by claping one Town on the top of another, most of the houses being of 5 and some of them of 6 storys. You may easily imagine that the streets being so narrow, the upper tooms are extream Dark, and what is an inconveniency much more intolerable in my Opinion, there is no house that has so few as 5 or 6 familys in it. The Apartments of the greatest Ladys and even of the Ministers of state are divided but by a Partition from that of a Tailor or a shoe-maker... Those that have houses of their own let out the rest of them to whoever will take 'em; thus the great stairs (which are all of stone) are as common and as dirty as the street. 'Tis true when you have once travelled through them, nothing can be more surprizingly magnificent than the Apartments. They are commonly a suitte of 8 or 10 large rooms, all inlaid, the doors and windows richly carved with Gilt, and the furniture such as is seldom seen in the Palaces of sovereign Princes in other Countrys: the Hangings of the finest Tapestry of Brussells, prodigious large looking glasses in silver frames, fine Japan Tables, the Beds, Chairs, Canopys and window Curtains of the richest Genoa Damask or Velvet, allmost covered with gold Lace or Embroidery – the whole mad Gay by Pictures and vast Jars of Japan china, and allmost in every room large Lustres of rock chrystal... I must own I never saw a place so perfectly delightful as the Fauxbourgs of Vienna. It is very large and almost wholly compos'd of delicious Palaces.

Letter to Lady Mar. 8 September 1716

Hester Lynch Piozzi

The streets of Vienna are not pretty at all, God knows; so narrow, so ill built, so crowded, many wares placed upon the ground where there is a little opening, seems a strange awkward disposition of things for sale; and the people cutting wood in the streets makes one half wild when walking; it is hardly possible to pass another strange custom, borrowed from Italy I trust, of shutting up their shops in the middle of the day; it must tend, one would think, but little to the promotion of that commerce which the sovereign professes to encourage, and I see no excuse for it *here* which can be made from heat, gaiety, or devotion.

Observations... in the Course of a Journey, 1789

Washington Irving

This is one of the most perplexing cities that I was ever in. It is extensive, irregular, crowded, dusty, dissipated, magnificent, and to me disagreeable. It has immense palaces, superb galleries of paintings, several theatres, public walks, and drives crowded with equipages. In short, everything bears the stamp of luxury and ostentation; for here is assembled and concentrated all the wealth, fashion and nobility of the Austrian empire, and everyone strives to eclipse his neighbour. The gentlemen all dress in the English fashion, and in walking the fashionable lounges you would imagine yourself surrounded by Bond Street dandies. The ladies dress in the Parisian mode, the equipages are in the English style though more gaudy; with all this, however, there is a mixture of foreign costumes, that gives a very motley look to the population in the streets. You meet here with Greeks, Turks, Polonaise, Jews, Sclavonians, Croats, Hungarians, Tyroleans, all in the dress of their several countries; and you hear all kinds of languages spoken around you . . . here the people think only of sensual gratifications.

Letter to his sister, 10 November 1822

A clever thing said by Lord Dudley, on some Vienna lady remarking impudently to him,'What wretchedly bad French you all speak in London!' 'It is true, Madame, (he answered), we have not enjoyed the advantage of having the French twice in our capital.'

Thomas Moore

Diary 1829

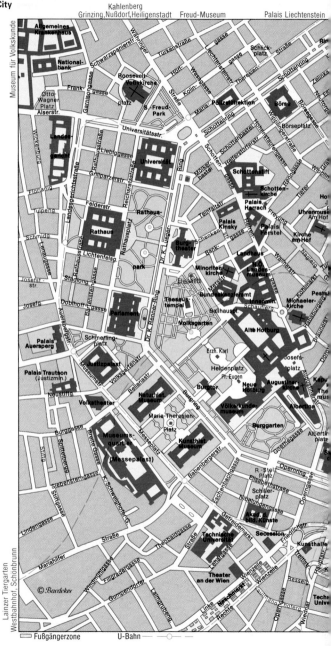

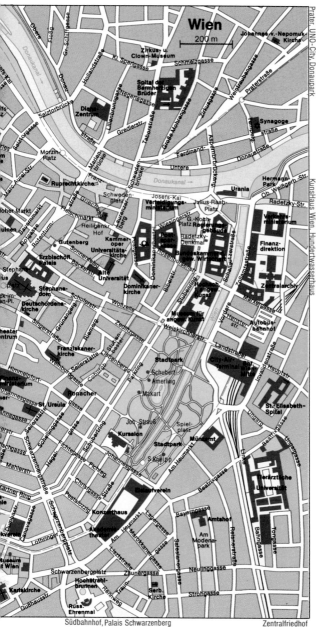

Südbahnhof, Palais Schwarzenberg
Belvedere, Museum des 20. Jh. s.

Zentralfriedhof

Vienna from A to Z

Suggestions for making the most of a short stay in Vienna may be found under the headings "City Sightseeing" and "Sightseeing Programme" in the Practical Information section at the end of this guide book.

★Akademie der Bildenden Künste (Academy of Fine Arts)   C 4

The Academy of Fine Arts is an institution of international importance for the training of painters, sculptors, graphic artists, stage-designers and architects. It also has a major print collection and impressive picture gallery. Peter von Strudel, the founder of the Academy, started the first art school in his house called "Strudelhof" in 1692. He was inspired by Italian examples. In 1876 it transferred to new premises on the Schillerplatz; they were designed by Theophil Hansen in Italian Renaissance style. Among former pupils of the Academy are such Viennese painters as Friedrich von Amerling, Ferdinand Georg Waldmüller, Leopold Kupelweiser, Moritz von Schwind, Egon Schiele, Albert Paris Gütersloh, Ernst Fuchs, Wolfgang Hutter, Rudolf Hausner and Anton Lehmden. Professors of the architecture faculty have left their mark on the appearance of the city; practically all the architects responsible for the buildings on the Ring were professors at the Academy, including Theophil Hansen, who also designed the Musikvereinsgebäude and the Parliament (see entries). In more recent years Professors Friedensreich Hundertwasser (see Hundertwasser Haus) and Fritz Wotruba (1907–75) (see Wotruba Kirche) have added their own creations. Adolf Hitler applied for admission to the Academy in 1907 but he failed the entrance examination.

Open: Mon., Wed., Fri. 9am–4pm, Tue., Thur. 9am–6pm; opening times in July and August tel. 5 88 16–166.

Location
1, Schillerplatz 3

Underground station
Karlsplatz
(U1, U2, U4)

Bus
57A, 59A

Trams
1, 2, D, J, 62, 65

Library

Print Room

Before going up to the Print Room on the mezzanine, visitors should pause on the ground floor and take a look at the Aula, a classical hall for ceremonies with an arcaded gallery all round. On its ceiling is a painting by Anselm Feuerbach, "The Fall of the Titans".

   The Print Room, adjacent to the Library on the mezzanine, has a collection of 30,000 drawings and water-colours, 25,000 engravings and etchings, unique architectural drawings from the Clerk of the Works' Office at St Stephen's Cathedral, more than 300 nature studies by Friedrich Gauermann and 415 water-colours of flowers by the miniature-painter Michael Daffinger. Also noteworthy are prints by the German Romanticists Friedrich Overbeck, Heinrich Reinhold and the Olivier brothers.

Opening times
Mon., Wed.
10am–noon;
Tue., Thur.
2–6pm;
Feb., Easter,
July–Oct., only by
prior arrangement
tel. 5 88 16 225

Picture Gallery

The Picture Gallery (west wing of the first floor) was originally intended as a "teaching aid" in order to train students in observation and feeling for style. However, the Academy was not only a school of art but also an institution and thus during the 18th c. the collection was increased by "accepted works". These were pictures which every student had to submit when applying to be a member of the Academy. In 1822 when the stock of

Opening times
Tue., Thur., Fri.
10am–2pm; Wed.
10am–1pm, 3–6pm;
Sat., Sun.
9am–1pm

◀ Baroque memorial to Maria Theresa

pictures was increased by the acquisition of the collection of the late President of the Academy, Anton Graf Lamberg-Sprinzenstein, the first step towards the foundation of a gallery of international importance had finally been taken. Even today, when the collection is being increased by purchase and by gifts, the picture gallery of the Academy is characterised by the fact that at least one work of almost all the artists associated with it is included. The exhibition begins in Room 4, Rooms 1, 2 and 3 are used for administrative purposes.

Room 4
15th and 16th c.;
Dutch and German
artists

Examples of 15th c. painting include a panel by Simone da Bologna depicting the Holy Trinity and Saints, as decoration for a late 15th c. altarpiece, and "The Miracle of Saint Nicholas" (c. 1455) by Giovanni di Paolo, probably also from an altar. Dierck Bouts's "Coronation of the Virgin" represents early Dutch art of the 15th c. One of the most important works in the collection is a triptych by Hieronymus Bosch (after 1504) of the "Last Judgment between Heaven and Hell". An important early work by Hans Baldung-Grien is "The Holy Family in the Open Air" (c. 1512). "The Holy Family" and "Lucretia" (1532) are major works by Lucas Cranach the Elder.

Room 5
16th c. and
Baroque;
Italian and Spanish
artists

The classical ideal of Italian Renaissance painting is captured in "The Madonna and Child with Angels" (c. 1480) from the workshop of Botticelli. Pictures of the Venetian School include the "Reclining Venus" from the workshop of Giorgione and one of Titian's last works "Tarquin and Lucretia" (c. 1575). "The Deliverance of Peter" (c. 1650) by Mattia Preti and "Still Life" (1675) by Guiseppe Antonio Recco represent the Italian Baroque; works of the Spanish Baroque include sketches by Carreno de Mirandas for an altarpiece of the First Mass of St John (c. 1666) and Murillo's "Boys Playing Dice".

Room 6
17th c.; Flemish
artists

Works by Peter Paul Rubens, with the magnificent sketches for his ceiling-painting (subsequently destroyed by fire) for the Jesuit Church in Antwerp. Van Dyck, who worked as an independent artist in Rubens' studio, is represented by a self-portrait and the sketch of an "Assumption of the Virgin". "Paul and Barnabas in Lystra" (1645) is by Jacob Jordaens, also associated with Rubens.

Rooms 7–9
17th c.; Dutch
artists

Works by David Vinckboons, Pieter Codde, Dirck Hals, Adriaen van Ostade, Cornelis Bega and Cornelis Saftleben typify Dutch genre painting. Architectural paintings are by Hendrick C. van Vliet and Jan van der Heyden. Portraits include Pieter de Hooch's "Dutch Family" (c. 1600) and Rembrandt's "Young Woman in an Easy Chair" (1632). Landscapes include works by Jan van Goyen, Jacob van Ruisdael and Cornelis Vroom and some Italianised landscapes; the still-life works are by Jan Weenix and Jan Davidsz de Heem.

Room 10

Works by Giovanni Battista Tiepolo, Alessandro Magnasco and Gianpaolo Pannini. The paintings of Francesco Guardi: eight Venetian "Vedutas" and two altarpieces, are among the greatest works of art in the Academy's collection. The "Artist's Studio" (c. 1747) is a major work of Pierre Gubleyras. Austrian painting includes a portrait of the Empress Maria Theresa (1759) by Martin Van Meytens, a director of the Academy, and works by Daniel Gran, Franz Anton Maulbertsch and Johann Martin Schmidt (Kremser Schmidt), the last of the great Baroque painters.

Room 11
19th and 20th c.;
Austrian artists

Works by Friedrich Heinrich Füger, Johann Peter Krafft, Hubert Maurer and Josef Abel represent Austrian Classicism. Biedermeier painting is represented by Ferdinand Georg Waldmüller, Friedrich von Amerling and Josef Danhauser, whose painting "The Pupil's Room" shows a classroom in the former academy building.

Room 12
Student collection
and temporary
exhibits

Works by Herbert Boeckl, Fritz Wotruba, A. P. Gütersloh, Sergius Pauser, Franz Elsner, Gustav Hessing and by previous professors of the Academy, including Friedensreich Hundertwasser, Anto Lehmden, Josef Mikl and Arnulf Rainer.

Schiller Memorial

The square in front of the Academy of Fine Arts used to be called the Kalkmarkt, but it was changed to Schillerplatz (Schiller Square) in 1876. At the same time the Schiller Memorial, the work of Johann Schiller from Dresden, was unveiled. The plinth is of red granite. The allegorical bronze figures represent the Four Ages of Man, and the reliefs portray Genius, Poetry, Truth and Learning.

On the monument Schiller is shown standing with Goethe sitting to one side. It is said that the admirers of Schiller were furious about this, but Franz Josef I is supposed to have spoken in favour of portraying Goethe sitting: "Let the old fellow be comfortable. . . ."

Albertina   C 4

The Albertina possesses 45,000 drawings and water-colours, about 1½ million printed sheets of graphic material covering a period of half a millennium and 35,000 books – it is the world's most comprehensive collection of graphic material. The collection was founded in 1786 by Maria Theresa's son-in-law, Duke Albert of Saxony-Tescha. Since 1795 it has been housed in the former Taroucca Palace. Between 1801 and 1804 the building was altered by Louis von Montoyer. The Albertina as we know it today resulted from the amalgamation, after the First World War, of the collections of Duke Albert and the print room of the Imperial Library. Since June 1994 the Albertina has been closed for refurbishment which should take until 1998. Information on the temporary special exhibitions which are held elsewhere can be obtained by telephoning 534 83–0.

Location
1, Augustinerstr. 1

Underground station
Karlsplatz
(U1, U2, U4)

Trams
1, 2, J, 62, 65

Closed for refurbishment

Contents
Drawings

All major European schools are represented in the drawings.

German School: after the 15th c. – 145 drawings by Dürer who is more fully represented in the Albertina than anywhere else, works by Holbein the Elder, Baldung Grien, Cranach the Elder, Altdorfer, Kölderer, Menzel, Spitzweg, Feuerbach, Liebermann, Nolde and Kollwitz.

Austrian School: from the 18th c. onwards, including von Rottmayr, Troger, Kremser-Schmidt, Schwind, Daffinger, Amerling, Alt, Gauermann, Makart, Klimt, Schiele and Kubin.

Italian School: from the Early Renaissance onwards, including Pisanello, Fra Angelico, Lippi, Mantegna, Leonardo, Titian, 43 drawings by Raphael, Michelangelo, Tintoretto, Veronese, Guardi, Canaletto and Tiepolo.

Flemish School: from the 15th c. onwards, including drawings by Van Leyden, Brueghel the Elder, de Mompaer, Van Dyck and a collection of sketches by Rubens.

Dutch School: city schools from the 17th c. onwards, including drawings by Both, Asselijn, Van Goyen, Ruysdael, de Hooch and 70 drawings from all Rembrandt's creative periods.

French School: from the 16th c. onwards, including examples of work by Clouet, Bellange and Callot, choice drawings by Poussin and Lorrain, works by Watteau, Liotard and Fragonard, and by Picasso, Matisse and Chagall.

English School: from the second half of the 17th c. onwards, with drawings by Hogarth, Reynolds, Gainsborough and Romney.

The Special Collections, available only to experts, include architectural drawings (8,000 sheets), miniatures, views of Austria and Vienna, historic prints, illustrated books (Including those belonging to Waldmüller, Stifter, Gauermann, Schwind and Schiele).

The Print Collection includes the world's largest collection of 15th c. single-sheet xylographs, Dürer's woodcuts and copper engravings, Rembrandt's etchings, original work by Menzel, woodcuts by Munch, first impressions by Goya and works by Picasso and Chagall. The majority of the collection

Print Collection

Albrechtsrampe

A reminder of war and Fascism

Equestrian statue of Archduke Albrecht

consisits of original graphics. Special collections include historical papers and collections of playing cards, caricatures, illustrated books and portfolios, views, posters and original printing plates from the time of Dürer.

Austrian Film Museum
Performances
Mon.–Sat.
6pm and 8pm

The Albertina also houses the Austrian Film Museum which does not have exhibitions but shows classic and avant-garde films from October to May. Programmes can be found in the daily papers and weekly brochure of events.

Albertinaplatz
Memorial against war and fascism

A monument against war and fascism by the Austrian artist Alfred Hrdlicka dominates the square. Erected in 1988–91 it commemorates the victims of the Nazi regime and those killed in the air-raid shelters below Albertinaplatz during the Second World War.

The stone "Gateway of Violence" symbolises the terror of the Nazi dictatorship, the marble Orpheus stands for the doom of war, the bronze sculpture of a Jew scrubbing the pavement is a reminder of March 12th 1938 when, following the annexation of Austria by the Nazis, Jewish citizens were forced to scrub off the pro-Austrian slogans painted on the streets.

Albrechtsrampe   C 4

Location
1, Albertinaplatz

Underground station
Karlsplatz
(U1, U2, U4)

The ramp is now just the remains of the old, once-mighty Augustinian priory, on the site of some former city fortifications.

The bastion was destroyed in 1858, and the ramp that remained was severely damaged by bombing in 1945. It was converted into open-air steps in 1952.

The ramp is dominated by an equestrian statue (1899) by Kaspar von Zumbusch of the Field-Marshal Archduke Albrecht (1817–95), the victor of the battle of Custozza (1866).

By the "ground floor" of what remains of the ramp stands the Danubius Fountain (also called the "Albrecht Fountain"). It, too, has survived only in a fragmentary state. The fountain was a gift to the city of Vienna from Franz Joseph I, and when it was unveiled in 1869, the allegorical figures of Danubius and Vindobona in the middle were surrounded by 10 more figures in alcoves. All of white Carrara marble, they personified the Rivers Theiss, Raab, Enns, Traun, Inn, Save, March, Salzach, Mur and Drau. Most of these figures by Johann Meixner have been returned to their alcoves.

Danubius
Fountain

★Alte Backstube (Old Bakehouse)   B3

From 1701 to 1963 Austrian specialities such as Kaiserschmarrn were baked in the old bakehouse and even today the aroma of fresh croissants, bread rolls and strudel is still inviting. Since 1965 it has been partly an offshoot of the Josefstadt Regional Museum with displays illustrating the crafts and trades of the area and partly a unique gastronomical business.

Location
8, Lange Gasse 34
Tel. 4 06 11 01

Underground station
Lerchenfelder Strasse (U2)

Bus
13A

All sorts of objects connected with baking are on show – dough troughs, weights, measures and the old baking ovens. These all date from 1701. It was at that period that a well-to-do baker built for himself one of the finest Baroque houses in Vienna. The bakery has been restored meticulously to its original form, and a café has been installed here. The wine bar was once the flour store and the "snug" was the coachman's room. (Open: Tue.–Sat. 9am–midnight, Sun. 2pm–midnight; closed in August.)

The Alte Backstube, famous for its croissants and strudel

Altes Rathaus (Old Town Hall; Museum of Austrian Resistance) B 4

Location
1, Wipplingerstr. 8
Staircase 3

Underground station
Stephansplatz,
Schwedenplatz
(U1, U3, U4)

Trams
1, 2

Opening times
Mon., Wed., Thur.
9am–5pm

The Old Town Hall, opposite the Böhmische Hofkanzlei (see entry), houses the archive of the Austrian Resistance Movement. In the Resistance Museum are exhibits illustrating the active revolt against Austrian Fascism (1934–38) and of the resistance and persecution under the National Socialists in Austria (1938–45).

Although the decision to set up the Museum of Austrian Resistance in the Old Town Hall has little to do with the history of the building, there are nevertheless parallels. The Old Town Hall was originally the house of a rebel, Otto Heimo.

After Emperor Albrecht I was murdered in 1309 a number of influential Viennese citizens including Heimo resolved to resist the Habsburg rulers. However the plot was discovered, the conspirators punished and their property confiscated. Duke Frederick the Fair gave Heimo's house to the municipality in 1316. The building remained the town hall until 1885 and during this time was on several occasions altered, enlarged and partly rebuilt. It received its Baroque façade about 1700 and the portals with the sculptures of "Fides publica" and "Pietas" by Johann Martin Fischer are also 18th c. The Andromeda Fountain with a lead relief of Perseus and Andromeda in the courtyard is one of Raphael Donner's last works, dating from 1741.

Memorial to the victims of the Austrian Resistance

A memorial to the Austrian resistance fighters and victims of the Nazi regime can be found five minutes away at No. 6 Salztorgasse.

Open: Mon. 2–5pm, Thur., Fri. 9am–noon and 2–5pm.

Museum of Austrian Resistance   *. . . in the Altes Rathaus*

Amalienburg

See Hofburg

Am Hof

B 4

Am Hof is the largest square in the city centre. The Romans set up camp on this site (remains of buildings may be seen at Am Hof, open: Sat., Sun. 11am–1pm). The Babenbergs judged this the right place to build their first palace (1135–50), and Walther von der Vogelweide sang the glories of the glittering festivities there: "That is the wondrous court at Vienna" (plaque on wall of Länderbank 2). Emperor Barbarossa stopped off here on the third crusade in 1189, the Habsburg-Yargellon double wedding was celebrated here and the Jesuits performed plays in front of their church at Am Hof. Later the Ducal Court was replaced by the Mint of the ruling princes.

Location
1st District

Underground station
Stephansplatz (U1, U3),
Herrengasse (U3)

Trams
1, 2, D

In 1667 the Corinthian column with the bronze figure of the Virgin treading the serpent underfoot was erected in the middle of the square. Four putti symbolise the Virgin's protection against war, plague, hunger and heresy.

Virgin's Column

The square is dominated by the remarkable Early Baroque west façade of the former Jesuit church dedicated to the Nine Choirs of Angels. In 1782 Pius IV pronounced his blessing "Urbi et Orbi" from the balcony above the entrance. It was from the same balcony that Emperor Francis II proclaimed the dissolution of the Holy Roman Empire of the German nation in 1806. The Gothic rectangular church was built in the 14th c., reconstucted in the Baroque style in the 17th c. and provided, probably by Carlo Carlone, with its façade which dominated the square in 1662. Inside, the organ-casing is notable, as are the Maulbertsch frescoes (second side chapel on the left),

Church of the Nine Choirs of Angels

Burghers' Armoury

Am Hof

41

the Lady Chapel altar, and the ceiling paintings by Andrea Pozzo in the Ignatius Chapel.

Märkleinische House	Among the most noteworthy houses around Am Hof is the Märkleinische House, named after its original owner who commissioned it to be built to a design by Johann Lukas von Hildebrandt. Today it houses the headquarters of the Vienna Fire Brigade and the Fire Service Museum (Feuerwehrmuseum). (Open: Sun., public hols. 9am–noon; Mon.–Sat. by prior arrangement, tel. 5 31 99.) The development of the Vienna Fire Brigade is brought to life with a display of fire engines, fire-fighting equipment, uniforms, figures, documents and paintings.
Former Burghers' Armoury	The former Burghers' Armoury (No. 10), built in 1530 and enlarged and extensively rebuilt by Anton Ospel in 1731, is a fine example of Baroque architecture. Mattielli's allegorical figures of Strength and Stamina balancing an enormous globe provide the crowning glory of this magnificent façade.
Urbani House	The Baroque Urbani House (No. 12) was designed by pupil of Hildebrandt. The Urbanikeller in the basement is a popular wine cellar with an excellent wine list.
Palais Collalto	The Palais Collalto (No. 13) was built in 1680; the façade towards Am Hof was redesigned in 1715 and 1725, the façade on the Schulhof re-fashioned in a classical style in 1804. A tablet on this building commemorates the fact that Mozart made his first public appearance here in 1762.

Annakirche (church)   C 4

Location 1, Annagasse 3b **Underground station** Stephansplatz (U1, U3)	The Church of St Anne in Annagasse was built in the 15th c. in the Gothic style. It was founded by Elisabeth Wartenauer, the wife of a burgher of Vienna. In the 17th c. the original church was rebuilt, and in 1715 it was refurbished in the Baroque style. It belonged successively to the Poor Clares and to the Jesuits, before being handed over in 1897 to the Oblates of St Francis of Assisi. The church has a ceiling painting and a picture above the High Altar, both by Daniel Gran. The wood-carving of Anne, above the first altar on the left, is ascribed to the Nuremberg Master, Veit Stoss, the original can be seen in the Dom and Diözesan Museum (see entry). Devotion to St Anne has deep roots in Vienna. The church has in its keeping as a precious relic the hand of the Saint in a rich Baroque setting which is exhibited every year on July 26th for her followers.
Annagasse	Annagasse, which turns off right from Kärntnerstrasse (see entry), is a narrow thoroughfare which is a reminder of what Vienna looked like in the 18th c. The lane existed as early as the 14th c., when it was called "Pippingerstrasse", and there was a chapel already on the site now occupied by the Annakirche. There are some fine old houses here: the 17th c. Esterhazy Palace, (No. 2), Kremsmünsterhof (No. 4), Herzogenburgerhof (No. 6), Hotel Maibergerhof (No. 7), Deybel- or Täublerhof (No. 8) which was a school for artists and engravers before the Academy of Fine Arts (see Akademie der Bildenden Künste) was opened, "Zum Blauen Karpfen" hotel, rebuilt by Ehmann in 1814 (No. 14) with noteworthy reliefs by Josef Klieber and the renowned hotel "Zum Römischen Kaiser" (No. 16).

Augarten (park)   A 5

Location 2, Obere Augartenstr. 1–3	Vienna's oldest park, the Augarten, covers 52ha/140 acres between the Danube Canal and the North-west Station. In it still stand the ruins of the Alte Favorita, the Augarten Palace and the Josephsstöckl. The park was laid out as an Imperial pleasure garden in the 17th c., and reconstructed to plans

Augarten procelain manufactory

by Jean Trehet. In 1775, at the desire of Emperor Joseph II, it was opened to the people of Vienna "as a place dedicated to the enjoyment of all men".

Bus
5A

The "Alte Favorita", Leopold I's garden palace, was set on fire by the Turks in 1683. Joseph I had the Garden Pavilion erected on part of the ruins, and it was here that from 1782 the famous musical matinées took place, under the direction first of Mozart, then also of Beethoven (original performance of the Kreutzer sonata) and Strauss' father, and illustrious evenings with Wagner and Liszt.

Trams
31, 32, N

The Augarten porcelain factory is at present housed in the former Garden Pavilion. It was founded in 1718 and has belonged to the city since 1924. Its traditional dinner services, bearing the names Pacquier, Liechtenstain, Prince Eugene and Maria Theresa are known the world over. The most popular articles made for export are porcelain Lippizaner horses in the various haute école positions and Viennese types based on original models dating back to the era of Maria Theresa.

★Porcelain factory
tours Mon.–Fri.
9.30am

Since 1948 the Augarten Palace has been the boarding-school of the Vienna Boys' Choir which consists of 96 "sparrows" in four choirs. A Privy Councillor had this fine mansion built towards the end of the 17th c., to plans produced by Johann Bernhard Fischer von Erlach. In 1780 it was purchased by Emperor Joseph II who, however, personally preferred to reside in the modest Kaiser Joseph-Stöckl. The latter was built for him in 1781 by Isidor Carnevale. Nowadays this building houses the "transitional"

Augartenpalais and Josephsstöckl

members of the Vienna Boys' Choir, that is to say choristers who have to move on when their voices have broken.

★Augustinerkirche (church)   C 4

Location
1, Augustinerstr. 3

Underground station
Stephansplatz
(U1, U3),
Herrengasse (U3)

Bus
57A, 59A

Trams
1, 2, D, J

This triple-naved church was the scene of great weddings: in 1810 the Archduchess Marie Louise was married here to Napoleon I, who was so short of time that he had to be represented by a proxy, Archduke Karl. In 1854 Emperor Franz Joseph wedded Elisabeth (Sissi) of Bavaria here, and in 1881 the legendary and unfortunate Crown Prince Rudolf married Stefanie of Belgium. The church was built for the Augustinian Canons. Between 1330 and 1339 Dietrich Ladtner von Pirn constructed an aisle-less oblong church in Gothic style. The aisle-less choir was added about 1400, and the tower was built on in 1652. The chapel of St George dates from 1351, and the Loretto Chapel from 1724. The church was refurbished in Baroque style later, but all this was swept away in 1785 when J. F. Hetendorf von Hohenberg carried out a restoration at the behest of Joseph II, bringing back the Gothic style.

Tour

Walking around the church visitors will note – in addition to the features mentioned below – the icon to the left of the entrance, the chancel and the High Altar.

Loretto Chapel

The Loretto Chapel was once adorned with silver, but that had to be melted down during the Napoleonic Wars. The beautiful wrought-iron railing dates from the 18th c.

Heart Vault

In the Heart Vault the hearts of the Habsburgs are contained in small silver urns. The earliest is the heart of Matthias who died in 1619. Here rest the hearts of nine emperors, eight empresses, one king, one queen, fourteen archdukes, fourteen archduchesses and two dukes. The bones are interred in the Imperial Vault of the Kapuzinerkirche (see entry), the internal organs in the catacombs of the Stephansdom (see entry).

Chapel of St George

The Chapel of St George was built in the 14th c. by Duke Otto the Merry as a meeting-place for the knightly Order of St George. Later it was converted into a mortuary chapel, and the victor of Kolin, the Imperial Count Daun, lies buried here, as does Maria Theresa's physician, Gerard van Swieten. The marble tomb of Leopold II (1799) is empty. The Emperor lies in the Imperial Vault in the Kapuzinerkirche (see entry).

Christinen-denkmal

The Christinendenkmal is a monument opposite the entrance. It is considered to be the most important piece of sculpture in the church. Antonio Canova's famous marble tomb for the Duchess of Saxony-Tescha, the daughter of Maria Theresa, dates from 1801 to 1805. Beneath the apex of the flat pyramid up against the surface of the wall, the spirit of blessedness bears the Archduchess's medallion. Her body, however, lies in the Imperial Vault in the Kapuzinerkirche (see entry).

Organ

The organ, like the pews, comes from the Schwarzspanierkirche (the Black Spaniard Church) which was destroyed in a storm. This organ, which was used at the first performance of Bruckner's Mass in F minor, was restored between 1974 and 1976.

Austria Center Vienna   B 5

See UNO City

Bäckerstrasse   B 5

Location
1, Off Lugeck

In this street, where bakers once lived, visitors will find old mansions and ancient doorways with coats of arms and signs on houses that have been handed down over the ages. Among the most notable houses are: No. 7 with a courtyard with Renaissance arcading and, on the first floor, a small collection of fine metalwork which the Viennese painter F. Amerling brought together. No. 8 is the former Seilern Palace which was built in 1722 in J. L. von Hildebrandt's style. No. 12 dates from the 15th and 16th c. and has a remarkable Renaissance oriel on its first floor. Once upon a time the house was called "Wo die Kuh am Brett spielt" (Where the cow plays chequers) and was painted all over; No. 14 was built in 1558, and altered in 1700. The Baroque residence at No. 16 was built in 1712 and formerly housed a tavern called the "Schmauswaberl", a much loved eating-place for the students of the nearby university as the food was left over from the court kitchens and very cheap.

Underground station
Stephansplatz (U1, U3), Stubentor (U3)

★Baden (near Vienna)

Excursion

The spa town of Baden (pop. 29,500) lies on the eastern edge of the Vienna Woods at a height of between 200 and 250m/656 and 820ft at the foot of the Valley of the Helenen, a protected area, surounded by extensive vineyards and woods. It owes its origins to the discovery of the sulphur springs; 14 springs produce almost 5 million litres a day at an average temperature of 36°C.

The spa of "Aquae" was known by the Romans who sought relief and cures from illnesses here. Baden was first mentioned in 869 under the name of "Padaun", it received its charter in 1480. It became especially popular in the 19th c. when all of Vienna met here following the presence of the Habsburg Court every summer from 1803 to 1834. Celebrated artists were among the Viennese society who gathered here. Mozart wrote his "Ave Verum" for the choirmaster of the parish church of St Stephan and Beethoven spent 15 summers here at Rathausgasse, where he composed his Ninth Symphony which he completed in 1823–24. Schubert, Liszt, Raimund, Stifter, Alt, Daffinger, Waldmüller and Schwind were frequent visitors to Baden. Lanner, Ziehrer and Strauss gave concerts in the Spa Gardens, and it was here that Grillparzer composed "Das Goldene Vliess" (The Golden Fleece).

Today people go to Baden to bathe in the large hot baths in Helenen-strasse or one of the other indoor or outdoor pools, to attend the open-air performances in the Summer Arena in the Spa Park, to gamble in the

Location
26km/16miles south

Electric Baden Railway
From Oper

Express train
From Südbahnhof

Bus
from Westbahnhof

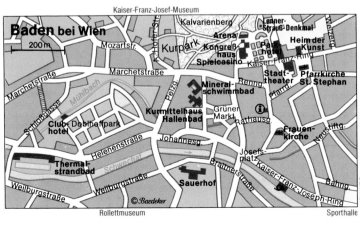

Kaiser-Franz-Josef-Museum

Rollettmuseum

Sporthalle

Casino in the Walddorfertstrasse, to attend the trotting races, to play golf or walk, to drink in the old inns or dine in the gourmet restaurants.

Sights
Interesting sights include the Trinity Column in the main square (1714), the Town Hall built in 1815, the Kaiserhaus (Imperial House) finished in 1792, where the Emperor resided each summer, with a noteworthy collection of weights and measures (open: 2nd and 4th Thur. in month 10am–noon). The Museum in the Attemsvilla on the Erherzog-Rainer Ring contains old Baden dolls and toys (open: Tue.–Sun. 4–6pm; Sat., Sun. 9–11am), the Kaiser-Franz Josef Museum in Hochstr. 51 houses a display of craftwork and folk art (open: Apr.–Oct. Tue.–Sun. 1–7pm), the Rollettmuseum on Weikersdorfer Platz has exhibitions of the municipal collections (open: May–Oct. Wed., Sat. 3–6pm, Sun. 9am–noon). The Beethoven House in 10 Rathausgasse is open Tue.–Sun. 4–6pm, and also Sat., Sun. 9–11am.

Ballhausplatz   B4

Location
1st District

Underground station
Volkstheater
(U2, U3)

Bundes-
kanzleramt

For more than 250 years Austrian history was made at Ballhausplatz; today the seat of the Austrian government and its Ministry of Foreign Affairs is at Ballhausplatz 2.

Austria's policies were not resolved in the ministry but at Ballhausplatz according to Robert Musil in his novel "The Man without Qualities".

The Bundeskanzleramt (Office of the Federal Chancellor), formerly the Privy Court Chancellery, was erected here between 1717 and 1719 to plans by Lucas von Hildebrandt. It was enlarged by Nikolaus Pacassi in 1766 and made even bigger when the State Archive Building was added in 1902. After damage in the war, restoration was completed in 1950.

In the Privy Court Chancellery powerful chancellors such as Kaunitz under Maria Theresa, and Prince Metternich under Franz I and Ferdinand I determined the fate of the country. In 1814 and 1815 the Congress of Vienna met here for its deliberations after Napoleon's downfall. It was here, too, that the ultimatum to Serbia which led to the outbreak of the First World War was conceived and here, also, that Federal Chancellor Dolfuss was murdered in his office in 1934. In 1938 Federal Chancellor von Schuschnigg concluded in his famous farewell address with the words: "May God protect Austria". In 1940 Baldur von Schirach, Hitler's Governor in the Vienna District, moved into Ballhausplatz. The Federal Government and Ministry of Foreign Affairs have been housed here once more since 1945.

Basiliskenhaus   B 5

Location
1, Schönlatern-
gasse 7

Underground station
Stephansplatz
(U1, U3)

The Basiliskenhaus is also called the "House with the Red Cross", it is known to have existed as early as 1212. It is one of the oldest houses in Vienna. It was damaged by bombing in 1944, and has been restored in 16th c. style.

There is a sandstone figure of a basilisk in a niche in the second storey of the façade. Legend has it that a monster – half hen, half toad – hatched from an egg, lived in a deep well and made people ill with its poisonous breath or killed them by looking at them. One day an apprentice baker in love with a pretty baker's daughter took heart and bravely held a mirror up to the monster, which was so shocked at its appearance that it burst and turned to pieces of stone.

Beethoven Monument   C 5

Location
1, Beethovenplatz

The Beethoven Monument is the work of the Westphalian sculptor Kaspar von Zumbusch and dates from 1880. It stands in a little square in front of the

Office of the Federal Chancellor

Akademisches Gymnasium, one of the oldest and best humanistic schools in Vienna founded by the Jesuits in 1552, and former pupils include Arthur Schnitzler and Peter Altenberg. At the feet of the seated figure of the composer may be seen Prometheus in chains with the eagle pecking at his flesh. On the right stands Victory proffering a triumphal wreath, and all round are nine putti, representing Beethoven's nine symphonies. Formerly Beethoven's statue faced away from the River Wien, but since the little river was covered over it has faced the water.

Underground station
Stadtpark (U4)

★★ Belvedere Palaces· Austrian Galleries · C 5

There are two Baroque palaces built for Prince Eugene, the Unteres (Lower) Belvedere and the Oberes (Upper) Belvedere. They now house the three museums of the Austrian Gallery: the Museum of Medieval Art, the Austrian Baroque Museum and the Museum of 19th and 20th c. Austrian Art. In 1995 the palaces are to undergo complete renovation with the 19th and 20th c. galleries being redesigned so that the temporary closure of some exhibitions is possible during this period. From the Oberes Belvedere there is access to the Alpine Garden (see Botanical Gardens).

With the Château of Versailles in mind, Prince Eugene, who defeated the Turks, had a summer residence built on the abandoned slope of the Glacis by the Rennweg. Work began in 1700, and Lucas von Hildebrandt devoted 10 years to what was to be his masterpiece. In 1716 the Unteres Belvedere, where Prince Eugene actually lived, was completed. It was only in 1724 that the Oberes Belvedere with its reception rooms was finished. It stands on higher ground. Both palaces are linked by a magnificent garden. Dominique Gerard, a landscape gardener from Paris, designed them in accord with Hildebrandt's overall concept of a terraced park laid out along an axis with cascades and symmetrical flights of stairs and with hedges and paths

Location
Unteres Belvedere:
3, Rennweg 6;
Oberes Belvedere:
3, Prinz-Eugen-Str. 27

Underground station
Karlsplatz
(U1, U2, U4),
Taubstummen-gasse (U1)

Trams
D, 71

Opening times
Tue.–Sun.
10am–5pm

47

Lower Belvedere – Prince Eugene's summer palace

forming the sides. The sculptures adorning the pools lead symbolically up from the bottom. At the foot can be seen the Underworld with Pluto and Prosperina in the bosquets, then Neptune and Thetis, the deities of water, in the area where the cascades play, together with Apollo and Hercules. From the terrace in front of the Oberes Belvedere there is a wonderful view down over the garden which drops away, and out over the towers of Vienna Woods.

After the death of the Prince who remained a bachelor all his life, his heiress – "frightful Victoria", as the Viennese called her, – sold off the entire property without a second thought. The Imperial Court acquired the buildings and the gardens in 1752. A table in the curator's wing of the Upper Belvedere commemorates the death here of Anton Bruckner in 1896. The Emperor had placed the quarters at the disposal of the Court Organist and Composer as a mark of his respect. Franz Ferdinand, the heir to the throne, lived in the Belvedere between 1894 and 1914, and he was living here at the time of his tragic visit to Sarajevo. It was in the Marble Chamber of the Oberes Belvedere that, on May 15th 1955, the Foreign Ministers of France, Great Britain, the Soviet Union, the United States and Austria signed the Austrian State Treaty which restored Austria's independence.

Museum of Medieval Art (Unteres Belvedere)

The Museum of Austrian Medieval Art is housed in the Orangery of the Unteres Belvedere. The collection included masterpieces of sculpture and panel-painting from the end of the 12th c. to the early 16th c., though there is some emphasis on 15th c. works. The oldest exhibit is the Romanesque Stammerberg Crucifix. It dates from the end of the 12th c. and is thought to be the oldest surviving example of Tyrolean wood-carving.

The collections of the museum are divided into five sections.

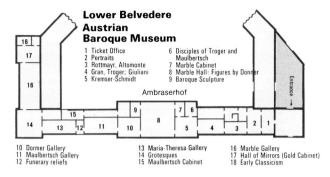

Lower Belvedere
Austrian
Baroque Museum

1 Ticket Office
2 Portraits
3 Rottmayr, Altomonte
4 Gran, Troger; Giuliani
5 Kremser-Schmidt

6 Disciples of Troger and Maulbertsch
7 Marble Cabinet
8 Marble Hall: Figures by Donner
9 Baroque Sculpture

Ambraserhof

10 Dormer Gallery
11 Maulbertsch Gallery
12 Funerary reliefs

13 Maria-Theresa Gallery
14 Grotesques
15 Maulbertsch Cabinet

16 Marble Gallery
17 Hall of Mirrors (Gold Cabinet)
18 Early Classicism

In the first are works by the "masters of the altarpieces", including four stone figures by the Salzburg Master of Grosslobming (c. 1375–85) and a Madonna and Child on a throne (end 12th c.), the second oldest exhibit in the museum. In the second section the outstanding exhibits are the Crucifixion scenes, so-called "Wiltener Crucifixion" and the entire centre panel of Conrad Laib's 1449 Crucifixion reredos. The main work of the third section is the colourful "Znaimer Altar". Also there are five pictures by the Tyrolean painter and carver Michael Pacher and seven pictures by Rueland Frueauf the Elder. Among the works by Pacher owned by the museum are parts of the High Altar from the Franciscans' Church in Salzburg. Important exhibits in the fourth section include a pair of pictures: "Pietá" and "The Adoration of the Kings"; they once formed part of the original reredos in four sections of the Schottenkirche in Vienna and date from 1469. In the fifth section, as well as Marx Reichlich's pictures of the Life of the Virgin and parts of the Waldauf reredos from near Hall, the pictures by Urban Görtschacher, including an "Ecce Homo" of 1508, are especially noteworthy, as are those by the masters of the Krainburg Altar.

Baroque Museum (Unteres Belvedere)

The Austrian Baroque Museum has been housed since 1923 in Prince Eugene's residence, the Unteres Belvedere. It contains a collection of paintings and sculptures from the great age of the Baroque style in Austria executed between 1683 and 1780. The museum was reopened in 1953 after the Second World War and rebuilt in 1974 with extensive renovation taking place in 1994. The most important rooms in the museum are the Rottmayr Room (Room 3): Johann Michel Rottmayr painted figures like those of Rubens in bright, light colours. On show are two of his early works, "The Praising of the Name of Jesus" and "The Sacrifice of Iphigeneia". The picture "Susannah and the Elders" in the same room is by Martin Altomone.

Closed 1994 for renovation

The Troger Gallery (Room 4): Paul Troger represents the pinnacle of Austrian Baroque painting. His "Christ on the Mount of Olives" is one of the most sensitive works of European Baroque. Sketches for secular monumental paintings by Daniel Gran are on display.

Kremser-Schmidt Collection (Room 5): Martin Johann Schmidt devoted himself almost exclusively to religious painting, but there are two of his secular paintings here. "Venus in Vulcan's Forge" and "The Judgment of Midas" were the two works he painted when he sought admission to the Viennese Academy.

Marble Room (Room 8): This two-storey high chamber with its extremely rich stucco decoration and its painted ceiling by M. Altomonte which depicts the Triumph of Prince Eugene, the conqueror of the Turks, is the finest room in the Unteres Belvedere. In the middle stand the original figures made by George Raphael Donner for the Providentia Fountain in the Neuer Markt (see entry).

Donner Gallery (Room 10): In what used to be Prince Eugen's bedroom, with a painted ceiling by M. Altomonte, may be seen Donner's reliefs for the piscina at St Stephen's Cathedral, statuettes of Venus and Mercury, statues of Charles VI and of a nymph.

Maulbertsch Gallery (Room 11): Franz Anton Maulbertsch brought the Austrian Baroque tradition to its culmination. Some notion of the power of his monumental paintings is given by such works of his as the "Allegory of the Jesuits' Mission to the Whole World" and "Saint Narcissus".

Maulbertsch Cabinet (Room 15): Here hang some small-scale pictures and sketches by Maulbertsch.

Marble Gallery (Room 16): The former audience chamber portrays, like the Marble Hall, the Apotheosis of Prince Eugene. The life-size figures of Greek deities in the alcoves are the work of the Venetian artist Domenico Parodi.

Gold Chamber (Room 17) also called the "Hall of Mirrors": this is a grandiose room with massive mirrors in golden frames which seem to make the room go on for ever. Here stands Balthasar Permoser's "Apotheosis of Prince Eugene", a marble sculpture carved in Dresden in 1721. It was commissioned by Prince Eugene himself.

Gallery of the 19th and 20th c. (Oberes Belvedere)

This gallery which is housed in the Upper Belvedere is devoted to Austrian art of the 19th and 20th c. It offers an excellent survey of Austrian artistic endeavour from the end of the Baroque era to the present day, taking in the art of the early 19th c., of the period when the Ringstrasse was being developed, and the so-called "Jugendstil", the characteristic Austrian version of Art Nouveau which developed at the end of the 19th c. The collection was started in 1916, and it has had its present form since 1953. Owing to the current renovations which will probably last until the autumn of 1995 the permanent exhibition can only be shown in part.

Ground floor

The ground floor is devoted to Austrian art of the 20th c. The period between the wars is represented by Oskar Kokoschka, Oskar Laske, pain-

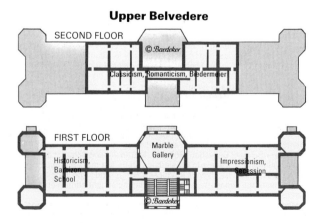

Upper Belvedere

SECOND FLOOR

© *Baedeker*

Classicism, Romanticism, Biedermeier

FIRST FLOOR

Marble Gallery

Historicism, Barbizon School

Impressionism, Secession

© *Baedeker*

ters of the Nötscher Circle (Anton Kolig, Franz Wiegele), Herbert Boeckl, Josef Dubrowsky, Anton Faistauer, Albert Paris Gütersloh aand Rudolf Wacker. Among the post-war movements are Austrian Informel, the Viennese School of Fantastic Realism and the New Painting of the Eighties.

The first floor is reserved for Historism, the Barbizon School, the Impressionists, the French Impressionists and the Viennese Secession. On display are Hans Makart ("Bacchus and Ariadne"), Hans Canon, Franz Defregger ("The Last Commandment"), Anton Romako ("Admiral Tegetthoff in the Sea Battle at Lissa"), August von Pettenkofen ("Horse Market in Szolnok"), Leopold Carl Müller, Camille Corot, Constant Troyon, Emil Jakob Schindler ("Steamer at Kaisermühlen"), Tina Blau ("Spring in Pater"), Olga Wissinger-Florian, Theodor von Hermann ("Znaim in the Snow"), Karl Schuch, Edouard Manet, Claude Monet ("The Garden at Givenchy"), Carl Moll ("The Sweet Market in Vienna"), Vincent van Gogh ("The Plain at Auvers") and the main representatives of Viennese Art Nouveau Gustav Klimt ("The Kiss") and Giovanni Segantini ("The Angry Mothers").

First Floor

On the second floor works of Classicism, Romanticism and Biedermeier are displayed. Historical, mythological and religious themes pervade the works of Heinrich Füger ("The Death of Germanicus"), Johann Peter Krafft ("Withdrawal of Emperor Franz I after the Paris Peace of 1814"), Jacques Louis David ("Napoleon at St Bernhard 1801"), Moritz von Schwind ("Rübezahl", 1851; "Erlkönig", about 1930) and Leopold Kupelwieser ("The Journey of the Three Holy Kings", 1825). One of the greatest landscape artists Ferdinand Georg Waldmüller (1793–1865), the master of Viennese Biedermeier, who became famous through his consummerate skill in the handling of light ("Great Prater Landscape"). Other landscapes are by Carl Blechan, Rudolf von Ait ("The Stephansdom at Stock-im-Eisen Platz", 1832), Caspar David Friedrich ("Rocky Landscape in the Elbsand Mountains", about 1832), Friedrich Gauermann ("Landscape at Miesenbach" about 1830), Joseph Anton Koch, Joseph Rebell, Ludwig Ferdinand Schnorr von Carolsfeld ("Broad Scot's pine at Mödling", 1838), Franz Steinfeld and Adalbert Stifter. Among the portait painters are Friedrich Amerling, the favourite Biedermeier artist with the nobility and the self-important middle classes ("Rudolf von Arthaber and his Children", 1857), Moritz Michael Daffinger, Franz Eybl, Friedrich Heinrich Füger, François Pascal Simon Gérard ("The Family of Count Moritz von Fries"), Angelika Kaufmann, Johann Baptist Lampi the Elder and Ferdinand Georg Waldmüller ("The Eltz Family"). This genre is represented by Ferdinand Georg Waldmüller ("Perchtoldsdorf Peasant Wedding"), Josef Danhauser ("Wine Women and Song"), Peter Fendi, Friedrich Amerling ("The Fisher Boy"), Michael Neder ("The Coachmann's Fight"), Carl Spitzweg and Carl Schindler. Still lifes by Waldmüller, Petter, Lauer and Knapp are also noteworthy.

Second Floor

Blutgasse

B 5

The Blutgasse District, just behind St Stephen's Dom (see entry) is one of the oldest and most interesting parts of the city. The medieval houses, forming a complex of seven old buildings (others include Fähnrichshof Nos. 3–9), were restored and improved in 1965 in exemplary historical fashion. Where lovers of Schubert used to meet in the café whose name was altered to "Zur lustigen Blunze", there are now dwellings and artists' studios. The name "Blutgasse" (Blood Lane) is without historical warrant. According to legend, however, when the French Chivalric Order of Knights Templar was dissolved here, so many templars were slain that the narrow lane ran with their blood.

Location
1, off Singerstrasse

Underground station
Stephansplatz
(U1, U3)

The Blutgasse District also has one of Vienna's special architectural features: the "Durchhäuser" (passage houses). The passages lead through one or more courtyards to the next street, passing from Blutgasse through

Durchhäuser

picturesque galleried courtyards (the Viennese "Pawlatsch") into Fährichshof and further into Singerstrasse.

Böhmische Hofkanzlei (Bohemium Court Chancellery)   B 4

Location
1, Wipplingerstrasse 7

Underground station
Stephansplatz
(U1, U3)

The buildings of the the former Bohemian Court Chancellery now serve as the seat of the Constitutional and Administrative Court. The original dates from 1708 to 1714. J. B. Fisher von Erlach designed this Baroque palace, and Lorenzo Mattielli was responsible for the many sculptures. In 1752 Maria Theresa commissioned Matthias Gerl to enlarge the building. The building was badly damaged in the war, and large-scale reconstruction was necessary (1946–51). A pedestrian passage was added in 1948.

Botanischer Garten (botanical gardens)   C 5

Location
3, Mechelgasse 2
(near Rennweg)
or Landstrasser
Gürtel 1 (entrance
to the Belvedere,
then right)

Underground station
Südtiroler Platz
(U1)

Trams
71, D, O

The chief attractions of the Botanical Gardens are its succulents and its orchids as well as the important collection of Australian plants housed in the Sundial House.

The garden, originally only for medicinal plants, was laid out by Maria Theresa in 1757 on the advice of her physician G. van Swieten. It is said that when one of the plants failed to bring the Empress any relief from an illness she ordered the physician and botanist Nikolaus von Jacquin to forget about the medicinal plants and turn the place into a botanical garden which she gave to the university.

Open: 9am until dusk; tours: May and Sept, Wed. 4.30pm, June–Aug., every 2nd Wed. in month 4.30pm.

Alpine Garden

Between the garden of the Belvedere Palaces (see entry) and the Botanical Gardens is a large Alpine Garden with a comprehensive display of rare plants which is open in fine weather (April–July: 10am–6pm, Sat., Sun., pub. hols. 9am–6pm).

Bundeskanzleramt

See Ballhausplatz

Burggarten (park)   C 4

Location
1, Opernring/
Burgring

Underground station
Mariahilfer Str.
(U2)

Bus
57A, 59A

Trams
1, 2, D, J, 62, 65

In 1809 Napoleon had the bastions of the Burg blown up which meant that at last there was room for an Imperial garden, generally called the "Promenade". Later the Neue Burg (see Hofburg) was erected on part of the site. The Burggarten has been open to the public since 1919. In the park stand famous monuments to Mozart, Francis I and Franz Joseph I.

The Mozart Memorial of 1896 is a master-work in marble by Victor Tilgner. The plinth is embellished with the various members of the Mozart family and with two reliefs from "Don Giovanni". The monument used to stand in Albertina Platz, was seriously damaged in the last war, taken away and then in 1953, after full restoration re-erected in the Burggarten.

The equestrian statue of the Emperor Francis I, by Moll, was erected in 1781 in the Paradiesgartel on the bastion. It was later moved to the present spot.

During the Emperor's lifetime Vienna had no statue of Franz Joseph I, and then the Republic was not interested in erecting one. This memorial

Marble statue of Mozart

was erected as late as 1957, almost as an act of subversion. To general surprise, there were no unfortunate political consequences.

★★Burgtheater   B 4

This theatre, "Die Burg" as the Viennese call it, is the stage with the richest traditions in the German-speaking lands. For a long time it was also the most important. The Classical style of the Burgtheater and the German spoken by the players exerted a decisive influence on the development of the German stage, and even now an engagement to play at the Burgtheater is still a high point in the artistic career of an actor or actress. Many famous names have played here.

The theatre was founded by Emperor Joseph II in 1776 as a "Court Theatre" intended to be a National Theatre. It was later called the "Court and National Theatre" with "Imperial Royal Court Theatre" above the entrance. In 1888 a new theatre was built on the instructions of Franz Joseph I on the Ring to designs by Hasenauer and Semper for the huge sum of 10 million guilders. When the Viennese voiced criticisms of the new theatre, Gottfried Semper retorted that "every theatre has to be rebuilt after 60 years or it is bound to burn down after that period". Right on time the Burgtheater was burned down within 57 years, when it caught fire in 1945. The auditorium was completely destroyed, and it was not until October 15th 1955 that the theatre could reopen with Grillparzer's "König Ottokars Glück und Ende" (King Ottokar's Prosperity and Demise).

The building is 136m/445ft long and the middle section is 95m/320ft across. The height of the façade is 27m/88ft. In the auditorium there are seats for 1285 and standing room for 105. The season runs from September to June.

The exterior of the Burgtheater is impressive on account of the numerous decorative figures, colossal groups, scenes and busts by the sculptors

Location
1, Dr Karl-Lueger Ring 2

Underground station
Herrengasse (U3), Rathaus (U2)

Trams
1, 2, D, J

Tours
July, Aug.:
Mon.–Sat.
1, 2, 3pm;
Sept.–Oct.,
Apr.–Jun.:
Tue., Thur.
4pm, Sun. 3pm;
Nov.–Mar. upon
request, tel.
5 14 44–26 13

Tilgner, Weyr and Kundman. The interior has costly decoration in the French Baroque style. The staircase has frescoes by Gustav and Ernst Klimt and by Franz Matsch.

Tickets

Information: tel. 5 14 44–29 59; postal reservations: Österreichischer Bundestheaterverband, A-1010 Vienna, Hanuschgasse 3, fax 5 14 44–29 69 (up to 10 days in advance); telephone bookings by credit card: tel. 5 13 15 13 (up to 6 days in advance); Vienna Ticket Service, A-1043 Vienna, Postfach 160, tel. 5 87 98 43, fax. 5 87 98 44.

Carnuntum

See Petronell Carnuntum

Danube (Donau)   A 5

General and History

The Danube, which is almost 300m/330yds wide flows for 24km/15 miles through Vienna from north-west to south-east. In times past, this, the second largest river of Europe, brought great problems to the city. The river meandered considerably – every rise in its level caused catastrophic flooding and it often formed new channels. Naturally the first efforts to control the waters were concentrated on the channels nearest the city and in 1598 the so-called "Danube Canal" was regulated. This flowed for 17km/10 miles between Nussdorf and Pratespitz; it was navigable and commercially important. With the introduction of larger vessels and with the growth of Vienna along the right bank of the main river and its expansion on the plain to the east it became necessary to regulate the main stream. Between 1868 and 1876 the river was straightened and provided on the east with a

DDSG ships moored at Schwedenplatz

400m/440 yard-wide flood channel. Further measures, begun in 1975 and now almost finished, will complete the protection against flooding. Parallel to the main river a relief channel, the "New Danube" has been excavated in what has been a useful flood-plain, forming an elongated island, called "Spaghetti Island" (see Danube Island). The Danube is now in four parts; the main stream, the New Danube, the Danube Canal and the Old Danube, the last named being made up of the cut-off remains of various arms of the old course of the river before 1870.

Below the Reichsbrücke the river is flanked by broad meadows which have been converted into a park-like area in the Prater and in the Lobau have been declared a nature reserve. From here to the Czech and Slovak republics' border the Eastern National Park is to be established. Within an overall civic plan Vienna will convert the Danube area into a scenically attractive region (see General, Redevelopment of the Danube).

Redevelopment area

The river is spanned by two railway bridges, Nordbahn- and Stadtlauer Ostbahnbrücke; five road bridges, Nordbrücke, Florisdorfer Brücke (renovated 1977–78), Brigittenauer Brücke, Reichsbrücke, which collapsed in 1976 and was fully restored by 1980, and the Praterbrücke as well as two service tunnels. There are also two small ferries.

Bridges and ferries

See Facts and Figures, Transport.

Port

Danube City   north-east beyond A 6

The 1995 World Exhibition would have provided many facilities for future use afterwards but was rejected in a referendum. It was planned to stage it near UNO City and it could have been the impetus to develop this bridgehead into a second city centre. This role is now to be taken by Danube City near the UNO City. It is to be built partly on the land designated for the World Exhibition partly on a covered section of the motorway by the banks of the Danube. Danube City will not only provide offices and shops and free the Altstadt from the rising pressure of rents, it will also include the Viennese University of Economics, other cultural facilities and become a lively multi-purpose centre. A direct and rapid underground link and the development of a municipal axis between both centres should guarantee that the Altstadt is not undermined as a centre.

Location and function

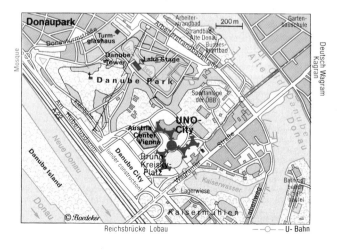

55

Architectural concept

The Danube City will contrast sharply with the Altstadt. It will have 150m/492ft-high blocks as new landmarks on the other bank of the Danube with offices and shops on the lower floors, and flats on the upper floors with views of the Danube, the Altstadt and the Viennese Woods. The principle of just an outline plan for an entire district is a revolutionary idea. It divides up the available land into square parcels 42 × 42m/137 × 137ft, determines the building height (with a slope down to the Danube) and the maximum building space per plot. It also determines that motorised traffic should be on ground level with pedestrians, shops and house entrances on "first floor" level platforms and bridges supported by stilts. The design of the individual plots can otherwise be left up to the individual owners and the period. Thus an entire district has not been planned at once, it has been left to necessity which buildings actually fit in with the plan in the course of time. Numerous prominent Austrian and international architects are currently engaged in planning the individual units. The first large-scale project began in 1994 and its flats are already taken.

Danube Island (Donauinsel)   A 6

Location
Between Klosterneuburg and the oil port Lobau

Vienna has to thank the scheme for the regulation of the Danube for the creation of Danube Island, the popular recreation area, which lies between the relief channel, the New Danube, and the main river. The island extends over 700ha/1730 acres and includes woodland areas of grass, stretches of water and several kilometres of bathing beaches. At high tide, when the New Danube functions as a flood protection and the locks are opened, there is a bathing ban for two weeks afterwards. By then the water has become clean enough to swim in again.

A brochure giving details of each section of the Danube and its recreational facilities is available from the tourist information office (see Practial Information, Information).

North Section

S-Bahn stations
Strandbäder (S1, S2, S3)

Bus 33B

Trams 31, 32

This is a paradise for yachtsmen and surfers as the wind coming from the Vienna Woods blows most strongly here. There are surfing schools and yacht harbours; bicycles can be hired as can rowing, paddle and electric boats (motor boats are not permitted on the New Danube). There are good facilities for swimming and sunbathing and, as in the other parts of the island, restaurants and cafeterias.

Ferry
DDSG landing stage
Nussdorf

There are parking facilities at the main access point (via Langenzersdorf); at the north yacht harbour (vie Scheydgasse); on the Überfuhrstrasse and by the Florisdorfer bridge. There are cycle paths on the Florisdorfer bridge, on the Jedleseer footbridge and on the main access road.

Central Section

S-Bahn station
Strandbäder (S1, S2, S3)

Underground station
Donauinsel (U1)

Bus
80B, 91A, 18A

As befits their function as a flood barrier, the banks of Danube Island are reinforced with boulders and concrete, but in a few places suitable for bathing a layer of fine gravel covers the stones and there are special areas with shallow water for children. Full-size football pitches, an 800m/880 yard-long water ski-lift and a water chute are available and there is a school for diving, sailing and canoeing. Further attractions include a roller-skating rink and a "fun" cycle area. Cyclists can reach the island via the Nordbahn and Brigitenauer bridges, the Reichsbrücke, the Praterbrücke and Weir 1. There are parking facilities by the Reichsbrücke and in Raffineriestrasse.

South Section

Here there are facilities for naturists and the handicapped. A 1500m/ 1650 yard-long cyclodrome provides a venue for cycle, roller-skating and wheelchair races.

Sites are available for summer barbecues, and anglers can find peaceful spots for their sports (a fishing permit is necessary) – some of the best fishing in Vienna is from the banks of the Danube.

The "Toter Grund" (dead ground) with its pools and reeds is a protected area in this part of the island.

There are parking facilities along the left bank of the New Danube with display boards showing the number of free spaces.

Visitors can reach the south section of the island by ferry from the right bank of the Danube at Lindmayer's restaurant (Dammhaufen 50) and visit the "Peace Pagoda" at the same time. The pagoda was erected at the restaurant by Elisabeth Lindmayer, the proprietor's daughter, who is Buddhist. In 1982 two monks of the Michidatsu Fujii Order visited her; members of their order had already erected some 70 peace pagodas in Japan, Sri Lanka, India and the US during their pilgrimage for world peace.
   Elisabeth Lindmayer had the first peace pagoda in Europe erected on the banks of the Danube in 1983. The bell-shaped pagoda is a monument rather than a temple and contains an almost 3m/10ft high seated statue of Buddha under a dome decorated with a band of ornaments and reliefs.

S-Bahn station
Lobau, Stadtlauer Brücke (S80)

Bus
18A, 80B, 91A

Tram 21

Ferries
at the Lindmayer and Ronesch restaurants (right bank), WALULISO (New Danube): also for cyclists

Peace Pagoda

★★Demel (café)   B 4

Demel was once the Royal and Imperial pastry-cook's. Now it is the choicest and most expensive café in Vienna. All cooked dishes and cakes are prepared by hand to traditional recipes. In the kitchen machinery is hardly used at all. Even Emperor Franz Joseph sent for cakes and pralines from Demel during his tête-à-têtes with his lover, while his unhappy wife Sissi was addicted to their legendary violet sorbet. The age-old battle between "Sacher" and "Demel" for the right to describe their own Sachertorte, which is exported throughout the world, as "the real thing" is still unsettled.
   The firm's unmistakable trademark are its waitresses, known as "Demelinerinnen", made famous in a song by Helmut Qualtinger, and who always wear modest black dresses with lace collars and still address the customers very formally with "Haben schon gewählt?" (Has Madam already made her choice?).
   The over 200-year-long history of this illustrious establishment began in 1785 when it was founded by the Württemberg confectioner, Ludwig Dehne, by the Danube. His heirs gave the business to the apprentice Christoph Demel, whose family acquired the Stadtpalais and made it the first house on the square. In 1917 it was taken over by the ignominious Anna – she had divorced a Demel to marry his brother soon afterwards – who ran it successfully for four decades. Her successor, Klara Demel, married a Baron Berzeviczy who showed little interest in the traditional firm and sold it following the death of his wife. From 1972 Udo Proksch ran it and established the notorious Club 45 before the "Lucona" affair which resulted in his being put behind bars for the rest of his life for six murders following the sinking of the freighter. In 1993 it was sold to the German Günter Wichmann who swore an oath of disclosure forcing the confectionery into bankruptcy and into the hands of its creditors. Despite continual rumours of closure visitors can still enjoy their coffee, strudel,

Location
1, Kohlmarkt 14

Underground station
Stephansplatz (U1, U3), Herrengasse (U3)

Opening times
Mon.–Sat. 9am–7pm; Sun. 10am–7pm

Demel's, formerly pastry-cooks to kings and emperors

sachertorte or hearty snacks at the inviting marble tables of this noble emporium of pastries.

Kohlmarkt

The pedestrianised Kohlmarkt links Michaelerplatz and Graben (see entries). Wood and coal was once sold on the site of these luxurious shops and elegant boutiques. Two of these, Nos. 7 and 8/10, have façades designed by Hans Hollein in post-Modernist style decorated boldly in metal and marble. The fine Art Nouveau (No. 9) Artaria Publishing House where Chopin lived during his stay in Vienna is interesting.

Grosses
Michaelerhaus

Opposite the Demel café stands the Grosses Michaelerhaus with its attractive courtyard built by the Barnabites around 1720. The poet Pietro Metastasio (1698–1782) lived and died here and Joseph Haydn lived in the attic for several years. Today the Royal and Imperial pastry-cook's sells its delicious produce in "Vis-à-Vis"; the adjoining restaurant's speciality is seafood.

Deutschmeisterdenkmal (monument)   B 4

Location
1, Deutsch-
meisterplatz

In 1986, to celebrate and honour the second centenary of the Viennese garrison regiment, the K. and K. Hoch- und Deutschmeister Nr. 4 (The Fourth Royal and Imperial High and German Masters), money was raised for a memorial. It was inaugurated in 1906.

Johann Benk made the bronze figures. Under an ensign bearing the standard of the regiment are gathered "Vindobono" and "Landshut grenadier" and the "true comrade". Two reliefs recall the regiment's baptism of fire at Zenta in 1696 and the Battle of Kolin of 1757.

On November 1st 1918 Egon Erwin Kisch formed the "Red Guard" in front of this memorial.

Underground station
Schottenring
(U2, U4)

Trams
1, 2, 31, 32, D

Deutschordenshaus and Deutschordenskirche   B 4
(Teutonic Order house and church)

The Teutonic Order was called to Vienna by Duke Leopold VI at the beginning of the 13th c. The Order started constructing its premises, which probably included a chapel, a little later. In the 14th c. the Gothic church dedicated to St Elisabeth was incorporated into the buildings. In 1667 Carlo Carlone erected a new building which included a church. Between 1720 and 1725 this building was given the appearance which it has kept to the present day. The architect was Anton Erhard Martinelli.

In the Middle Ages the Teutonic Order was devoted to colonial and military activity ruling from the 12th c. large areas of what was later to be East Prussia; now it is a spiritual Order concerned with religious matters and also with service in hospitals and the care of the young and the old. Since 1923 the High Masters of the Order have always been priests of the Order.

Location
1, Singerstrasse 7

Underground station
Stephansplatz
(U1, U3)

The Deutschordenskirche was remodelled between 1720–22 to harmonise with the 14th c. Gothic work. It was restored in 1868 and 1947. The interior of the church is decorated with coats of arms and banners. Among the most precious objects are the Flemish reredos (1520) and the epitaph of Jobst Truchsess von Wetzhausen (1524).

Church

When Napoleon declared the Teutonic Order to be disbanded it moved its headquarters to Vienna where the treasure has been ever since, the result of the passion for collecting of several High Masters. The Treasury of the Order is in four rooms. In the first are Insignia of the Order and coins. The enthronement ring of High Master Hermann von Salza which is on show dates from the 13th c. The second room is dedicated to chalices and other Mass vessels from the 14th to the 16th c. together with cutlery made from exotic materials. The third room houses the art collection of High Master Archduke Maximilian III (1602–18): silver and gold reliefs, ornaments, Oriental parade arms, clocks and astronomical equipment, the fourth room contains miniatures, rosaries, precious glasses, armour and 15th c. panel paintings (open: May–Oct. Mon., Tue.–Sun. 10am–noon, Wed., Fri., Sat. 3–5pm; Nov.–Apr. Mon., Thur., Sat. 10am–noon, Wed., Fri., Sat. 3–5pm).

Treasury

Dogenhof (Doge's Palace)   B 5

The Doge's Palace is a typical example of architectural taste at the end of the 19th c. It is inspired by the Ca d'Oro in Venice and is decorated with a stone lion of St Mark. Emperor Franz Joseph I wanted to designate for each of the various ethnic groups in the monarchy a specific part of Vienna and to let them create there an environment in which they would feel at home. Thus an Italian colony was supposed to grow up in Leopoldstadt. Not a lot came of the idea, and the Dogenhof stands now as a rather odd historical curiosity amid the other houses on Praterstrasse.

Location
2, Praterstr. 70

Underground station
Nestroyplatz (U1)

Bus 5A

Early Baroque door of the Dominikanerkirche

★Dominikanerkirche   B 5
(church; officially the Rosary Basilica ad. S. Mariam Rotundam)

Location
1, Postgasse 4

Underground station
Stubentor (U3)

Bus
74A

Trams
1, 2

The Dominicans were called to Vienna in 1226 and they consecrated their first church as early as 1237. After a series of fires work began on the construction of a Gothic church between 1283 and 1302. This suffered severe damage in the First Turkish Siege of 1529. The present church, the third, was built between 1631 and 1632 and is one of the most beautiful Early Baroque churches in Vienna. It was promoted to the rank of a "minor basilica" in 1927, bearing the name "Rosary Basilica ad. S. Mariam Rotundam".

The frescoes in the nave are by Matthias Rauchmiller (17th c.); those in the crossing are by Franz Geyling (1836), and those in the choir by Carpoforo Tencala (1676). All the wall and ceiling paintings in the side-chapels date from the 17th c. The subject of the picture above the High Altar, "The Virgin as Queen of the Rosary" by Leopold Kupelweiser (1839), refers to the institution of the Festival of the Rosary by Pope Gregory XIII. The chapels date from the 17th c. and 18th c. The oldest is the Thomas Aquinas Chapel with a painting above the altar dated 1638. The most important is the Vincent Chapel. Its altar-piece, "St Vincent raising a Man from the Dead", was painted by Françoise Roettiers in 1726.

★Dom- and Diözesanmuseum (Cathedral and Diocesan Museum)   B 5

Location
1, Rotenturmstr. 2
(entrance
Stephansplatz 6)

The Cathedral and Diocesan Museum stands in Zwettlerhof, adjacent to the Archbishop's Palace. Founded in 1932, it was remodelled in 1973 and extended in 1985. It displays religious art from the Middle Ages to the present day.

The Treasury contains the most valuable items from St Stephen's (see Stephansdom), including two Syrian glass vessels of the 13th and early 14th c., the St Andrew's Cross reliquary and an important 14th c. reliquary which was refashioned in 1514. Mementoes of Duke Rudolph IV the Benefactor, who had the church rebuilt in Gothic style, include the Chapter Seal, an antique medieval cameo and his portrait and funeral shroud. Other valuable exhibits include a monstrance with a pattern of rays by Ignaz Würth (1784), enamelled 12th c. tablets (with scenes from the Old Testament), a Carolingian 9th c. evangelistary with all its sides decorated with representations of the Evangelists, and the sword of St Ulrich (10th c.).

Pre-eminent among the Gothic painted panels are the Upper St Veit Altar, based on a sketch by Dürer, and the "Man of Sorrows" by Lukas Cranach. Among Gothic sculptures are a relief of the "Descent from the Cross" and the Erlach and Therberg Madonnas (14th c.).

The most valuable of the many early 15th and 16th c. sculptures are the Madonna of the Shrine (early 15th c.) and the Anna Selbdritt group by Veit Stoss.

Pictures from the 16th, 17th, 18th and early 19th c. complete the exhibits. The most noteworthy Baroque works are by Paul Troger ("St Cassian"), A. Maulbertsch ("Golgotha"), Kremsesr-Schmidt ("St Sippe") and Jan von Hemessen ("Christ bearing the Cross").

Underground station
Stephansplatz
(U1, U3)

Opening times
Tue., Wed., Fri., Sat.
10am–4pm, Thur.
10am–6pm,
Sun.,pub. hols.
10am–1pm

★Donaupark and Donauturm   north-east beyond A 6
(Danube Park and Tower)

The Danube Park borders UNO City and occupies 1 million sq.m/250 acres which makes it the second largest park in Vienna. It was laid out in 1964 in connection with the Vienna International Garden Show (WIG '64) at a cost of 7 million schillings. The Danube Park railway, a narrow-gauge line, runs

Location
22, Danube/Old
Danube

View from the Giant Wheel, showing the Danube Tower and UNO-City

Dorotheum

Underground station
Alte Donau (U1)

S-Bahn station
Strandbäder
(S1, S2, S3)

Bus
20B, 90A, 91A, 92A

around the gardens. There is an artificial lake (Lake Iris) on the bank of which stands a theatre which seats 4,000.

The Danube Tower is 252m/825ft high, which makes it the tallest building in Vienna. It was opened in 1964 and restored in 1991. It weighs 17,600 tons, and it is 31m/100ft in diameter at the base. Two express lifts ascend to 165m/540ft in 45 seconds. They lead to the viewing-chamber and to the two revolving restaurants. The rates at which they revolve around the axis of the tower can both be regulated so that a cycle takes either 26, 39 or 52 minutes.

★Dorotheum   C 4

Location
1, Dorothee
Gasse 17

Underground station
Stephansplatz
(U1, U3)

The Dorotheum is one of the largest pawnbroking institutions in the world. The Viennese call it either "Tante Dorothee" or just "Pfandl" (The Pawn). The origins of the Dorotheum go back to 1707 when the Emperor Joseph I founded an office for pawnbroking. It was moved in 1787 into the Dorothea Monastery which was empty at the time and these premises later underwent large-scale construction in neo-Baroque style.

There are 2,400 auctions a year, dealing with over 700,000 objects. In Vienna alone the Dorotheum has 16 branches. In the main building there are sections for furniture, carpets, pictures, small objects, furs, objets d'art, stamps, books and jewellery. The four major art auctions, in March, June, September and November, attract experts from all over the world. The Dorotheum is worth a visit if only for its exciting atmosphere. Auctions take place Mon.–Fri. at 2pm and Sat. at 10am, open sales Mon.–Fri. 10am–6pm, viewing Mon.–Fri. 10am–6pm, Sat. 8.30am–noon. There are many antique shops to browse through in the neighbouring streets.

Dreifaltigkeitskirche (Church of the Holy Trinity)   B 3

Location
8, Alserstr. 17

Underground station
Schottentor (U2)

Trams
5, 44

The Dreifaltigkeitskirche, dedicated to the Holy Trinity, is commonly called the "Alserkirche" in Vienna. It stands opposite the front of the General Hospital, and sick people and those on the way to recovery used to hang thousands of votive tablets in the cloister and in the Anthony Chapel. The church, which was completed in 1727 was taken over by the Minorites in 1784. In its exterior form it is an Early Baroque building with a façade flanked by twin towers and a high domed roof. The interior of the church dates primarily from the 18th and 19th c. An exception to this generalisation is a 16th c. wooden Crucifix larger than life-size and the "Weeping Madonna" by the Spanish Baroque Master, Pedro de Mena y Mendrano. He carved this bust out of mahogany and pine in 1662–63; it may be seen in the Johann Nepomunk Chapel. On March 29th 1827 the body of Beethoven was brought to this church. One year later, just a few weeks before his own death, Schubert wrote the hymn "Glaube, Liebe, Hoffnung" (Faith, Love and Hope) for the consecration of the church's bells.

★Ephesus Museum   C 4

Location
1, Heldenplatz,
Neue Burg
(entrance
behind the
Prinz Eugen
monument)

Around the turn of the century Austrian archaeologists excavating at Ephesus on the coast of Asia Minor brought to light interesting statues, reliefs and bronzes from this ancient trading city. They became a gift from the Sultan to the Emperor in Vienna and in 1978 were housed in the Ephesus Museum in Neue Burg (see Hofburg).

Among the most remarkable exhibits is the 2m/6½ft-high bronze of an athlete composed of 234 fragments (Roman copy of a Greek original, second half of the 4th c. B.C.). The Parthian Memorial, a nearly 40m/130ft-long frieze with life-size figures in relief commemorating Lucius Verus

Finds from Samothrace in the Ephesus Museum

(d. 169), the co-regent and adoptive brother of Emperor Marcus Aurelius, was erected after the victorious conclusion of the war against the Parthians (161–165). Also noteworthy are the "Hercules fighting with the Centaurs" and the "Boy with a Goose" (Roman copy in marble of an Hellenistic original). Particularly interesting among the architectural remains are the fragments of an altar of a Shrine to Artemis (4th c. B.C.), of an octagon (second half of the 1st c. A.D.), of a so-called "Round House" (second half of 1st c. A.D.) and of the Great Theatre (mid 1st c. A.D.) with erotic reliefs and a frieze of masks. A 8 × 4m/26 × 13ft model of Ephesus creates an imposing impression of its size and grandeur which was made of countless little pieces of wood and cost 1.3 million schillings.

Considerable discoveries from the Aegean island of Samothrace which complete the collection were excavated by the Archaeological Institute in 1873 and 1875. These include Victory figures, pediment sculptures (from the Hellenistic Hieron), Ionic capitals (from the Ptolemaion), frieze of lotus fronds (from the Arsinoeion) and a gable-end from the Propylon.

Underground station
Mariahilfer
Strasse (U2)

Bus
57A

Trams
1, 2 D, J

Opening times
Mon., Wed.–Sun.
10am–6pm

Fiakermuseum

B 3

In the "Fiakerhaus", built in 1852, the Viennese landau-drivers have set out in three rooms an exhibition tracing in prints, photographs, pictures and models, the 300-year history of their trade. The bronze in the garden of the Fiakerhaus is a reminder of the project to erect a "Fiaker Fountain" commemorating Vienna's landaus; it was finished at the beginning of the war but was never set up.

The first licence to a carriage to ply for hire was granted in Vienna in 1693, 71 years later than in Paris. Towards the end of the 19th c. there were, however, 70 ranks. A hundred years ago a 5km/3 mile ride in a landau cost only about 1½ guilders. All the same that provided a large enough income

Location
17, Veronikagasse
12, 2nd floor

Underground station
Josefstädter
Strasse (U6)

Trams
44, J

63

The "Zeugl" (landau), a Viennese institution

Opening times
1st Wed. in month
10am–1pm

and Viennese landau-drivers paid for the Schrammel brothers to take music lessons, while the Fiaker Ball, with "Fiaker Milli" as queen of the dance was the high point of the carnival.

Today there are only about four dozen "Fiaker". They ply for hire in Stephansplatz, taking visitors round the sights of the city centre. A few drivers still wear the traditional costume of Pepita trousers, a velvet jacket and a hard hat called a "Stösser".

★ Figarohaus (Mozart Memorial Rooms)   B 5

Location
1, Schulerstr. 8
(entrance in
Domgasse 5)

**Underground
station**
Stephansplatz
(U1, U3)

Opening times
Tue.–Sun.
9am–12.15pm
and 1–4.30pm

Figarohaus stands on Schulerstrasse which leads out of Stephansplatz (see entry). For three years, from 1784 to 1787, Mozart lived here with his wife and son on the first floor of this typical Old Viennese house near St Stephen's Cathedral (see entry). These were his happiest years, and it was here that he wrote "The Marriage of Figaro". For a short while Beethoven was his pupil and it was while he was resident here that Mozart was appointed Imperial Chamber Composer. Mozart's rooms in what was then called "Camesina House" have been set out as a permanent memorial. Visitors can see the room (with a fine stucco ceiling) where Mozart worked, pictures and prints, figurines and the first German libretto of the "Marriage of Figaro". The house where he died, Rauhensteingasse 8, no longer exists, his grave is in St Marx Cemetery (see Practical Information, Cemeteries).

★ Franziskanerplatz   C 5

Location
1, Singerstrasse/
Weihburggasse

Franziskanerplatz with the Franciscan monastery and church has 17th and 18th c. buildings all round and is one of the most attractive squares in Vienna. The Moses Fountain, with its jaws like the base of a lion, used to

Kleines Café on Franziskanerplatz

stand in the courtyard of No. 6 "Zum grünen Löwen" (The Green Lion). Johann Martin Fischer designed the lead statue of Moses striking water from the rock. In 1798 it was placed on the base of the fountain which had been brought here. The country coaches used to set out from the former "Zum grünen Löwen" in the days of Emperor Joseph. It was possible to travel 160km/100 miles and more out of the city into the country by these coaches. Nowadays people meet in the little café for a chat or coffee while shopping.

Underground station
Stephansplatz
(U1, U3)

The Church of St Jerome at present standing on this idyllic old-world square is the only church in Vienna to possess a Renaissance façade. The interior is, however, decorated and fitted out in Baroque style. A 14th c. Poor Clares convent formerly occupied the site where this church was constructed between 1603 and 1611. Father Bonaventura Daum was responsible for the designs of the new building. The tower was added in 1614. In the interior the High Altar by Andrea Pozzo dating from 1707 is particularly notable as is a venerated picture of the Madonna and Child from about 1550 which probably came from Grünberg in Bohemia. Behind the altar is the monks' choir which is reached by passing through the sacristy. The Capristan Altar (second altar on the left) has a painting the "Martyrdom of St Capristan" by Franz Wagenschön. The Francis Altar (fourth altar on the left) contains a picture of the church's patron saint by Johann George Schmidt, and on the Crucifixion Altar (third altar on right) is a "Crucifixion" by Carlo Carlone (first half of the 18th c.). The carved Baroque organ of 1643 is the oldest organ in Vienna. It has folding doors which are in part painted, in part carved, with the figures of saints on them. According to legend, the Madonna on the reredos, popularly called the Madonna with the Axe, was being struck down by iconoclasts, but the axe remained firmly attached. Soldiers took this indestructable image of the Virgin with them on their campaign against the Turks and ascribed to it their victory at Pest in Hungary.

Franziskaner-
kirche
(St Jerome)

In Sigmund Freud's waiting-room

★Freud Museum   B 4

Location
9, Berggasse 19

Underground station
Rossauer Lände
(U4), Schottenring
(U2)

Bus
40A

Trams
D

Opening times
daily 9am–4pm

Sigmund Freud lived in the house at 19 Berggasse for almost half a century, from 1891 to 1938. It was here that he wrote his theories including "Dreams and their Meaning" (1900) and received the official announcement in 1902 that the Emperor had awarded him an honorary Professorship.

Of the fifteen rooms in the house, only Freud's "working" rooms are open to the public: the vestibule, waiting room, treatment room and study have been turned into a museum by the Sigmund Freud Society in 1971 and contain some original furnishings, documents and photographs. The vestibule and waiting room have been almost exactly recreated, down to the hat and cane in the cloakroom and the plush upholstery from the turn of the century.

The Psychological Wednesday Society which became the Vienna Psychoanalytical Association met here until 1908. Among the displays in the museum are items from Freud's collection of antiquities which his daughter Anna Freud donated to the Society; the majority of the pieces used to be kept in the study. A film narrated by Anna Freud tells the story of the life of the Freud family.

Freyung   B 4

Location
1st District

The Freyung is a triangular space near the Schottenkloster (see Schottenstift). The name Freyung ("free place") refers to the fact that, like St Stephen's (see Stephansdom) it had the right of receiving and protecting any who were being pursued, except those who had shed blood. In olden days a Punch and Judy show stood on Freyung, and later on there was a gallows where quick justice was meted out to traitors. Mountebanks, hucksters and sweetmeat-sellers had their pitches here. It was only in the 17th and 18th c. that the buildings were erected which form the setting for Freyung today: Palais Ferstel (No. 2), Harrach Palace (No. 3; currently being refurbished by Oskar Schmidt as an exhibition centre of contemporary art) and the Baroque Kinsky Palace (No. 4). The art forum of Bank Austria (No. 1) has interesting temporary exhibitions (open: daily 10am–6pm, Wed. until 9pm).

Underground station
Schottentor (U2), Herrengasse (U3)

Trams
1, 2, D, J

In the middle of the square is the Austria Fountain which is a work of Ludwig Schwantaler. It was cast by Ferdinand Miller in the Munich bronze foundry and unveiled on Freyung in 1846. Its allegorical bronze figures represent Austria and the main rivers of the monarchy as it then existed, the Po, Elbe, Weischel and Danube. There may be some truth in the Viennese chronicles which state that Alma von Goethe, the granddaughter of the poet, was the model for the figure of Austria at the age of seventeen, shortly before her death. After the bronze figure was completed, Schwanthaler is said to have had it filled with cigarettes in Munich to smuggle them into Vienna. The figure was set in place so quickly on arrival, however, that he never had the chance to "empty" Austria and the cigarettes may still be there to this day.

Austria Brunnen

The palace with its beautiful façade and magnificent staircase was built between 1713 and 1726 to a design by Johann Lukas von Hildebrandt. It was commissioned by Count Daun, the father of the legendary commander in the seven year war against Friedrich II of Prussia.

Palais Kinsky

The Palais Ferstel, which Heinrich Ferstel, architect of the Votivkirche (see entry) and the University (see entry), built in 1856–60 for the National Bank, has a distinct Italianate air. Until 1877 the Stock Exchange was housed here. For years the building was neglected but has been restored exactly as it

★ **Palais Ferstel**

Colourful Easter market on the Freyung

Arcade in the Palais Ferstel

Enchanting Fountain of the Danube Sprites

was in the elaborate "Ringstrasse" style as an exclusive venue for conferences and banquets. A glass-roofed shopping arcade containing the fountain of the Danube sprites by Anton Fernkorn, leads to the Herrengasse.

★Café Central

The Café Central (open: Mon.–Sat. 8am–10pm) was reopened in 1986 in the Palais Ferstel. On entering the café from Herrengasse the visitor will find himself greeted by the writer Peter Altenberg – not, of course, in person but as a life-size model. Altenberg was a regular patron and often gave as his address "Vienna 1, Café Central". Other "regulars" who brought "renown" to the café and turned it into a Viennese institution were Egon Friedell, Franz Werfel, Stefan Zweig, Karl Kraus, Leo Trotzky and Alfred Polgar, who even wrote a theory on the Café Central. Today the café displays its wonderful vaulted ceiling and beautifully restored marble columns to visitors who may find it a pleasant place to stop and relax from the rigours of sightseeing.

Gardekirche (church)   C 5

Location
3, Rennweg 5a

Underground station
Karlsplatz
(U1, U2, U4)

Trams
71

This square church was built in 1755–63 during Maria Theresa's reign by Nikolaus Pacassi to serve as the church of the Imperial Hospital. In 1782 it was handed over to the Polish Life Guards. It was altered again between 1890 and 1898.

In 1897 it became the Polish national church dedicated to the Crucified Saviour. The painting above the High Altar in the attractive central section of the building with its light Late Rococo decoration is by Peter Strudel and dates from 1712. Strudel was the founder of the Akademie der Bildenden Künste (see entry).

Geymüller-Schlössl (Sobek Clock Collection)

beyond A 1/2

This small palace was built in 1808 for the banker J. J. Geymüller. It is now the home of the Sobek Collection of old Viennese clocks, and is a separate department of the Austrian Museum of Applied Arts (see entry). Dr Franz Sobek acquired the property in 1947 saving the mansion and Biedermeier-style garden from decay. There are seven rooms decorated in Empire and early 19th c. style. On show are about 160 clocks – Old Viennese pedestal clocks, case clocks and wall clocks. The oldest are Baroque clocks, but most of the exhibits come from the period 1780–1850.

Location
18, Pötzlein-dorfer Str. 102

Trams
41

On the ground floor there are art exhibitions from the early 19th c. (Open: Mar.–Nov.: Tue., Wed., Fri.–Sun. 10am–5pm; tours Sun. 3pm.)

Graben

B 4

Graben, a wide-open space which is half street and half square, is the hub of the great city of Vienna. In 1950 it was the first place to have fluorescent lighting. In 1971 it became the first pedestrian zone, and soon afterwards cafés took over for the summer months what was formerly a major thoroughfare. Graben was once the city moat around the Roman camp, then it became the flower and vegetable market, and from the 17th c. on it was the scene of Court festivities. There are two old fountains, the Joseph Fountain and the Leopold Fountain. Both were altered many times and lead figures by Johann Martin Fischer were added in 1804. Of the many Baroque buildings that surrounded the Graben in the 18th c. only the Bartolotti-Partenfeld Palace (No. 11) remains.

Location
1st District

Underground station
Stephansplatz
(U1, U3)

The shop façade of the jewellers Caesar's by Hollein has long been on the itinerary of tourists interested in art. With its polished granite slab and a mass of metal pipes it is reminiscent of the decorative style of the early Seventies. Other famous shops and boutiques are nearby.

Shops

Also of interest in the Graben are the subterranean Art Nouveau toilets. They were built in 1905 by Adolf Loos and have been renovated to reveal their true glory. The cubicles are lined with wood and marble panels and have gilded fittings.

Curiosity

In the middle of the Graben stands the famous Plague Pillar. This 21m/70ft tall Baroque pillar (also called the "Trinity Pillar") owes its existence to a vow made by Emperor Leopold I. He swore that when the plague ceased he would pay for the erection of a pillar which would reach up to heavens. The plague of 1679 cost 75,000 Viennese their lives, other estimates even reach 150,000. The first plague pillar was erected in the same year. The construction of the definitive Plague Pillar by Matthias Rauchmiller was begun in 1681, continued after his death, which occurred in 1686, by J.B. Fischer von Erlach, and completed in 1693 by Locovico Burnacini. The figure of the Emperor kneeling in prayer is the work of Paul Strudel, that of the Trinity was modelled by Johann Kilian of Augsburg.

★Pestsäule
(Plague pillar)

In 1400 a wealthy cloth merchant, Michael Menschein, had the great hall on the first floor of the house at Tuchlauben 19 (near the Graben square) decorated with frescoes depicting the Minnesänger Neidhart's poetry. In 1715/16 the house was refashioned in the Baroque style and most of the paintings were destroyed and the rest covered with a thick layer of plaster. The frescoes were discovered by accident during renovation work in 1979 and took three years to restore. They are the oldest secular wall paintings in Vienna and an important example of popular art in the late Middle Ages. The walls of the 15 × 7.5m/50 × 25ft hall were originally completely covered; the frescoes depict typical scenes from Neidhart's songs in the cycle of the four seasons.

Neidhart Frescoes
Tuchlauben 19

Opening times
(Tue.–Sun.
9am–12.15pm,
1–4.30pm)

Graben – a popular rendezvous in the heart of the city

Griechenbeisl, an historic inn with ''Lieber Augustin'' on the façade

★Griechenbeisl (inn)   B 5

This historic inn with the figure of "lieber Augustin" on the façade gives rise to the story that some anonymous ballad singer wrote the mocking song "Lieber Augustin" during the plague in 1679 having survived spending the night drunk in the plague grave. In the 15th c. it was called "Zum roten Dach" becoming "Griechenbeisl" in the 18th c. Among the many famous persons to frequent the inn were Wagner, Beethoven, Schubert, Strauss, Brahms, Waldmüller, Grillparzer, Nestroy, Schwind and Count Zeppelin. It has been proved that Mark Twain wrote "The Million Pound Note" in a room at Griechenbeisl. The walls of the Mark Twain Room are completely covered with the autographs of famous artists.

Daily 10am–1pm.

Location
1, Fleischmarkt 11
Tel. 5 33 19 77

Underground station
Schwedenplatz
(U1, U4)

Trams
1, 2, N, 21

Opening times

★Grinzing   north beyond A 3

The little village of Grinzing is first mentioned in records in 1114. It was destroyed by the Turks in 1529 and there was a great fire in 1604. The village was destroyed again by the Turks in 1683, and in 1809 by the French. Nowadays there is another type of destruction caused by the erection of buildings on the vineyards. In order to counter this building it is possible for individuals to purchase 1 sq.m/1sq.yd of land with a vine and the right to the produce. Prominent owners of Grinzing vines include the Pope, Dalia Lama, Jimmy Carter and Sophia Loren.

With its old houses and lanes, nestling in gardens and vineyards, the name Grinzing still to many people all over the world is synonymous with

Location
19th District

Underground station/Bus
U4 or U65
to terminus
Heiligenstadt,
then bus 38A

Tram 38

Grinzing, synonomous with the Viennese "Heurige"

"Viennese Heurige". the word "Heurige" has two meanings: wine made from grapes most recently gathered and thus new wine, but also the place where that wine is drunk. Establishments which are open place branches of spruce over their entrances, and a sign is hung out. Genuine "Heurige" serve only their own wine, and they are open each year for only from three weeks to a maximum of six months. The large "Heurige" in Grinzing and the so-called "Nobel Heurige" are for the most part only pseudo-Heurige. They serve hot and cold meals and their wines often come from Lower Austria. An evening in one of the wine-gardens with a glass of wine surrounded by the wonderful countryside among the vineyards is certainly to be recommended as are walks around nearby Kahlenberg (see entry) and Leopoldsberg (see entry).

Gumpoldskirchen   Excursion

Location
Between Mödling and Baden, 18km/ 11 miles south of Vienna

Train
Gumpoldskirchen (S1, R10)

Bus
from Vienna Central bus station

Amid the vineyards, at the foot of the Anniger, lies Gumpoldkirchen, which is famous for its wine.

There is evidence that wine has been made here for a thousand years, perhaps even for twice as long. Gumpoldskirchen wines – Zierfandler, Rotgipfler and Neuburger – were the first alcoholic beverages to take to the air in the Zeppelin and graced the choice table on the occasion of the coronation of Queen Elizabeth in London.

Visitors generally go to Gumpoldskirchen to drink the new wine in one of the many inns.

The Renaissance Town Hall and the picturesque old houses of the burghers are also noteworthy.

Haydn Museum (with Brahms Memorial Room)   C 3

Location
6, Haydngasse 19

Underground station
Zieglergasse (U3), Westbahnhof (U3, U6)

Bus 57A

Opening times
Tue.–Sun. 9am–12.15pm, 1–4.30pm

Joseph Haydn acquired the single-storey house in the little street known as Steingasse (which later received the name Haydngasse) in 1793. He lived here until his death, and it was here he wrote his oratorios "The Creation" and "The Seasons".

When he died in 1809 shortly after the second occupation of Vienna by the French, Napoleon ordered the posting of a Guard of Honour outside his house.

The museum here was opened in 1899. Among the objects on display are letters, manuscripts and personal possessions as well as two pianos and the deathmask of the composer.

Also in the house is a memorial room to Brahms, with mementoes and furniture from the composer's last home and a pictorial record of his later life and works.

Heeresgeschichtliches Museum (Museum of Military History)   D 5

Location
3, Arsenalstrasse, Objekt 18

Underground station
Südtiroler Platz (U1)

The Museum of Military History is housed in the oldest building in Vienna to have been designed specifically as a museum. It contains valuable collections of militaria and historical relics concerned with the history of the army and of warfare in Austria from the outbreak of the Thirty Years' War to the First World War. It was Emperor Franz Joseph I who commissioned the museum and Ludwig Förster and Theophil Hansen who, between 1850 and 1857, erected a building inspired by Byzantine architectural styles.

Car in which Archduke was assassinated

1920s training aircraft

Ground floor

On the ground floor are the Hall of the Field Marshals, the Navy Room to the left, the Emperor Franz Joseph Room and the Heavy Artillery Room to the right. The Hall of the Field Marshals contains 36 life-size marble statues of Austrian rulers and military commanders. The Navy Room has an impressive collection of model ships which recount the history of the Imperial (later the Royal and Imperial) Navy. The exhibits include a model of the "Novara" which circumnavigated the globe and a model of the longitudinal section (to a scale of 1:25) of the Austrian Navy's First World War battleship "Viribitus Unitis" which was launched in 1911. The Franz Joseph Room recalls the era of the Emperor with portraits, the insignia of the family Orders, pennants and uniforms. In an adjoining room stands the motor car in which the heir to the throne, Archduke Franz Ferdinand, and his wife tragically lost their lives when attacked by an assassin in Sarajevo on June 28th 1914. Other mementoes are the Archduke's uniform, pictures and documents. The Heavy Artillery Room has a display of the monarchy's heaviest guns from the period between 1859 and 1916. The most impressive is an M16 38cm/15in. motorised howitzer. The Artillery Halls, Objekte 2 and 17, contain the largest collection of guns in the world. Most of them date from the 16th and 18th c.

First Floor

The first floor houses the Commemorative Rooms: the Radetzky Room and the Archduke Charles Room are on the right, and on the left is the Prince Eugene Room and the Maria Theresa Room. The Hall of Fame is a domed chamber with frescoes illustrating the most important military events in Austrian history. The Radetzky Room is devoted to the period between Napoleon's downfall and the 1848 Revolutions and to the memory of Field Marshal Radetzky. Relics of the Duke of Reichstadt, Napoleon's son, are displayed in a showcase. The Archduke Charles Room recalls the Napoleonic era by means of pictures by Peter Krafft. There is a hot-air balloon (a

S Bahn station
Südbahnhof
(S1, S2, S3, S7, S15)

Bus
13A, 69A

Opening times
Mon.–Thur., Sat., Sun. 10am–4pm

73

"Montgolfière") which was captured from the French, and a Russian officer's greatcoat which Napoleon is said to have worn when he was exiled to Elba. The Prince Eugene Room has a display of weapons and armour from the period of the Thirty Years' War and the wars against the Turks. There are also 15 battle scenes by the Court Painter Peter Sneyer. Mementoes of Prince Eugene include his breastplate, his Marshal's baton and his shroud. The Maria Theresa Room illustrates the events of the War of the Spanish Succession and the last wars against the Turks. The Turkish Tent of State was probably captured at Peterwardein in 1716. The mortar did great service at the Siege of Belgrade in 1717. The central showcase shows the institution of the Order of Maria Theresa after the Battle of Kolin in 1757.

Heiligenkreuz

Excursion

Location
34km/19 miles
south-west of
Vienna

The prettiest route to Heligenkreuz goes through the village of Perchtoldsdorf with its vineyards and Trinity Pillar by J. B. Fischer von Erlach on the Main square, the friendly little town of Mödling and through the Hinterbrühl Valley (with an underground grotto by the lake and the historic Höldrichsmühle Inn).

**★Heiligenkreuz
monastery**

Bus
from Wien-Mitte
(1092, 1093, 1094)

Austria's second oldest Cistercian abbey, founded in 1133, takes its name from the relic of a cross which an Austrian duke presented to the monks of the monastery. The collegiate church, the last resting place of several members of the House of Babenberg, was built in the 12th c. The buildings were renovated in the 17th and 18th c. and enlarged by the addition of a large courtyard with a two-storey arcade and a gate-tower. The richly decorated Trinity Column and the Joseph Fountain are modelled on the work of the Venetian Baroque sculptor Giovanni Giuliani (1663–1744) who lived in the monastery from 1711 until his death. On the west façade of the triple-naved church is a group of three windows typical of Cistercian churches. The Romanesque long house, with massive pillars, is in stark contrast to the bright Gothic choir with valuable 13th c. stained glass windows. The richly carved choir stalls are 18th c. On the south side of the church are the cloisters built between 1220–50 in the transitional style from Romanesque to Gothic which can only be seen as part of a tour. The 300 pillars are made of red marble. Also interesting are the grave stones and the tracery windows overlooking the cloisters, mostly grey-coloured. In the adjoining Chapter House can be seen the gravestone of Frederick II, the last Babenberg Duke, who fell in battle against the Hungarians in 1246. In the west wing of the courtyard are illustrations from the 13th to 16th c. together with 150 clay models by the Venetian Baroque sculptor Giuliani. The well-stocked monastery library contains precious hand-written medieval manuscripts.

Mayerling
hunting lodge

About 6km/4 miles south-west of Heilienkreuz is Schloss Mayerling, now a Carmelite convent. Crown Prince Rudolf of Austria and his lover Maria Vetsera committed suicide here on January 1st 1889 – the exact details are still unknown. The room of the unfortunate prince, who is buried in the Capuchin vault, was later turned into a Death Chapel.

Heiligenkreuzerhof

B 5

Location
1, Schönlatern-
gasse 5

**Underground
station**
Stephansplatz
(U1, U3)

The present Heiligenkreuzerhof complex, consisting of the abbey church, the prelacy, the counting-house and the courtyard, lies in the historic quarter between Schönlaterngasse (see entry) and Grasshofgasse. The Heiligenkreuzerhof was erected between 1659 and 1676 at the behest of the Abbots of the Monastery of Heiligenkreuz (see entry). Considerable alterations were made in 1746 when the complex took on the appearance it has at present. The counting-house was not built until 1754. The Baroque

Heiligenkreuzerhof

painter Martino Altomonte lived here in the monastery until his death in 1745. He spent his declining years here and painted the picture above the High Altar in the Bernard Chapel near the prelacy in 1730. The wonderful Baroque room is used for weddings.

Heiligenstadt — north beyond A 3/4

Heiligenstadt, incorporated in Döbling in 1892, is the oldest and prettiest of the Viennese wine-producing villages.

Location
19th District

Its narrow winding streets have helped to keep it free from too much bustle. In the area around Probusgasse and Armbrustergasse it is still possible to see how the place used to look, with its vineyards and Empire and early 19th c. houses.

Underground station
Heiligenstadt (U4, U6)

St Jacob's Church on the Pfarrplatz was built in Romanesque times on Roman foundations; although frequently destroyed, altered and rebuilt, it is still worth seeing.

S Bahn station
Heiligenstadt (S9)

Tram D

Beethoven stayed in Heiligenstadt on several occasions including the autumn of 1802 while working on his Second Symphony. He wrote his "Heiligenstadt Testament", a letter to his brothers Carl and Johann which he never sent, at 6 Probusgasse. The house is under the administration of the Vienna City Historical Museum (open: Tue.–Sun. 9am–12.15pm and 1–4.30pm). In 1817 he was once more living in Heiligenstadt, this time at 2 Pfarrplatz, where he worked on his Pastoral Symphony.

★Beethoven memorial

★Historisches Museum der Stadt Wien (Vienna City Historical Museum) — C 4

Founded in 1888, the Vienna City Historical Museum was first housed in the New Town Hall but was transferred to Karlspaltz in 1959. The extensive

Location
4, Karlsplatz 8

St Jacob, the patron saint of Heiligenstadt   *A "Heurige" in the town*

**Underground
station**
Karlsplatz
(U1, U2, U4)

Bus
4A, 59A

Trams
1, 2, D, J, 62, 65
71

Opening times
Tue.–Sun.
9am–4.30pm

collections display clearly the history of the city of Vienna throughout
various periods.

Ground floor
Neolithic Period–Time of Tribal Migrations. Finds from the Stone Age,
Bronze and Iron Ages and the time of the Tribal Migrations. The most
important exhibits are a painted Sequani gravestone (2nd c.), a Roman
altar and an ancient treasury.

Middle Ages and Late Middle Ages. Views of the city and plans illustrating its development. The Albertinischer Plan is considered to be the oldest
plan of the city of Vienna. There are stone fragments and valuable architectural remains from St Stephen's Cathedral. These were removed during
restoration and carefully preserved. Among them are an early Gothic Anna
Selbdritt (about 1320), three larger-than-life size pairs of Princes (about
1360–65), Gothic stained glass from the Duke's Chapel and the remains of
an altar of lime wood (14th c.)

Collections of weapons from armouries and arsenal. Among the exhibits
are suits of armour, shields, spears and halberds, and also the oldest Italian
horse armour and the funeral arms of Frederick III.

First floor
History of Vienna in the 16th c. to early 19th c. The 16th c. was a warlike
century, and the exhibits include weapons, armour, such as the gilt armour
of Imperial princes, ensigns, orders and battle princes.

Counter Reformation to the Great War against the Turks. The life of
Vienna in the 17th c. is represented in portraits, medallions, coats of arms
and etchings and engravings. An exceptional suit of armour recalls the
Thirty Years' War, and the Turkish ensigns are mementos of Prince
Eugene's victory over the Turks at Zenta.

The transition from Baroque to Classicism and City life in the 18th c. The
views of Vienna by Delsenbach are particularly interesting, as are the guild

Historical Museum of the City of Vienna

From c. 1800 to the Present Day

SECOND FLOOR

SECOND FLOOR
1 Pompeian Salon
2 First half of the 19th c.
3 Second half of the 19th c.
4 1848 Revolution
5 Grillparzer's Apartments
6 Theatre
7 Model of city as in 1898
8 Loos's living-room
9 Otto Wagner
10 Painting about 1900
11 20th c.

From 1500 to c. 1800

FIRST FLOOR

FIRST FLOOR
1–4 History of the City from the
16th to the beginning
of the 19th c.: weapons,
Turkish Siege; views of city,
pictures, porcelain, etc.
5 Model of the Inner City in
1852–54
6–7 Castle of Laxenburg

Neolithic Period to 1500

GROUND FLOOR

GROUND FLOOR
1 Prehistory, Roman period,
Tribal Migrations, temporary
exhibitions
2–4 Middle Ages (maps of the city,
views, architectural fragments
from St Stephen's Cathedral
stained glass), Weapons and
armour
Temporary exhibitions

booths, the old house signs and traders' signs and the Baroque paintings, sculptures and prints.

Second floor
Napoleonic era. Medallions from the reign of Francis II. The Caprara Grey-müller Empire Salon. This "Pompeian Salon" with its gold, white and pastel shades, tells us about the environment in which the nobility lived about 1800.

The Congress of Vienna, the early 19th c. (Biedermeier period), pre-1848 period and Revolution. There are a great number of paintings here with all the Viennese painters of the Biedermeier period represented (Fendi, Schindler, Danhauser, Gauermann, Rieter, Waldmüller and Amerling). There are displays of the fashions of the day, glass and porcelain, a survey of Viennese Biedermeier period social games, Lanner's giraffe piano and Fanny Elssler's butterfly grand piano. The time of the Revolution is evoked in prints and paintings, and weapons of the National Guard are on show.

Foundation period (mid 19th c.). This is illustrated by portraits and relics, in handicrafts and busts. Theatrical life of the period is evoked, as well.

Franz Grillparzer's Apartments. When the house at 21 Spiegelgasse was demolished, everything was brought here and the apartments were set up with careful attention to detail. The living room of the architect Loos. This is one of the most outstanding examples of Viennese interior design from the early 20th c.

Jugendstil (Viennese Art Nouveau). The most important exhibits include paintings by Klimt and Schiele and designs by Kolo Moser. There is also a sculpture by Rodin.

Vienna between the wars and during the Second World War. Documentation concerning the history of the period and modern art. There are works by Wotruba. Kokoschka, Herbert Böckl, Rudolf Hausner and Albert Paris Gütersloh.

History in pictures: mainly portraits of important personalities.

★★Hofburg   B/C 4

Location
1, Michaelerplatz 1,
Burgring

Underground station
Stephansplatz
(U1, U3),
Herrengasse
(U3), Maria-
hilfer Strasse
(U2)

Bus
48A, 57A

Trams
1, 2, D, J

The Imperial Castle in the inner city was for more than six centuries the seat of the ruler of Austria. From here the Habsburgs ruled until the end of the First World War in 1918. European history was written in this seat of power, from here Empress Maria Theresa carried out her policies and bewailed the military defeats against Prussia's Frederick the Great. It was here that Joseph II introduced his progressive reforms and Franz Joseph ruled for 68 years until the downfall of his empire. For two and a half centuries until 1806 it was the seat of the German Emperor and today it is the official seat of the Austrian Head of State. The Federal President of Austria exercises his office and carries out representative functions in rooms once belonging to Maria Theresa and Joseph II.

The complex consists of ten major buildings and in them may be seen the reflection of the 700-year-long architectural history of the Hofburg. Nearly every Austrian ruler since 1275 ordered additions or alterations to be made to the palace. Accordingly in the Hofburg examples may be seen of architecture in a great variety of styles – Gothic, Renaissance, Baroque, Rococo, Classicism and the early 1870s. Together with its squares and gardens the entire Hofburg complex occupies an area of some 240,000sq.m/59 acres. This "city within a city" comprises 18 ranges of buildings, 54 major staircases, 19 courtyards and 2,600 rooms. Some 5000 people are employed here.

In November 1992 a major fire damaged a large part of the Hofburg, notably the 18th c. Redoutensäle (Redoubt Rooms). The frescoes in the Reading Room of the National Library were also partly damaged in the attempts to extinguish the fire, as was part of the Court Riding School but this was repaired by 1994. During the repair work, which is expected to last

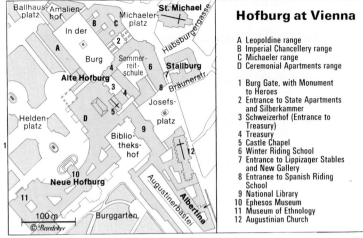

Hofburg at Vienna

A Leopoldine range
B Imperial Chancellery range
C Michaeler range
D Ceremonial Apartments range

1 Burg Gate, with Monument to Heroes
2 Entrance to State Apartments and Silberkammer
3 Schweizerhof (Entrance to Treasury)
4 Treasury
5 Castle Chapel
6 Winter Riding School
7 Entrance to Lippizaner Stables and New Gallery
8 Entranee to Spanish Riding School
9 National Library
10 Ephesos Museum
11 Museum of Ethnology
12 Augustinian Church

until 1997, the access to the Winter Riding School is via a temporary entrance in the square.

Castle layout

Schweizerhof or Schweizertrakt is the name commonly given to the Alte Burg (Old Castle). There is evidence that it has been here since 1279. Ferdinand I had the buildings reconstructed in the style of a Renaissance castle between about 1547 and 1552. The massive Schweizertor (Swiss Gate) dates from this period. All the emperors resided in the Burg from Ferdinand I's time until 1916.

Alte Burg

The present chapel castle was constructed on the orders of Emperor Ferdinand III between 1447 and 1449. In the 17th and 18th c. there were alterations and additions in the Baroque style. More changes were made in the 19th c. when the interior was reconverted to the Gothic style in 1802. Maria Theresa had the old wooden altars replaced by marble ones, but the present High Altar dates from 1802. The tabernacle contains Ferdinand II's miraculous cross; according to legend it inspired him with courage during the Wars of Religion. The Burgkapelle is now a much-favoured and distinguished setting for weddings. The cynics say that the thirteen 500-year-old wooden statues of the "Helpers in time of need" – the fourteenth was removed to make space for the pulpit – are in the right place in a church used in marriages. (Tours: Tue., Thur. 2.30–3.30pm every 15 mins., except Jul. to mid.-Sept and mid.-Dec. to mid.-Jan.)

Burgkapelle

The boys' choir was originally founded to sing in the Burgkapelle used by the Imperial Court. The Vienna Boys' Choir developed from this and together with members of the State Opera Choir sing at Sunday Mass and on religious holidays (9.15am except July–mid.-Sept.; pre-booking essential, tel. 5 33 99 27).

Vienna Boys' Choir

The Inner Courtyard was used by the Emperor Maximilian II as a tilt-yard as early as 1545. Later it was the site of tourneys, festivities and executions. In 1846 a monument was erected to the memory of Emperor Francis II. On its plinth may be read a line from his will: "My life is for my peoples".

Innerer Burghof

Memorial to Emperor Francis II in the Inner Courtyard

Stallburg

In 1558 Emperor Ferdinand I ordered the construction of a Renaissance palace, one of the most important Renaissance buildings in Vienna, for the particular use of his son Maximilian. When Maximilian became Emperor and moved into the Hofburg, Maximilian's palace was converted into Court mews. Since the time of Charles VI the stables for the Lipizzaner horses of the Spanish Riding School (see entry) have occupied the ground floor. (Not open to the public.)

Amalienburg

Following the example of his father, Maximilian II had a palace built between 1575 and 1577 for the particualr use of his son. He was called Rudolf, hence the name Rudolfsburg. The upper floor was added in the 17th c. and the tower rebuilt. In the 18th c., however, the name was changed to Amalienburg when the Empress Wilhelmine Amalie lived here during her widowhood. The rooms were later used by the Empress Elizabeth and Tsar Alexander I were furnished as State Apartments.

Leopoldinischer Trakt

The Leopoldinischertrakt is a range of Baroque buildings, constructed at the behest of Emperor Leopold I, Maria Theresa's grandfather, which connects the Schweizerhof and the Amalienburg. The buildings were erected between 1660 and 1680 and were occupied by Maria Theresa and her husband Francis Stephen of Lorraine. Their apartments together with those of Joseph II opposite them, now form part of the Presidential Chancellery. The Austrian President works in what was formerly Joseph II's study.

Reichskanzlertrakt

The Imperial Chancellery range constitutes the north-east wing linking the Schweizerhof and the Amalienburg. It was designed by Hildebrandt in 1723 and completed by J. E. Fischer von Erlach, who gave it the Baroque façade in 1730. Some of its rooms are set out as State Apartments.

Winterreitschule

The Winter Riding School, where the Spanish Riding School gives its equestrian displays, was the scene of numerous glittering events, especially during the Congress of Vienna in 1814 and 1815. This handsome white room was designed by J. E. Fischer von Erlach at the behest of Emperor Charles VI. The coffered ceiling spans an arena in which the horses exercise and which is 55m/175ft long and 18m/60ft wide. The gallery is borne on 46 pillars. The arena may be visited in July and August.

The Michaeler range was the site of the Hofburg Theatre until 1888. After its demolition Emperor Franz Joseph I went back to the old plan drawn up by J. E. Fischer von Erlach and ordered the construction of a range of buildings linking the Reichskanzleitrakt and the Winterreitschule. This was done between 1889 and 1893. The grandiose Michaelertor (Michael Gate) which is flanked by figures of Hercules leads into the domed chamber. The figures in the niches symbolise the mottoes of various rulers: "Constantia et Fortitudine" (With Constance and Fortitude – Emperor Charles VI), "Justitia et Clementia" (Justice and Mercy – Maria Theresa), "Virtuete et Exemplo" (By Might and Example – Joseph II) and "Viribus Unitus" (With all our Strength United – Franz Joseph I). In the hallway are the entrances to the Silver Room and to the State Apartments.

Michaelertrakt

In 1804 Francis I ordered the reconstruction of the oldest part of the castle to provide a ceremonial suite in Classical style. The area of the chamber is 1000sq.m/1220 sq.yd. The magnificent coffered ceiling is supported on 24 Corinthian columns. It served as throne-room and ballroom.

Hoftafel und Festsaaltrakt

It was here that the Habsburgs formally renounced their rights to the throne in the event of a morganatic marriage (i.e. a marriage to a partner of lower social status). Nowadays the chamber is part of the Hofburg Congress Centre. Each year it provided the fitting setting for the Imperial Ball on New Year's Eve.

Congress Centre

The Heldenplatz (Heroes' Square) was originally the parade ground. After the erection of the two statues, one of Prince Eugenen who defended the

Heldenplatz

The Michaeler range of the Hofburg

On the Heldenplatz, where the landaus begin their nostalgic tour

Turks and the other to Archduke Charles who won the Battle of Aspern, it was given the name Heldenplatz. Both statues are the work of Anton Fernkorn. In the square the fiakers await passengers who wish to take a guided tour of Vienna in a traditional manner.

Äusseres Burgtor

The Outer Gate of the palace was built exclusively by soldiers as in Roman times to plans drawn up by Peter Nobile. It was inaugurated in 1824 on the anniversary of the Battle of Leipzig at which Napoleon was at last defeated and converted into a memorial to heroes in 1933.

Neue Burg

Plans for a vast Imperial Forum and a gigantic New Palace were drawn up by the architects Karl Hasenauer and Gottfried Semper. Emperor Franz Joseph I, however, gave his approval only to the building of a new wing to the palace, and the over-all plan was never carried out. Work on the interior of the New Burg went on until 1926. It has only once been the scene of historic events: it was here that Hitler proclaimed the annexation of Austria in 1938 while the first Austrian resistance fighters were being taken to the German concentration camps. Nowadays museums are housed here: the Museum für Volkerkunde, Ephesus Museum, the Sammlung alter Musikinstrumente (see entries), the Waffen-Sammlung, as well as the new Reading Room and the Archives of the Austrian National Library (see Österreichisch Nationalbibliothek).

Silberkammer (Closed until 1995)

Entrance through the Domed Chamber in Michaelertrakt (Michaelerplatz)

The ceremonial and everyday tableware of the Imperial Court is on display in the so-called "Silver Chamber" where restoration work should be completed by the end of 1994.

Among the treasures in the collection are 18th c. East Asian porcelain, the formal dinner service of the time of Franz Joseph, now used at State receptions, a silver travelling service of the Empress Elisabeth Christine, wife of Charles VI (Paris 1717/1718), three particularly fine 18th c. services of tableware in Sèvres porcelain, gift of the French Court, 18th c. cutlery (Vienna, Paris), the Milanese table centre, nearly 10m/30ft long, made of meticulously carved and gilded bronze, the Meissen service (c. 1775), Viennese Empire service (early 19th c.). The most important service in the collection is the Ruby service for Imperial grand occasions, with settings for 140 guests. It is decorated with silver which was given a gold hue by heat treatment. It was made by a Parisian goldsmith in the early 19th c.. There are also smaller glass services (c. 1850) and plates decorated with pictures and flowers (1800–30), 19th c. tableware, vases decorated with historical scenes, the "English service" which Queen Victoria gave to the Emperor Franz Joseph and a Romantic period service in Neo-Gothic style (Vienna 1821–24).

Imperial Apartments

The State Apartments open to the public in the Hofburg comprise the Franz Joseph Apartments in the Reichskanzleitrakt together with Elisabeth and Alexander's apartments in the Amalienburg.

Entrance
Through the Domed Chamber in the Michaelertrakt

Tours
Mon.–Sat. 9am–4pm, Sun. 9am–noon

It is not possible for visitors to see the living-quarters and ceremonial apartments of Empress Maria Theresa and of her son Emperor Joseph II (the Leopoldinischertrakt) because they comprise the official residence of the Austrian President.

The furnishing of most rooms remains unaltered.

Here the Emperor used to take his meals with his staff officers. The Flemish gobelins currently being restored represent the heroic deeds of Hercules; in their place hang 17th c. Brussels tapestries depicting the myth of Perseus and Andromeda.

Franz-Joseph Apartments
Dining Room

This was where the Court used to meet for conversation after meals in front of the Rococo ceramic stove which was fuelled from the corridor. The 17th c. Brussels tapestries depicting scenes from the life of Emperor Augustus are being restored and in their place are Flemish tapestries from Oudenarde (16th c.) showing the life of King David.

Circle Room

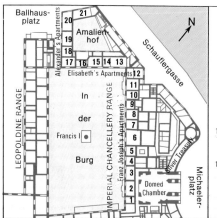

State Apartments in the Hofburg

1 Antechamber
2 Dining-room
3 Circle Room
4 Smoking-room
5 Guardroom
6 Large Audience Chamber
7 Emperor's Audience Chamber
8 Council Chamber
9 Study
10 Bedroom
11/12 Salons
13 Living-room, Bedroom
14 Dressing-room, Gymnastics Room
15/16 Salons
17 Linking Room
18 Antechamber
19 Red Salon
20 Crown Prince Rudolf's Study
21 Banqueting Hall

Hofburg

Smoking Room	The tapestries represent scenes from Graeco-Roman history.
Guard Room	In the guard room of the Imperial Life Guards the most interesting exhibit is a model of the old Hofburg.
Large audience chamber	This was the waiting-room for the audiences which took place twice a week. The Bohemian crystal candelabrum with 80 candles is particularly fine as is the Biedermeier painting by Peter Krafft.
Emperor's Audience Room	On a lectern lies a list of people coming to an audience on January 10th 1910. It is said that audiences were conducted with everybody standing. Even the Emperor stood by his desk when he received those who came to an audience.
Council Chamber	It was in this room that the Emperor discussed matters with the Privy Councillors and his Ministers. It is furnished in Empire style.
Study	The rose-wood furniture is in the Louis XV style. The study contains the bust and sabre of Field-Marshal Radetsky who was one of the small select band permitted to appear unannounced before the Emperor.
Bedroom	Franz Joseph I lived simply. He slept in a modest iron bed and took his bath in a wooden tub which was placed in the bedroom. He died at Schönbrunn (see entry).
Large Salon	This room has rose-wood furniture with bronze fittings. Francis Xavier Winterhalter's famous picture shows the Empress Elisabeth in a fine gown with jewelled stars in her hair.
Small Salon	In the former breakfast room may be seen one of the few portraits of Maximilian of Mexico, the Emperor's brother, and a bust of Admiral Tegetoff who brought back from Mexico the body of this unfortunate Prince.
Elisabeth's Apartments Living Room	This is one of the prettiest rooms on the Hofburg. It served as living room and bedroom, with its bureau, reading desk, neo-Gothic altar of Carrera marble and bed. The Spartan iron bed was pushed away during the daytime.
Gymnastics Room	Elisabeth was fanatical about keeping slim and was a superb horsewoman. She, therefore had gymnastic equipment fitted in her dressing-room which, moreover, she used regularly, much to the disgust of the Court.
Large salon	Everything here is splendid. There is Louis XIV furniture, large Sèvres porcelain vases, Romantic landscape paintings and Antonio Canova's marble statue of Napoleon's sister.
Small salon	The showcases contain mementoes of the Empress who was assassinated in Geneva in 1898. There is a photograph of the gown she was wearing on the day she met her death.
Antechamber	The pictures are by Martin van Meytens, Maria Theresa's Court Painter; they portray her children. There is also a life-size statue of the 15-year-old Empress Elisabeth and some fine vases made of Sèvres porcelain.
Alexander Apartments	These take their name from Tsar Alexander I who occupied the rooms during the Congress of Vienna.
Linking Room	The busts are of the last Austrian emperor, Emperor Charles I, and of his consort, Empress Zita.
Red salon	It is also called the "Boucher Salon" because the tapestries were worked by François Boucher. They were presented to Emperor Joseph II by Marie-Antoinette. After 1916 it became Emperor Charles I's Audience Chamber.

A photograph shows the unhappy Crown Prince and there are two portraits of Crown Princess Stefanie and Archduke Franz Ferdinand.

Crown prince
Rudolf Memorial
Room

The Brussels tapestries are 18th c. A special feature of the canopied "Highest Table" which is bedecked with gold and silver is the placing of all the cutlery on the right-hand side of the plate, in accordance with Spanish Court Etiquette.

Banqueting
Room

Secular and Sacred Treasuries

The Treasuries – reopened in 1987 after four years of restoration – contain in 21 rooms the Imperial regalia and relics of the Holy Roman Empire of the German Nation, coronation and chivalric insignia, badges of rank, secular and sacred treasures, and ornaments and mementoes formerly owned by the Habsburgs. It is all of incalculable artistic, historic and material value.

Opening times
Mon., Wed.–Fri.
10am–6pm;
Sat., Sun.
9am–6pm

The origins of the Treasury go back to Ferdinand I's "Kunstkammer" (art chamber). From the 16th c. onwards all the emperors brought their treasures here and kept them in various rooms in the Hofburg. During Charles VI's reign the treasury was moved to the ground floor of the palace. The iron door at the entrance bears the date 1712 and the Emperor's monogram.

After leaving room 8 of the Secular Treasury the visitor passes through the Robes Corridor into the 5 rooms housing the Sacred exhibits. Then, beginning with Room 9, the visitor returns to the Secular Treasury.

The Secular Treasury is housed in 16 rooms, with the collections organised on a thematic basis.

**Secular
Treasury**

Insignia of hereditary fealty. This applied to the Habsburg monarchs who as rulers of Austria had the rank of Archduke until 1804, whereas in the Holy Roman Empire they ruled as Emperors and Kings. The Imperial orb (second half of the 15th c.) was borne by the Emperor Matthias. the sceptre (mid 14th c.) belonged to Charles VI, and the sword of investiture, used at fealty ceremonies, belonged to Maximilian I.

Room 1

The Habsburgs, who remained Holy Roman Emperors until 1806, had their own private insignia made, since the insignia of the Empire was kept in Nuremberg from 1424. On view are the Imperial Crown ("Kaiserliche Hauskrone") of Rudolf II, made by the Court Jeweller Jan Vermeyen (1598–1602) together with the orb and sceptre made in Prague (1612–15).

Room 2

In 1804, with the rise of Napoleon, the Holy Roman Empire came to an end and Francis II proclaimed the hereditary Austrian Empire. Exhibited is his

Room 3

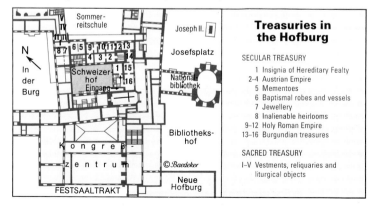

Treasuries in the Hofburg

SECULAR TREASURY

1 Insignia of Hereditary Fealty
2–4 Austrian Empire
5 Mementoes
6 Baptismal robes and vessels
7 Jewellery
8 Inalienable heirlooms
9–12 Holy Roman Empire
13–16 Burgundian treasures

SACRED TREASURY

I–V Vestments, reliquaries and liturgical objects

gold-embroidered mantel with an ermine collar he wore in 1830 when his son was crowned King of Hungary. Also on view are civil orders; the Hungarian Order of St Stephen (1764), the Austrian Order of Leopold (1808) and the Order of the Iron Crown (1815).

Room 4	The Congress of Vienna awarded Austria the Lombardo-Venetian kingdom. The coronation regalia and sword are exhibited, together with a herald's tabard of this kingdom.
Room 5	Mementoes of Mary Louise, daughter of Francis I and consort of Napoleon I. These include a silver jewel box, a silver-gilt trivet presented by the City of Milan on the birth of her son (King of Rome, Duke of Reichsstadt), a silver-gilt cradle given by the city of Paris on the same occasion. There are also mementoes of the Emperor Maximilian of Mexico.
Room 6	Baptismal robes and vessels. Among the exhibits are the baptismal robes given by Maria Theresa. It is said that the Empress herself undertook some of the embroidery. There is also a gold christening flagon and spoon (1571) and a little jug from the Prague Court workshop.
Room 7	Jewellery. Only very little of the Imperial jewellery was preserved. On November 1st 1918 the senior Chamberlain, Count Berchtold, took the Habsburgs private jewellery out of the country at the command of Charles I. On view are the Colombian emerald (2,680 carats), hollowed out to form a salt-cellar and polished (1641) and the hyacinth "la bella" (416 carats), set as a double eagle into enamel, flanked by an opal and an amethyst. A small genealogical tree presents sixteen portraits of the Habsburgs in chalcedony cameos; there are displays of 19th c. jewellery and insignia. There is also the "Golden Rose", a Papal decoration given in 1819 to Carolina Augusta, fourth wife of Francis I, two Turkish sabres used by Charles VI and Maria Theresa at the Hungarian coronation and the crown of Stephen Bocskay who became King of Hungary in 1605.
Room 8	Two items left by King Ferdinand I (1564) were considered so valuable that the Habsburgs raised them to the status of "inalienable heirlooms". They are an agate dish of the 4th c., the largest of its kind that is known and which was once considered to be the vessel of the Holy Grail, and the 243cm/96in. long narwhal's horn which in the Middle Ages was believed to be the horn of the legendary unicorn, a symbol of Christ.
Room 9	Holy Roman Empire. The presence of the regalia of the Electoral Prince of Bohemia is explained by the fact that from the 14th c. the elected king was also King of Bohemia and, therefore, the duties of the electoral office were delegated to a deputy at the coronation festivities. Also on show are pictures and documents of the coronation of Joseph II (1764).
Room 10	Holy Roman Empire. Robes which formed part of the Imperial regalia from the 13th c. came into the possession of the Hohenstaufens; they were presumably used at the coronation of Frederick II and were assigned in 1246 to the Imperial treasury. They include the coronation mantel of King Roger II, made 1133–34, an indigo tunic of the same period, a white robe of 1181 which corresponded to the outer garment of the Byzantine emperor and which was later worn as an alb, red silk stockings of the last Norman king, William II, sumptuous shoes and gloves and a gold-woven sword belt from Sicily. Two items were added in the 14th c. – the eagle dalmatic which was worn instead of the blue tunic, and a stole.
Room 11	Imperial Jewels and Coronation Insignia of the Holy Roman Empire. On view are the Imperial Crown (2nd half of 10th c.), the Sacred Lance, the Processional Cross and the Imperial Cross (1024–25), the orb (end of 12th c.), the Gothic sceptre, the Aspergillum used for sprinkling holy water on the altar and the Imperial Cross (renewed c. 1200). Also exhibited are the

Imperial Gospel, a Carolingian purple codex (end of 8th c.), on which the new ruler took the oath and the sword (first half 10th c.) formerly a relic of Charles the Great with which kings were girded at their coronation.

Here can be seen the sacred relics belonging to the Imperial Treasury. | Room 12

Treasures of the Burgundians. These comprise the treasures of the Order of the Golden Fleece and the inheritance of Maria of Burgundy who married the future Emperor Maximilian. On show are the insignia of the Order, coats of arms and Mass vesels (between 1425 and 1475) as well as the Cross (about 1400) of the Order of the Golden Fleece on which the oath was taken and Philip the Good's Court cup (c. 1453–67). | Rooms 13–16

The five rooms of the Sacred Treasury exhibit liturgical objects, reliquaries and robes which were used at the Imperial Court. | **Sacred Treasury**

18th c. robes and the silver-gilt replica of the Am Hof Maria Column (see Am Hof). | Room I

Medieval objects and the reliquary cross of the Hungarian King Ludwig the Great (between 1370 and 1382). St Stephen's purse, the oldest item in the Sacred Treasury (late 11th or early 12th c.), a Gothic goblet belonging to the Emperor Frederick III (1438). Also to be seen is a collection of reliquaries and small altars of ebony with silver or gold decoration (late 16th–17th c.). | Room II

As well as cut gem stones, Augsburg silver work and rock-crystal there are valuable carvings including crucifixes (Giambologna, Guglielmo della Porta), a crucifixion group (Geremias Geisebrunn), an ebony tempietto (Christoph Angermair). | Room III

Among the most impressive items are the reliquary which holds the nail which is said to have pierced the right hand of Christ, two reliquary altars (1660–80) which belonged to the Emperor Leopold I and the monstrance containing the fragments of the Cross, which were preserved in a miraculous fashion in 1668 when the Hofburg caught fire. | Room IV

18th and 19th c. works including 22 reliquary busts, some of them very large and made of silver, rosaries and a tempietto with one of Peter's teeth. | Room V

★Hoher Markt   B 4/5

The oldest square in Vienna is found on the edge of the textile district (called "Fetzenviertel" by the Viennese, meaning "the rag district"). It is rich with memories that go back to the very start of the city's history. The Romans called it the "old forum"; here stood the palace of the Commander of the Roman fortress of Vindobona, and it is here that Emperor Marcus Aurelius died. In the Middle Ages executions were carried out here. It was the Reuthof of the Babenbergers, the fish market and the trading-site favoured by the cloth-sellers. After the destruction resulting from the events of 1945 nearly all the houses in the Hoher Markt had to be rebuilt.

The focal point of the square is the Espousals Fountain donated by Leopold I. The decoration of the figures, showing the espousal of Mary and Joseph, is by Antonio Corradini. Johann B. Fischer von Erlach erected the original fountain which was made of wood. In 1792 it was remade in white marble by his son.

On the east side of the square it is impossible not to see the splendid clock of the Anker Insurance Company on the archway spanning Rotgasse. Every hour historical figures solemnly go past in order from 1 to 12: Emperor Marcus Aurelius, Charlemagne, Duke Leopold IV and Theodore of Byzantium, the poet Walter von der Vogelweide, King Rudolf I with his consort,

Location
1, Hoher Markt/
Rotenturm-Strasse-
Wipplingerstrasse

Underground station
Stephansplatz
(U1, U3)
Schwedenplatz
(U1, U4)

Trams
1, 2

Anker Clock

Hotel Sacher

Espousals Fountain on the Hoher Markt

The Anker Clock, in Art Nouveau design

Anna of Hohenburg, Master Hans Puchsbaum, Emperor Maximilian I, Mayor A. von Liebenberg, Count Rüdiger von Starhemberg, Prince Eugene, Empress Maria Theresa with Emperor Francis I and Joseph Haydn. At noon all the figures form up and process, accompanied by music. This remarkable clock was built by the painter Franz von Matsch at the beginning of the First World War. It is dedicated to the "people of Vienna".

Roman ruins

A stairway by house No. 3 leads down to underground ruins dating from the Roman period. It is possible to see the footings of walls of houses for officers in the neighbourhood of the barracks of Vindobona (2nd and 3rd c.). There are also remains of a Germanic house (4th c.), as well as casts of reliefs, stamped tiles, remnants of a palisade and, in showcases, various remains (open: Tue.–Sun. 9am–12.15pm and 1–4.30pm).

★Hotel Sacher   C 4

Location
1, Philharmo-
nikerstr. 4

Underground station
Stephansplatz
(U1, U3),
Karlsplatz
(U1, U2, U4)

Trams
1, 2, D, J

Vienna's most famous old-world hotel still preserves its style and quality, with silk tablecloths, Biedermeier furniture from the mid 19th c. and valuable pictures. Important state receptions still take place in the nostalgic marble hall. Eduard Sacher had the hotel built in 1876. But his cigar-smoking wife Anna Sacher became more famous than he did. She used to allow unlimited credit to the offspring of rich parents – the so-called "Sacher lads" – until they came into their inheritances. She also organised those discreet little "séparées" which have survived at any rate in Arthur Schnitzler's "Abschiedssouper" (The Farewell Supper). Now the famous "separate rooms" have become little dining-rooms.

The legendary Sachertorte is said to have been created by one of Eduard Sacher's predecessors on the occasion of the Congress of Vienna in 1814 – however, the source of the original recipe is still contested in the courts by

Hotel Sacher, Vienna's famous hotel

The Hundertwasserhaus

its competitor Demel (see entry). The cakes are on sale in all sizes and boxes in a tiny shop around the corner in Kärtner Strasse.

★Hundertwasserhaus

B/C 6

At the request of the mayor of Vienna, Leopold Graz, the painter Friedensreich Hundertwasser let his imagination take over and designed the "nature and human-friendly" house on the corner of Löwengasse/Kegelstrasse in 1977. It was built between 1983–85 by the city administration as council housing, although the rents are not necessarily low. The main occupants are artists and intellectuals which pleased Hundertwasser "If privileged people move in here then it proves to me that the house is good". The brightly-coloured apartments can only be seen from the outside in consideration for the residents, in contrast to the nearby Kunsthaus Wien (see entry), also by Hundertwasser, which opened its doors in 1991.

There are 50 apartments of various sizes, outlook and structure in the complex which also contains a terrace café, doctor's surgery and health food store.

In line with the artist's economic principles only brick and wood were used in the complex, no plastic materials. Each apartment has its own colour and round the whole edifice runs a 5km/3mile-long ceramic band, joining the apartments and at the same time separating them by an individual colour. In general Hundertwasser follows the principle of "the tolerance of irregularity", so that all corners are rounded, the windows are of different sizes; internally bathrooms are irregularly tiled, corridor floors uneven and the walls wavy (on the lowest storey the wall provides a surface on which children can scribble and paint). The façades of the complex imitate those of the aristocratic palaces and houses on the Grand Canal in Venice. In addition a piece of the old house was incorporated into

Location
3, Kegelgasse/
Löwenstrasse

**Underground/
S-Bahn
station**
Wien/Mitte/
Landstrasse
(U3, U4, S7)

Tram
N

the façade so that the "spirit of the old house resettles into the new one" and places it under its protection.

Two golden "onion towers" surmount the building which according to Hundertwasser, raises the occupier to the status of a king. Lively elements are the coloured crooked pillars, the fountain and the figural decoration, all copies of originals.

Kalke
Village

Opposite the Hundertwasserhaus in Kegelgasse a turn-of-the-century house was converted by Peter Pelikan and Hundertwasser in 1990–91 into an irregularly-shaped shopping arcade in the artist's typical imaginative design.

★ Josefsplatz   C 4

Location
1, Augustiner-
strasse

Underground
station
Herrengasse (U3)

The Josefsplatz is deservedly called the finest square in Vienna. It is 200 years old, was built in a unified Late Baroque style and creates a fine impression. Round it stands the Österreichische National Bibliothek (see entry), the Winterreitschule (see Hofburg), the Palais Pálffy (see entry) and the Palais Pallavicini. A fire in the Redouten tract of the Hofburg (see entry) in 1992 required extensive rebuilding in the square which is now completed.

Palais
Pallavicini

The Palais Pallavicini (No. 5), now a club and conference centre, is a noble Classical building with a magnificent portal supported on caryatides and figures on the metopes dating from 1786 by F. A. Zauner. The Palais itself was built by Ferdinand von Hoheneberg in 1783–84.

Memorial to
Joseph II

The memorial in the middle of the square shows Maria Theresa's son, Joseph II; it is by A. Zauner and dates from 1795 to 1806. The reformer, clad

Joseph II, the great reformer

Portal of the Palais Pallavicini

in the garb of a Roman emperor, is shown blessing his people. The reliefs on the memorial celebrate Joseph's services to Austrian commerce and recall the many journeys he made abroad in order to benefit his people. The memorial became the spot where Viennese people loyal to the Imperial principle gathered in 1848 while the Revolution was in progress. It was their homage to an Emperor who had died half a century earlier.

★Josephinium (Institute of the History of Medicine)   B 4

The palatial Late Baroque Josephinium was built between 1783 and 1785 and designed by Isidor Canevale for the training of doctors and surgeons. It was remodelled in 1822. It was elevated to the status of military academy in 1854 and from 1918 it has housed the Institute of the History of Medicine and the Pharmacognostic Institute of Medicine. In the court of Honour there is a fountain with the figure of Hygeia and a lead statue by J. M. Fischer from 1787.

The world-famous collection of anatomical and obstetric models (anatomia plastica) in wax was commissioned by Joseph II from Tuscan sculptors and provide an unusual but fascinating collection for the study of the human body.

There is an experimental apothecary's collection which is protected for its historical significance and also a great collection of drugs and remedies.

Location
9, Währinger Str. 25/1

Underground station
Schottentor (U2)

Trams
37, 38, 40, 41, 42, 43, 44

Opening times
Mon.–Fri. 9am–3pm

Judenplatz   B 4

The Judenplatz (Jews' Square) was the centre of Vienna's Jewish Quarter from 1294 to 1421.

Here stood the rabbi's house, the hospital, school and synagogue, and here too Jewish traders, bankers and scholars went about their business until 1420 when the 800 inhabitants were driven away or murdered.

Haus "Zum grossen Jordan"
One of the most remarkable houses in the square is Haus "Zum grossen Jordan" (No. 2; 15th c.) which serves as a reminder of the 210 Jews who were burnt to death on the Gänseheide in 1421.
   A descendant of the original owner Jörg Jordan sold the house to the Jesuits, but it has been in private ownership since 1684. The building material from the synagogue which was demolished in 1421 was used to build the Old University. Towards the end of the 16th c. a Jewish community re-established itself in Vienna and was moved to Leopoldstadt (see entry) by Ferdinand II.

Also of interest are the Lessing Memorial by Siegfried Charoux, which was reproduced by the artist in 1968 based on the melted-down original from 1935, the Tailors' Guild House (No. 8) and the Böhmische Kanzlei (see entry) in Wipplinger Strasse whose rear façade bounds the Judenplatz on one side. From the west corner of the square Drahtgasse leads throught to Am Hof (see entry).

Location
1, Jordangasse/ Drahtgasse

Underground station
Schwedenplatz (U1, U4)

Trams 1, 2

Lessing Memorial

★Jüdisches Museum (Jewish Museum)   B 4

The new Jewish Museum was opened in mid-November 1993 by Vienna's mayor Helmut Zilk and the mayor of Jerusalem Teddy Kollek, who was born in Vienna.

Location
1, Dorotheer- gasse 11

Jüdisches Museum

Torah inscription in the Jewish Museum

Underground station
Stephansplatz
(U1, U3)

Opening times
Sun.–Fri.
10am–6pm
Thur. until 9pm

Tours
Thur. 7pm,
Sun. 11, 11.30am,
2, 3.30pm

The museum is housed in a classical Baroque palace in the Altstadt, which dates back to the 11th c. when it was separated from the neighbouring Dorotheer seminary. Aristocratic names are found in the register such as Harrach, Dietrichstein or Kaunitz. In 1823 it fell into the ownership of the banking house Arnstein and Eskeles which was one of the most respected institutions of its time and co-founder of the Austrian National Bank. The wives of the Imperial money-lenders, the sisters Cäcilie Eskeles and Fanny Arnstein from Berlin, ran elegant salons where Viennese society and famous poets, musicians, painters and intellectuals rubbed shoulders.

From 1827 the palace was owned by Count Nako de Szent Mikols; in 1896 the art dealer Hugo Miethke ran an art gallery here where, after 1900, Viennese artists such as Klimt, Scile, van Gogh and Picasso exhibited.

Since 1936 the Palais Eskeles has belonged to the Dorotheum (see entry) and for decades served as an exhibition hall for art auctions before it was given to the Jewish Museum to bring the history of the relationship between Jews and non-Jews in Austria and Europe closer to visitors and to provide a meeting-place where Jews and non-Jews can come together at symposia, films and musical events.

Exhibitions

The Viennese Jewish Museum has various temporary exhibitions on specific themes. As well as general Jewish topics, e.g. exhibitions on Jewish Vienna, eastern Jewry and Viennese salon culture, literature, architecture, photography and modern art are featured.

From 1996 a permanent Judaic Collection will be open to the public which will be based on three larger collections of inestimable worth already in existence: the Max Berger collection comprising over 10,000 works of art, the collection of the Israeli cultural community which was dispersed by the Nazis in 1938 and the Martin Schlaff collection, donated in 1993, of 5000 objects on the topic of anti-Semitism, making the complete exhibition unique in Europe.

★Kahlenberg

Kahlenberg stands 484m/1585ft high. It is, so to speak, Vienna's own "mountain" and virtually the last part of the Vienna Woods to the east. There is a magnificent view from the terrace with its fine Heurige restaurant. Nearby are the vineyards of Grinzing (see entry) and Nussdorf, and farther off, beyond the city and the Marchfeld, the Little Carpathians and the Schneeberg region. On the summit of the Kahlenberg stands a television tower and the recently restored 22m/72ft-high Stephanie Observatory (125 steps to the top; open Sun., pub. hols. 9am–6pm) which was a gift from Crown Princess Stephanie in the 1880s, designed by Fellner and Helmer who were the architects of the Viennese theatres and the Ringstrasse. It was from up here that in 1683 the relieving army of the Polish Prince Sobieski brought aid at the eleventh hour to the city of Vienna which was being besieged and almost overrun by the Turks for a second time. The event is commemorated by the Sobieski Chapel in the little Baroque Church of St Joseph.

Poets and composers have always had a soft spot for Kahlenberg. The fact that it was once called "Sow Hill", presumably on account of the numbers of wild boar in the dense oak woods, was forgotten long ago. Grillparzer wrote: "If you have seen the land all around from the top of Kahlenberg, you will understand what I have written and what I am".

Location
19th District

Underground station/Bus
Heiligenstadt (U4, U6), then bus 38A

Tram/Bus
Grinzing (38), then bus 38A

Kapuzinerkirche (church)

C4

The Capuchin Church dedicated to Our Lady of the Angels, is as befits a Mendicant Order vowed to poverty, modest, sober and almost totally lacking in ornamentation. Nothing visible reminds us that it was founded by an empress (Empress Anna) in 1618. The most precious work of art in the church is a "Pietà" near the altar in the right-hand transept. It is by Peter von Strudel, the Founder of the Academy of Fine Arts.

Location
1, Neuer Markt

Underground station
Stephansplatz (U1, U3)

★★Imperial Vault (Capuchin Vault)

On the left-hand side of the church is the entrance to the Imperial Vault. Beneath the Church of the Capuchins lie the Habsburg family vault where 138 members of the House lie buried. Since 1633 all the Austrian Emperors have been buried here, with just a few exceptions. (Ferdinand II was buried at Graz, Frederick III in St Stephen's Cathedral (see entry–Stephansdom), and Charles I, the last Emperor, at Funchal in Madeira where he had gone as an exile.) The coffins contain only the embalmed bodies without the internal organs (see Stephansdom) and the hearts (see Augustinerkirche).

The nine vaults are arranged in chronological order which makes it easy to trace the evolution of taste. Unfortunately the bronze caskets dating from the 17th and 18th c. have been attacked by decay, which necessitates extremely expensive conservation work.

Opening times
daily 9.30am–4pm

Emperor Matthias, who died in 1619, and Empress Anna, who died in 1618, are considered to be the inaugurators of the family vault. Originally they were laid to rest in the monastery of St Dorothea, and their bodies were the first to be transferred to the Imperial Vault in 1633.

Tombs
Founder's Vault

The Leopoldine Vault is called the Angel Vault for among the 16 bronze caskets are 12 in which children were laid to rest. Ferdinand III, who died in 1657, is also buried here. Balthasar Ferdinand Moll's casket for Elenore of Pfalz-Neuburg who died in 1720 made such a favourable impression on the Emperor that Moll, a Professor at the Academy for Fine Art, spent half the time of his remaining years working on sarcophagi.

Leopoldine Vault

Johann Lucas von Hildebrandt designed the sarcophagi for Leopold I (d. 1704) and for Joseph I (d. 1711). B. F. Moll designed the sarcophagus of

Caroline Vault

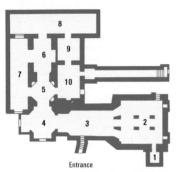

Entrance

Imperial (or Capuchin) Vault

1. FOUNDERS' VAULT (1622–33) – Emperor Matthias I (d. 1619), Empress Anna (d.1618)
2. LEOPOLDINE VAULT (1657 and 1701 – 16 sarcophagi, 12 for children
3. CAROLINE VAULT (1720) – 7 sarcophagi
4. MARIA THERESA VAULT (1754) – double sarcophagus for Empress Maria Theresa (d. 1780) and Francis of Lorraine (d. 1765)
5. FRANCIS II VAULT (1824)
6. FERDINAND VAULT (1842)
7. TUSCAN VAULT (1842)
8. NEW VAULT (1960–62 – 26 sarcophagi
9. FRANZ JOSEPH VAULT (1909) – Franz Joseph I (d. 1916), Empress Elisabeth (d. 1898), Ex Empress Zita (d. 1989)
10. Chapel: In the chapel is a memorial tablet to Emperor Charles I (d. 1922)

Charles VI (d. 1740); a magnificent work of art it rests on four lions and is decorated with the coat of arms of the Holy Roman Empire, Bohemia, Hungary and Castile.

Maria Theresa Vault

Jean-Nicholas Jadot de Ville Issey designed the domed chamber dominated by Moll's masterly double sarcophagus in the Rococo style for Maria Theresa, who died in 1780, and for Francis I, who died in 1765. The sarcophagus takes the form of a bed of state; at the head of the Imperial couple an angel of fame with trumpet and a crown of stars proclaims the triumph of faith. On the sides are numerous reliefs depicting scenes from Maria Theresa's life. It is also ornamented with four mourning figures and the crowns of Austria, Hungary, Bohemia and Jerusalem. Moll is also responsible for several Rococo sarcophagi for the children of the Imperial couple, though not for the excessively simple copper coffin for Emperor Joseph II who died in 1790. In a niche in the Maria Theresa Vault is the coffin of the Countess Karoline Fuchs-Mollart who died in 1754. She was responsible for the upbringing of Maria Theresa and is the only person buried here who was not a member of the Imperial House.

Frances II Vault

The last emperor of the Holy Roman Empire, Francis II who died in 1835, lies here surrounded by the graves of his four consorts. The Classical copper coffin is the work of Peter Nobile.

Ferdinand Vault

Ferdinand I, the Kindly, who died in 1875 and whose coffin stands on a pedestal, shares this chamber with 37 other members of the Habsburg family who are placed in niches in the walls.

Tuscan Vault

This vault for members of the Tuscan collateral branch of the Habsburg House is at present being altered.

New Vault

The New Vault was created between 1960 and 1962 and contains the sarcophagi of Emperor Maximilian of Mexico who was executed in 1867 and Marie Louise, Napoleon's wife, who died in 1847. The body of their son, the Duke of Reichstadt, was transferred to Paris where it was buried in the Invalides.

Franz Joseph Vault

In the Franz Joseph Vault, established in 1909, are buried Emperor Franz Joseph I (d. 1916), Crown Prince Rudolf, who committed suicide in the hunting-lodge at Mayerling in 1889, Empress Elisabeth ("Sissi") who was murdered in Geneva, and (in the vestibule) ex-Empress Zita von Habsburg (d. 1989)

Chapel

In the Chapel is a memorial tablet to Emperor Charles I, the last Emperor of Austria. He died in exile on the Portuguese island of Madeira in 1922.

★Karl Marx Hof

Karl Marx Hof is the symbol of the 398 housing complexes which were built between the wars by the social democratic city council (1919–34) and immortalised in a workers' song as the "little red brick to build a new world". There were 64,000 dwellings in total, but mainly in outlying districts and financed by taxes on luxury items such as champagne, the employment of servants and cars, and steep graduation of taxes on housing construction. The tenants, however, paid rents which were well within their means (5–8% of their wages) for the relatively small flats; gas and electricity rates were low and there was no charge for water. The scheme also offered excellent community facilities such as baths, laundries, community rooms, public houses, shops and libraries, nursery schools and paddling pools; but not least there were many green areas which made living in the "Welfare Palaces" more agreeable.

Karl Marx Hof, in its brick red and ochre colours, was built with 25 million bricks between 1927 and 1930 to a design by Karl Ehn and contains some 1,600 flats and communal facilities grouped around several inner courtyard gardens (about 80% of the Karl Marx complex is made up of parks and gardens). In February 1934 Karl Marx Hof was the centre of the riots between left-wing workers and right-wing extremists and was stormed by the army to suppress the uprising. Today it ranks as an historic monument.

Location
19, Heiligenstädter Strasse 82–92

Underground/ S-Bahn station
Heiligenstadt (U4, U6)

Tram
D

★★Karlskirche (church)

C4

The church dedicated to St Charles Borromeo was designed by J. B. Fischer von Erlach and his son. It is Vienna's most important religious building in the Baroque style. Emperor Charles VI vowed he would build it when the plague was raging in 1713, and in 1737 the church was dedicated to St Charles Borromeo, one of the saints evoked during plagues. In 1738 it was handed over to the Knights of Malta, and in 1783 it was declared an Imperial prebend.

The vast Baroque building is some 80m/262ft long and 60m/200ft wide. The dome rises to a height of 72m/235ft. It cost 304,000 guilders to build. All countries owing allegiance to the Crown had to contribute to the cost as a fine for the deliberate destruction of the chapel of the Austrian Embassy. There is much to be seen in the church with its tall oval central area, two major side-chapels and four smaller chapels in the corners.

Location
1, Karlsplatz

Underground station
Karlsplatz (U1, U2, U4)

Bus
4A, 59A

Trams
1, 2, D, J

The relief on the metope over the portal portrays the plague being overcome. The Latin inscription means: "I fulfill my vow in the presence of those who fear the Lord."

Porch

These are based on Trajan's Column at Rome. Their spiralling bands in relief depict scenes from the life of St Charles Borromeo. The pillars, which are 33m/110ft high are surmounted by the Imperial Crown over the lanterns.

Triumphal pillars

The light interior is dominated by Rottmayr's frescoes in the dome. They represent the apotheosis of St Charles and the petition that plague may be averted. On the left an angel with a flaming torch sets fire to Luther's Bible which has fallen to the ground.

Dome frescoes

Rottmayr painted the fresco on the organ-case. It depicts St Cecilia with angels making music.

Organ

The subject is the Ascent into Heaven of St Charles Borromeo. The sculptural decoration with clouds behind the High Altar is based on designs by J. B. Fischer von Erlach.

High altar

"Jesus and the Roman Captain" and "Healing of a Man Sick of the Palsy" by Daniel Gran; "Raising of the Young Man" by M. Altomonte; "St Luke" by van Schuppen.

Noteworthy Reredoses

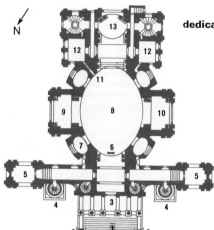

N

Karlskirche
dedicated to St Charles Borromeo

1 Stairway
2 Angel with bronze crosses
3 Porch in form of Greek portico with reliefs on the metopes
4 Triumphal pillars with spiral bands in relief
5 Campanile
6 Organ. Fresco ceiling above the organ-case by J. M. Rottmayr: it shows St Cecilia with the angels
7 Baptistery with stone dome
8 Dome with frescoes of the Apotheosis of St Charles Borromeo by J. M. Rottmayr (1725–30)
9 Reredos of the Assumption of the Virgin, by Sebastiani Ricci
10 Reredos of St Elisabeth of Thuringia by Daniel Gran (1736–37)
11 Pulpit
12 Vestries
13 High Altar by L. Mattielli

The painting of the Assumption of the Virgin on the left of the High Altar is by Sebastiani Ricci, and that of St Elisabeth of Thuringia to the right of the High Altar is by Daniel Gran.

Henry Moore sculpture

By the large pool in front of the church stands the Henry Moore sculpture "Hill Archer".

Karlsplatz   C4

Location
1st District

Underground station
Karlsplatz
(U1, U2, U4)

Bus 4A, 59A

Trams
1, 2, D, J

★**Otto Wagner Pavilions**

Art hall

The north side of the square is formed by the Handelsakademie, the Künstlerhaus (see entry) and the Musikverein (see entry) building, on the south side are the Karlskirche (see entry) and the Technical University, a building erected 1816–18 with an upper storey added later. On the east side stands the Historisches Museum (see entry) of the city of Vienna.

In the gardens in the southern part of Karlsplatz stand monuments to Johannes Brahms (1908), to Josef Ressel (1862), the inventor of the ship's screw, and to Josef Madersperger (1933), the inventor of the sewing-machine.

Karlsplatz, where important trams and underground routes converge, is one of the busiest squares in central Vienna. In 1977–78 the square was newly laid out and the striking station building of Otto Wagner re-erected. One of Wagner's 1901 pavilions, decorated with marble and gold leaf, now serves as an entrance to the U-Bahn station and also for minor temporary exhibitions of the Historical Museum (see entry); the other one becomes a café in summer.

On the west side at Treitlstrasse (no. 2) an exhibition hall for modern art with an area of 950sq.m/10,226sq.ft was opened in 1992 by Adolf Krischanitz (open: Mon., Wed.–Sun. 10am–6pm, Thur. 10am–8pm).

★Kärtner Strasse   C4

Vienna's most elegant shopping street leads from Stephansplatz (see entry) to the Staatsoper (see entry) on the Ring and ends at Karlsplatz (see

Karlskirche, designed by Fischer von Erlach, father and son

entry). Since 1974 it has been a pedestrian precinct as far as Walfischgasse, with lime trees, pavement cafés, traditional and fashionable shops, elegant boutiques and busy shopping arcades. It is named after the southern state of Kärnten (Carinthia) and seen from the Stephansdom (see entry) it runs in a southerly direction. Beneath the junction of Kärtner Strasse and the Ring lies the Opernpassage, Vienna's first underground pedestrian area opened in 1955 with shops and snack bars.

In contrast with the nearby side streets Kärtner Strasse, documented as early as 1257 under the name "Strata Carinthianorum" and widened in the Seventies, has very few historic buildings, most of them are 18th c., including Nos. 4, 6 and 17 with interesting façades. The oldest building is the Palais Esterházy (No. 41) from 1698 which houses Vienna's casino and the extravagant fashion house Adlmüller where Viennese high society purchase their clothes. Closeby are fashion shops with clothes by such famous designers as Jil Sander, Christian Dior, Pierre Cardin, Emanuel Ungaro, Burberrys, Daks and Fiorucci with prices to match. Traditional folk costumes, evening dresses, young fashion and sportswear are all represented. No. 26 the J. & L. Lobmeyr china and glass house has a glass museum on the upper floor which is open during business hours. The Viennese Tourist Board has its offices at No. 38. A relaxing break from shopping can be taken in the elegant surroundings of the café of the legendary Hotel Sacher (see entry) on the corner of Philharmonikerstrasse where a slice of the famous "Sachertorte" can be sampled.

Only the Maltese church still has a few features dating back to 1265. Inside there are numerous coats of arms of Knights of Malta as well as the 1806 stucco monument with Turkish figures on either hand to the memory of Jean de la Valette, the Grand Master who defended Malta against the Turks in 1565.

Location
1, Stephansplatz-Karlspaltz

Underground station
Stephansplatz (U1, U3),
Karlsplatz (U1, U2, U4)

Trams
1, 2, D, J

Maltese church

Kärnter Strasse – ideal for a stroll and a shopper's paradise

A glassware emporium in Kärnter Strasse

Artistic shop décor

Kirche am Steinhof (church)   west beyond B/C 1

The church, designed by Otto Wagner, was built between 1904 and 1907 in the grounds of the Vienna psychiatric hospital and is considered to be one of the most important buildings of the Art Nouveau style in Vienna. The church stands on the estate's highest point and its dome and flanking towers can be seen from some distance. The dome is, however, a fake structure; inside only shallow vaulting may be seen. The church interior is simple and light; the floors and walls are tiled in accordance with Wagner's aim to create "cleanliness", of light, air and function, in a church building. The glass mosaics in the windows were designed by Kolo Moser.

Location
14, Baumgartner
Höhe 1

Bus
48A

Tour
Sat. 3pm

Kirche Zur heiligsten Dreifaltigkeit

See Wotruba Kirche

Kleiner Bischofshof (Small Bishop's Palace)   B5

The former Small Bishop's Palace which later became the "Haus zum roten Kreuz" (House with the Red Cross) dates, in part, from the 15th c. Matthias Gerl gave it a new façade in 1761. The Madonna relief in a pretty Rococo frame with Turkish trophies on the wall is particulary noteworthy. The house belonged to Franz Georg Kolschitzky (d. 1694) who according to legend had set up the first Viennese coffee house here.

Location
1, Domgasse 6

**Underground
station**
Stephansplatz
(U1, U3)

★★Klosterneuburg   Excursion

Klosterneuburg (pop. 25,000) stands on the north-east edge of the Vienna Woods (See Practical Information, Excursions) and is separated from the Danube by a broad grassy island. It attracts many visitors mainly on account of its monastery which was founded by the Augustinian Canons. There is an extensive range of buildings high up above the Danube. It originated as a monastery founded by the Babenberg Margrave Leopold III ("The Pious") in the 12th c. In 1730 Emperor Charles VI embarked on a programme of large-scale new building, but this was stopped again in 1755. Work was only completed in 1842, and then on a reduced scale.

The buildings of the monastery comprise the monastery church with Romanesque features which was refurbished in Baroque style in the 17th c., the Leopold Chapel, a Romanesque-Gothic Cloister, the Leopold Courtyard and the monastery wine-vaults. The famous "Verdun Altar" in the Leopold Chapel is especially noteworthy. It is made up of 51 enamelled panels by the goldsmith Nikolaus of Verdun and dates from 1181. This reredos for a funerary chapel is among the finest examples of High Medieval goldsmith's and enameller's work. Following a fire in 1329 the panels were collected to form the present Gothic reredos. The Leopold Chapel leads into the beautiful Gothic Cloisters, the 600-year-old Freisinger Chapel and the monastery lapidarium where, with other examples of Romanesque and Gothic sculpture, the sandstone "Klosterneuburg Madonna", a life-size figure dating from about 1310 is preserved. The new monastery building erected during Charles VI's reign in the Baroque style has two copper domes, one of which is surmounted by the German Imperial Crown, the other by the Lower Austrian Archducal Bonnet. Among the features shown by guides when a conducted tour is taken are the Baroque main staircase, the Marble Hall with frescoes by Daniel Gran, the Imperial Apartment, the

Location
12km/7½miles
north-east of
Vienna on the
Danube

**Underground
station**
Heiligenstadt
(U4, U6)
then bus to
Klosterneuburg

Tours
Mon.–Sat.
9am–noon,
1–5pm;
Sun., pub. hols.
1.30 until dusk

Klosterneuburg
Sector of the Collegiate Canons

© Baedeker

A Imperial Courtyard in the New Building (Collegiate Museum on 2nd floor)	1 Main stairs (1723; Library above)	6 Collegiate Church
B Cloisters: Freisinger Chapel; Lapidarium	2 Marble Hall	7 Former tower
C Leopold Courtyard	3 Imperial Apartment	8 Collegiate Archives
	4 Prelate's Door	9 Fountain (1592)
	5 Leopold Chapel (Verdun Altar)	10 Mosmüller Wing (1620)
		11 Gothic Door
		12 Gothic Chapter House

Tapestry Room and the Treasury. The monastery museum has a rich collection including a Habsburg genealogy, the Albrechts Altar which was given in 1438 and valuable medieval pictures.

The monastery also possesses vineyards and famous wine-vaults. In the monastery cooperage, the "Thousand bucket barrel" dating from 1704, can be seen. Each year on St Leopold's Day, November 15th, there is a great barrel-rolling carnival.

Kafka Memorial

In nearby Kierling, the room in the former Hofmann sanitorium in which Kafka spent the last days of his life, has been turned into a memorial to the writer.

★★KunstHausWien (art gallery)   B 6

Location
3, Untere Weiss-gerberstr. 13

Trams
N, O

Opening times
daily 10am–7pm

In April 1991 the KunstHausWien opened its doors, a double monument to the architect and painter Friedensreich Hundertwasser: the museum being an exhibit in itself and an exhibition hall for the varied work of this rebel architect. The house, designed by Hundertwasser and Pelikan in the style of the nearby Hundertwasserhaus (see entry), was used from 1892 by the Thonet brothers as a workshop for their world-famous bow-wood furniture. There are over 100 different Thonet chairs to try out in the ground-level museum café.

The privately-owned KunstHausWien has on two floors about 300 paintings, graphics, tapestries and models of Hundertwasser's environmentally-friendly architectural projects, both fulfilled and unfulfilled, and two further floors dedicated to changing exhibitions of internationally famous artists' work. This fascinating architectural dream of forms and colours has a colourful tiled façade with different types of windows on a wavy chess-

KunstHausWien – a happy mixture of asymmetry, colour and greenery

board pattern background. In keeping with the natural feel the floor is uneven a "melody for the feet" designed to stimulate and "uplift" the visitor.

★★Kunsthistorisches Museum (Museum of Art History)   C 4

The Kunsthistorisches Museum, its mighty dome crowned by a bronze figure of Pallas Athene, houses one of the most important art collections in the world. It underwent restoration at the beginning of the Nineties. In the second half of the 19th c. it was realised that Vienna had no counterpart of the great art galleries of London and Amsterdam, particularly since the Imperial collections in Prince Eugene's former summer mansion had become far too large for those premises. Karl Hasenauer and Gottfried Semper were charged with the task of drawing up plans for two splendid museums, the Kunsthistorisches Museum and the Naturhistorisches Museum (see entry). Between 1871 and 1891 they erected the vast pair of buildings which form the left and right-hand sides of Maria-Theresien Platz. Though the state was close to bankruptcy, the architects were under instructions not to make economies, and they were able to use expensive materials and commission highly-rated artists with the decoration of the interior. Among those who worked on the embellishment of the Museum's interior were Viktor Tilgner, Hans Makart, Michael Munkacsy, the brothers Ernst and Gustav Klimt and Franz Matsch.

Location
1, Maria-Theresien Platz

Underground station
Volkstheater
(U2, U3)

Trams
1, 2, D, J, 52, 58

Opening times
Tue., Wed., Fri. 10am–6pm, Thur. 10am–9pm

Art Collections

The collections are divided into eight departments. The main building houses the Egyptian-Oriental Collection, the Collection of Antiquities, the

Museum of Art History

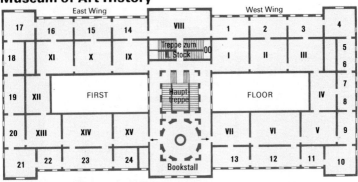

FIRST FLOOR
Picture Gallery

East Wing
Rooms
VIII 15th–16th c. Dutch
IX 16th c. Dutch
X P. Brueghel the Elder
XI 17th c. Flemish
XII Van Dyck
XIII Temporary Exhibitions
XIV Rubens
XV Rembrandt
Cabinets
14 Early Dutch
15 Cranach

16 Altdorfer, Huber
17 Old German masters
  (Dürer, Danube School)
18 Holbein the Younger,
  Clouet
19 Mannerists
20 Rubens
21 Teniers the Younger
22 Hals, Van Goyen
23 Ruisdael
24 Vermeer

West Wing
Rooms
I Titian
II Veronese
III Tintoretto, Basano
IV Tintoretto
V Caravaggio, Ribera
VI Reni, Fetti, Giordano
VII Crespi, Tiepolo
Cabinets
1 Mantegna, Vivarini
2 Bellini, Giogione
3 Corregio, Parmigianino

4 Raphael, Andrea del Sarto
5 Schiavone
6 Moretto, Marino
7 De Predis, Luini
8 Barocci, dell'Abate
9 Bronzino, Coello
10 Velázquez, Murillo
11 Poussin, Cortone
12 Fetti, Strozzi, Cavalline
13 Guardi, Canaletto

RAISED FIRST FLOOR

East Wing
Sculpture and Applied Arts Collection
Middle Ages
Rooms XXXIV–XXXVII
Renaissance
Rooms XXVIII–XXXII

Mannerism
Rooms XXIV–XXVII
Baroque and Rococo
Rooms XIX–XXII

West Wing
Egyptian
Oriental
Collection
Rooms I–VIII

Antiquities
Rooms IX–XVIII

Sculpture and Applied Arts Collection, the Collection of Paintings and the Collection of Coins. The Museum's other collections are found elsewhere: the Treasure in Schweizerhof of the Hofburg (see entry), the Sammlung Alter Musikinstrumente (Collection of Old Musical Instruments) (see entry), the Ephesos Museum (see entry) and the Waffensammlung (Weapon Collection) in der Neuen Burg (see entry) and the Wagenburg in Schloss Schönbrunn (see entry). The main building in Maria Theresien Platz has 51 rooms with the Egyptian-Oriental Collection and Collection of Paintings being the most highly-rated.

Room I: Cult of the dead. Large stone sarcophagi, (600–100 B.C.), painted wooden coffins (1100–100 B.C.); mummies with painted wrappings, partly gilded mummy masks, pearl-decorated faiences, entrail jugs, Uschebti (workers for the beyond) from assorted material and other tomb contents.

Egyptian-Oriental Collection
Raised first floor

Room II: Prehistoric and Early Egypt (5000–2635 B.C.) stone and clay pots, jewellery. Nubia and its connection with Egyptian culture; a selection of pots and jewellery from prehistory to the Meroitic period. Hyksos as a foreign ruler of Egypt (1650–1550 B.C.); Austrian excavations in Tell el Dab'a.

Room III: Animal cult. Mummified sacred animals; figures of animal gods; Apis stele from Sakkara.

Room IV: Representation of the development of old Egyptian writing, funerary papyrii.

Room V: Ptolemaic Age. Two heads of colossal statues of rulers (2nd c. B.C.), portrait of an old man (c. 250 B.C.). Late period (1080–332 B.C.). Sphinxes, statues, reliefs, bronzes; statue of Prince Nemarot (22nd Dynasty, about 900 B.C.), Sphinx of General Wah-ib-re (30th Dynasty, 350 B.C.), two large seated statues of the lion-headed goddess Mut from her temple in Karnak (18th Dynasty). Glazed tile relief representing a lion from Ischator in Babylon (around 580 B.C.).

Room VI: Everyday objects including furniture, clothes, jewellery, tools for working with stone and wood.

Room VIa: Old Kingdom. Cult chamber of Prince Kaninisut from Giza (5th Dynasty, about 2400 B.C.).

Room VII: New Kingdom (1550–1080 B.C.); statues of gods, kings and private citizens, grave steles, memorials, reliefs and vessels. Kings; portrait of Thutmosis III (18th Dynasty, c. 1460 B.C.), group statue of Haremhab and Horus (18th Dynasty, c. 1320 B.C.), upper section of a colossal statue of Sethos I (19th Dynasty, c. 1300 B.C.), huge elephantine stele of Amenophis II (1439–1413 B.C.). Statue of Siese (19th Dynasty, c. 1200 B.C.). Middle Kingdom (2134–1650 B.C.); statues and parts of statues from kings and private citizens, steles, small stone vessels; a life-size head of Sesostris III (12th Dynasty, c. 1860 B.C.) and the head of Amenemhet V (13th Dynasty, c. 1750 B.C.); among the rare treasure are a hippopotamus made of glazed and painted faïence, a burial gift from the 11th Dynasty (c. 2000 B.C.) and the almost life-size statue of Sebek-em-sauf from the 13th Dynasty (1720 B.C.).

Room VIII: Old Kingdom (2635–2155 B.C.); statues, architectural relics and vessels from private tombs of the 4th–6th Dynasty (c. 2500–2150 B.C.) in Giza. Of special interest and one of the finest examples extant is the "Head of a Man", c. 2450 B.C. sculpted from the finest limestone.

Room IX: Art from Cyprus. Bronze age pottery and sepulchral reliefs from Palmyra.

Antiquities
Raised first floor

Room X: Greek and Roman sculpture, including the precious bronze statue "The Youth of Helenenburg" (recent research has shown it to be a Renaissance copy of a missing Roman original) and a Head of Artemis (2nd c. B.C.).

Room XI: Earlier Greek and Roman sculpture including a Greek ruler and a magnificent Roman mosaic pavement (2nd c. B.C.).

Room XII: Greek bronzes and Minoan statuettes from Crete (end 2nd c. B.C.).

Room XIII: Etruscan art, including the clay statue of Athena from Rocca d'Aspromonte (5th c. B.C.)

Room XIV: Pottery decorated with pictures and reliefs, Tangara figures and an especially precious Ptolemaic cameo with the portraits of a Ptolemaic king and his consort (showcase 14).

Room XV: Roman art, portraits of Emperors, ceremonial utensils, miniature sculptures and cameos, including the world-famous "Gemma Augustea" (1st c. B.C.)

Room XVI: Art of Late Antiquity, individual finds from Austrian excavations, including marble portrait head from Ephesus.

Room XVII: Textiles from Egypt and early Christian handicrafts, including the Siebenburg golden treasure from Szilagysomlyo.

Room XVIII: Byzantine and Old Bulgarian work, including silver treasures from Galicia and Bukovina. The prime exhibit is the treasure from Nagyszentmiklós with 23 gold vessels.

Sculpture and Applied Arts

The sequence of the rooms is clear from the plan.

Room XXXVI: High and late Middle Ages. Ivory carving, rock-crystal vessels and two famous chalices, one from Wilten Abbey at Innsbruck, the other from St Peter's at Salzburg

Rooms XXXVII and XXXV: Clocks, scientific instruments and automata of the 16th and 17th c. including a rock-crystal clock by Jost Burgi, the heavenly globe by Georg Roll (1584) for Emperor Rudolf II and a Spanish automatic doll.

Room XXXIV: Late Medieval German Sculpture. Fine Nuremberg vessels, including the so-called Dürer and Maximilian cups. Gothic sculpture including the famous Krumau Madonna and a "Madonna and Child" by Tilman Riemenschneider.

Room XXXII: Florentine Early Renaissance. Many reliefs and busts from Donatello's and della Robbia's workshops; Settignano's "Laughing Boy" and Laurana's "Portrait of a young lady".

Room XXXI: 16th and 17th c. small bronzes, ivory work, rock-crystal and carved stone vessels.

Room XXX: Upper Italian Renaissance. Busts, plaques and bronzes by Antico (Venus Felix), Moderno and Riccio.

Room XXIX: Italian vessels of rock-crystal, lapis lazuli, jasper, etc; valuable 16th c. cameos; Spanish gold work.

Room XXVIII: German Renaissance. Wooden statuettes, inlay work and carving.

Room XXVII: 16th c. Italian bronzes. Many impressive works by Giambologna and Benvenuto Cellini's famous salt cellar.

Room XXVI: French 16th c. Mannerism with elegant vessels and Limoges display pieces.

Room XXV: German 16th c. Mannerism. Items from Archduke Ferdinand II's collection; rare Venetian jewellery; Tyrolean pottery, etc.

Room XXIV: Collection of carved stone vessels from the tomb of Rudolf II; fine gold and silver work, jewellery and cameos of the 16th and 17th c.; so-called Florentine mosaic.

Room XXII: High Baroque. Mainly miniature work, ebony statuettes, bronze busts and figurative reliefs made from Kelheim stone.

Room XX: Austria High Baroque and Rococo. Notable are the bust of Marie-Antoinette, Marie Theresa's gold breakfast service and the toilet seat of her husband, Francis II.

Room XIX: 17th c. carvings in crystal and quartz. Dionisio Miseroni's "Pyramide" a tower carved from a single rock-crystal for Emperor Ferdinand III. The tapestries on the walls are frequently changed as they are sensitive to light and dust.

The world-famous Picture Gallery is housed in 15 rooms and 24 cabinets. Room I: Works by Titian, "Ecce-Homo" and "Danae". **Picture Gallery** First floor

Room II: Representative works by Paolo Veronese ("Death of Lucretia", "Judith with the Head of Holofernes", etc.), scenes from the Old and New Testaments.

Room III: Venetian Mannerism, represented primarily by Tintoretto ("Susannah in the Bath") and Bassanno's family.

Room IV: Tintoretto

Room V: Works of the 17th c. chiaroscuro painting. The major work is "Madonna of the Rosary" by Michaelangelo Caravaggio.

Franz Hals: Study of a Man   *Portraits by Lucas Cranach the Younger*

Room VI: Christian themes from the Counter-Reformation era; Notable is the famous "Baptism of Christ" by Guido Reni.

Room VII: 18th c. Italian Baroque masters. Giambattista Tiepolo's scenes from Roman history are outstanding. View of Vienna by Bernado Bellotto, known as Canaletto.

Room VIII: Early Netherlands painting of the 15th and 16th c. Works by Rogier van der Weyden, Hans Memling, Joos van Cleves and two portraits by Jan van Eyck.

Room IX: 16th c. Netherlands painting. Genre pictures by Pieter Aertsen and a series depicting the Seasons by Lucas van Valckenborch.

Room X: A definitive collection of works by Peter Breughel the Elder, with about one third of the surviving works of the master, including "The Seasons", "Children Playing", "Tower of Babel", "Hunters Returning" and "The Peasant Wedding".

Room XI: 17th c. Flemish masters. Still-lifes by Frans Snyderss and Jacob Jordaens.

Room XII: Paintings by Rubens's pupil and collaborator Sir Anthony van Dyck, with his "Picture of a Younger Generation".

Room XIII and XIV: Peter Paul Rubens Collection. More than 30 of his works hang here, including many of his masterpieces.

Room XV: Dutch 17th and 18th c. painting, with pictures by Rembrandt and landscapes by Ruysdael.

The most important cabinets are:
Cabinet 2, with Bellini and the "Three Philosophers" by Giorgione
Cabinet 3, with Correggios "Kidnapping of Ganymed" and "Jupiter and Jo" together with Parmigianinos "Self-portrait in a Convex Mirror" and "The Fall of St Paul"
Cabinet 4, paintings by Raphael including "Madonna in Green" and pictures by Andrea del Sarto
Cabinet 10, works by Velasquez and an altar-painting by Murillo from Seville and only acquired in 1987
Cabinet 14, early Dutch painting
Cabinet 17, with eight major works by Dürer and Old German masters (incl. Danube School)
Cabinet 18, portraits by Hans Holbein
Cabinet 20, more paintings by Rubens
Cabinet 23, landscapes by Ruisdael
Cabinet 24, works by Vermeer

Secondary Gallery
Second floor

The Secondary Gallery reserved for temporary exhibitions is currently closed for rebuilding.

Coin Collection/ Coin Cabinet
Second floor

The Coin Collection is arranged in three rooms and is one of the largest and most important of its kind.

Room I: Development of money from natural forms of currency to modern forms of monetary transaction without cash. There is natural currency from Asia, Africa and America, stone money from Yap Island, money in the form of bars and rings, minted currency and rare old versions of paper money.

Room II: Medals. Exhibition of the artistic and cultural history of medals from the Roman era to the present day.

Room III: Modern medals, insignia of Orders and honorific badges.

Künstlerhaus (Artists' House)   C4

The Künstlerhaus (House of the Artists) is used for art exhibitions, cultural events and art festivals.

The most famous are the "Gschnas" festivals in spring. The Vienna Artists' Society, founded in 1861, had this building put up in 1865–68.

The marble standing figures by the entrance represent Diego Velásquez, Raphael Santi, Leonardo da Vinci, Michelangelo Buonarotti, Albrecht Dürer, Titian, Bramante and Peter Paul Rubens.

Location
1, Karlsplatz 5

Underground station
Karlsplatz
(U1, U2, U4)

Trams
1, 2, D, J

Lainzer Tiergarten (wildlife park)   south-west beyond D 1

The Lainzer Wildlife Park occupies 24·5sq.km/9½sq.miles of unspoiled landscape. Here the Vienna Woods have remained almost untouched, with oaks and beeches, roe-deer and red deer, wild boars, moufflons, fallow deer and aurochs. There are six other entrances apart from the Lainzer Tor, but they are not always open.

Once the hunting reserve of Emperor Joseph II, it was fenced off with a stone wall 24km/15 miles long built between 1782 and 1787 on the orders of Empress Maria Theresa. It has been open to the public since 1921, the property of the city of Vienna since 1937 and a conservation area since 1941. In September a Hunters' Fair is held near St Nicholas' Chapel in honour of St Eustace, patron saint of the hunt. In the park there are 80km/ 50 miles of footpaths, refreshment places and shelters, children's playgrounds and the 14m/46ft high Huburtuswarte observation tower on the Kaltenbründlberg (508m/1667ft above sea-level). Nature-lovers will be interested in the old oak trees on Johannser Kogel, some of which are more than 350 years old. In July and August the Lipizzaner horses of the Spanish Riding School (see entry) spend their "summer holidays" in the Hermes Villa Park.

This former hunting-lodge, built for Empress Elisabeth by Karl von Hasenauer in 1882–86, owes its name to the marble statue of Hermes in the garden. Having been partially restored to its original condition in the 1970s, the villa is now used by the Historisches Museum der Stadt Wien (see entry) for temporary exhibitions of 19th and 20th c. art (open: Wed.–Sun. and public holidays 9am–4.30pm).

Location
13, Hermesstrasse (entrance Lainzer Tor)

Trams and Bus
Tram 60 or 62 to Speisinger Strasse, then bus 60B

Opening times
Apr.–Oct.
Wed.–Sun. 8am–dusk;
Hermesvilla Park
Wed.–Sun.
9am–4.30pm

Hermes Villa

Landhaus (Provincial Government)   B 4

The official seat of the Lower Austrian Provincial Government is in the "Palace of the Lower Austrian Estates". The Estates acquired the former "Liechtensteinisches Freihaus" in 1513. In the 16th c. the building was completely renovated, and in the 19th c. it was restored to its original plan. In 1986 St. Pölten was designated as the provincial capital of Lower Austria, and a start made on constructing new government offices there, into which it is expected that the local authorities will move in 1996.

The Renaissance rooms in which Beethoven, Liszt and Schubert performed and where Abraham a Sancta Clara wrote his account of the plague in 1679, were restored in 1953. If a booking is made in advance it is possible to view the Hall of the Knights, the Hall of the Aldermen, the Hall of the Prelates, the great Debating Chamber and the parlours. The great Debating Chamber,

Location
1, Herrengasse 13

Underground station
Herrengasse (U3)

Opening times
Tours by prior arrangement
(tel. 531 10–0);
Chapel: Sun.
after mass

built *c.* 1570 in Renaissance style, boasts an elaborate coffered ceiling with a painting eulogising "Austria" (1710, by Antonio Beduzzi): it was in this chamber that the founding of the Republic was approved in 1918.

In the courtyard there is a 1571 tablet with an Imperial injunction that "nobody should venture to scuffle or fight or cause a disturbance in front of or within the chartered Landhaus". The decreed peace was, however, broken in 1848, when the Revolution actually started at the Landhaus.

Museum of the State of Lower Austria

Established in 1923 in the former Baroque Palace of Mollard-Cley at Herrengasse 9, the Museum of the State of Lower Austria (see Niederösterreichisches Landesmuseum) portrays the nature, art and cultural history of the region (open: Tue.–Fri. 9am–5pm, Sat. noon–5pm, Sun. 9.30am–1pm).

Laxenburg

Excursion

Location
15km/9 miles south of Vienna

Railway
from Wien-Mitte to Laxenburg-Biedermannsdorf (R61)

The little market town of Laxenburg (pop. 2000) lies amid the meadows bordering the Schwechat in the Vienna Basin. At one time the Court rode out to Laxenburg to escape from the heat of Vienna during the summer months, and the countryside around constituted the old hunting grounds of the Habsburgs. The park, laid out in 1780–90, has many old trees and other features characteristic of of the landscape gardening of the Romantic period, and is one of the most outstanding of its kind in Austria.

The medieval "Altes Schloss" in the park is of historical importance, because it was here that the Emperor Charles VI issued the "Pragmatic Sanction" which enabled his daughter Maria Theresa to succeed to the throne. It now houses the Austrian film archives, and film performances are put on at weekends during the summer months (May–Sept.).

Laxenburg: the Franzensburg in the Schlosspark

The Late Baroque "Neues Schloss", built *c.* 1752, is also known as the
Blauer Hof, after its first owner, the riding-master Sebastian Bloe. At the
time of the Empress Maria Theresa and the Congress of Vienna the palace
was a busy focus of court life. This was where the Empress, affectionately
known as Sissi, gave birth to her son, Crown Prince Rudolph, and in 1917
the last Austrian Emperor, Charles, received his brother-in-law Prince Six-
tus of Bourbon-Palma here to discuss possible peace terms.

Neues Schloss

Today the palace is the headquarters of the International Institute of
Applied Systems Analyses (IIASA). Every summer popular concerts and
theatrical performances are held in the old theatre.

In a dominant position on an island in the Grosser Teich (Great Pond)
stands the romantic Franzenburg (1798–1836), modelled on the Castle of
Habsburg in Switzerland. In the interior special mention should be made of
the Habsburger Saal (Habsburg Hall), the Lothringer Saal (Lorraine Hall),
the Spinning Room, the Capella Speciosa chapel (consecrated 1801) and
the Hungarian Coronation Room; in the courtyard (used for open-air theatrical performances) can be seen 37 busts of members of the Habsburg
family (open: Easter–Oct. daily 8am–6pm).

Franzenburg

Lehár Schlössl (Schikaneder Schlössl) north beyond A 4

Built in 1737 and extended in the first half of the 19th c., this Late Baroque
palace (Schlössl) was from 1802 to 1812 the home of the thespian, singer
and librettist of the "Magic Flute", Emanuel Schikaneder.

Location
19, Hackhofergasse
18

In 1932 Franz Lehár bought the house in which he later wrote "Guiditta";
one of the rooms has been turned into a small Lehár museum (visits by
prior arrangement only; tel. 3 71 82 13).

S-Bahn station
Nussdorf (S9)

Tram D

Leopoldstadt A/B 4–6

Leopolstadt, as District 2 of Vienna is known, together with Brigittenau
(District 20), forms an island running from north-west to south-east between the Danube Canal and the river. In pre-Revolutionary Vienna Leopoldstadt was the city's "leisure centre", boasting the best and largest
dance-halls (Sperl and Odeon), while its economic importance lay mainly
in the spheres of commerce and finance – the first Viennese savings bank
was established here in 1819. In 1865 the Nordbahnhof (North Station) was
opened and soon became very important as the major station where
immigrants arrived; in 1873 the Nordwestbahnhof took its place. Almost
60% of the old suburb, where most immigrants from Bohemia and Moravia
arrived, is now covered in green spaces and lakes. A port, exhibition-
grounds, a sports centre and the Prater nature park (see entry) having
become established here, Leopoldstadt has become an important centre,
while diverse classes and groups of society – upper, middle and working-
class, civil servants and self-employed, locals and foreigners – are all
closely integrated here.

Location
District 2

Since 1991 one of Leopoldstadt's oldest buildings, the "Seifensiederhaus"
(Soap Boiler's House) at Grosse Sperlgasse 24, first mentioned in the
records in 1685, has been the home of the Vienna Criminal Museum. The
history of crime in Vienna from the end of the Middle Ages until the present
day is documented in exhibits housed in 20 rooms. The exhibits cover the
judiciary, criminal law reforms and public executions, the assassination
attempt on the life of Emperor Franz Joseph in 1853, spectacular police
arrests and infamous criminals such as the poisoner Hofrichter and Hugo
Schenk, the poet and murderer of young girls. The gruesome curiosities
include a wheel on which criminals had their bones broken before they
were executed, pieces of equipment from a sadistic 19th c. exhibition,

Criminal Museum

Tram N, 21

Opening times
Tue.–Sun
10am–5pm

Jewish Vienna

The history of the Jews in Vienna is closely linked with Leopoldstadt. At one time most Jewish settlements were concentrated here, and before the Second World War almost a half of Vienna's 180,000 Jews lived in this district. Today there are only some 7000 Jewish citizens in the whole of the city, and few still live in the old Jewish quarter once inhabited by the ordinary man-in-the-street and which at one time formed as important a part of old Vienna as did the glittering life led by wealthy Jewish financiers, the influence of which can still be seen in the Biedermeier villa of Wertheimstein in Döbling. Many facets of the culture of this district have been preserved for posterity in such books as Grillparzer's "The Poor Minstrel", Joseph Roth's "Wandering Jews" and Heimito von Doderer's "Novel No. 7".

The comparatively peaceful period which Jews living in medieval Vienna enjoyed up to the early 14th c. was followed by a progressive worsening of conditions resulting from anti-Semitic decrees which had been issued at the Fourth Lateran Council of 1215 and which were now introduced into Vienna, with the result that the welfare of Jews in the city became increasingly dependent on the capricious whims of the reigning monarch. Finally, in 1420, Archduke Albrecht V made the Jews the scapegoat for his political and military mistakes, as a consequence of which all the inhabitants of the Judenplatz (Jews' Square) were expelled or murdered. During the 16th c. Jewish families again settled in Vienna, but it was 1620 before Ferdinand II offered them fresh economic security by reviving the old currency laws. Four years later the Emperor ordered a new ghetto to be built on the north bank of the Danube, and by 1660 this could boast three synagogues each with its own school, a large hospital, parish rooms and Vienna's first waste disposal system – the Christian inhabitants of the time were less well looked after. Among those who came to live in the Leopoldstadt ghetto were many families from the Polish Ukraine fleeing from the massacring Cossacks, and so Vienna soon came to play the role of mediator between western and eastern Judaism and continued to do so in the 19th and 20th c. When Leopold I ascended to the throne the pendulum again swung in the opposite direction, and in 1670, under pressure from his bigoted wife and from Bishop Leopold Kollonitsch, he expelled nearly 3000 Jewish citizens.

Jewish donations tablet c. 1857

The heyday of Jewish Vienna from the late 18th to the early 20th c. began in 1782 with Joseph II's Edict of Tolerance, which led to a large wave of immigrants, mainly from Eastern Europe. As Jews were allowed to purchase land only for the purpose of building factories Jewish financiers and money-lenders, with their vast capital, soon acquired a dominant position in Vienna's money market, and from 1796 many leading bankers were elevated to the peerage, including Barons von Arnstein and Eskeles as well as Baron Salomon von Rothschild – the second most powerful man of the first half of the 19th c. after Prince Metternich – and Jospeh von Weretheimer, one of the foremost spokesmen of Viennese liberal Judaism of the mid-19th c. At the same time a vibrant commercial centre developed in the inner city around Rotenturmstrasse, Graben and Tuchlauben, followed by the building of Jewish cultural centres and schools of religion. The Austro-

Hungarian Agreement (Ausgleich) of 1867 brought with it complete freedom of worship for both sections of the community. Following this equality of status under Emperor Franz Joseph I, "His Apostolic Majesty of the King of Jerusalem", who felt a genuine sympathy for the Jews, the Jewish proportion of the population rapidly increased from about 2% (6200) in 1857 to almost 11% (72,400) in 1880. About a third of them lived in Leopoldstadt, including small shopkeepers and craftsmen, labourers, students and artists, most being new arrivals from Hungary and the Sudetenland seeking a new life. They had little in common with the world of the well-to-do Jewish social climbers who by now had become absorbed into local society and lived mainly in Districts 1 and 9.

Jewish boundary stone of 1650

The late 19th c. was influenced by such men as Karl Lueger, Georg Ritter von Schönerer and Ernst Schneider and thus saw the re-introduction of malicious anti--Semitic campaigns and race-hatred. The words of hate which appeared in 1906–11 in the "Ostara-Heften" of Jörg Lanz von Liebenfels found an avid reader in the young Adolf Hitler, whose later "Final Solution to the Jewish Question" was a terrible follow-up to the ideology already expressed by Liebenfels. In this strained atmosphere the Zionist concept developed, something which had existed throughout the whole of the 19th c. in oppressed Eastern Europe and was now realised by Theodor Herzl and was to see the remigration of Jews to Jerusalem.

After the First World War pressures on the Jewish minority grew and, in spite of the efforts of such sincere men as Cardinal Theodor Innitzer and others, found increasing expression in anti-Semitic riots. After the incorporation (the "Anschluss") of Austria into the German Reich in 1938 the Jews in Vienna were left to the mercy of the brutal acts of the National Socialists. Arrests were made and Jewish property confiscated, synagogues and schools were destroyed, attacks on Jews became the norm, especially in Leopoldstadt, where most of them lived. The chief of the "Central Office of Jewish Emigration" in Vienna was the infamous Adolf Eichmann, who was responsible for expelling almost 225,000 Jews from the city by the end of 1939 accompanied by the payment of huge sums of money to the authorities, while at the same time the first deportations to concentration camps in Poland were under way. When emigration was finally prohibited in October 1941 the first "death trains" began to run from Vienna to Theresienstadt and Auschwitz, where by 1945 nearly 40,000 Viennese Jews had met their death.

In the years following the Second World War the "Mazzesinsel" remained deserted for a long period; today the quarter around Taborstrasse is a residential area just like many others, with only a few Jewish schools, synagogues and kosher restaurants as a reminder of the lost world of Viennese Jewry.

An insight into the past of Leopoldstadt can be obtained on one of the guided tours (see Practical Information, City sightseeing), which include a visit to the new Jewish Museum (Jüdisches Museum) in Dorotheergasse.

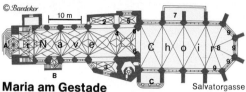

Maria am Gestade
('Maria Stiegen')

Salvatorgasse

A Main Doorway
  (West front)

B Baldachin Doorway
  (c. 1500)

C Choir Doorway
  (reliefs of 1350)

1 Organ gallery (c. 1515)
2 Joseph Altar (copy of 1878)
3 Clemens-Maria-Hofbauer Chapel
  with panels of the Gothic
  High Altar (1466)
4 Pulpit (c. 1820)
5 St Alphonse of Liguori
6 Column figures (c. 1370)
7 Perger Chapel (1520)
8 High Altar (c. 1846)
9 Choir window (14th/15th c.)

objects from a secret late 19th c. bordello, forgers' utensils, wax reconstructions of murder victims as well as photographs, large quantities of evidence material and detailed press reports on more than 300 criminal cases.

★Maria am Gestade (church)   B 4

Location
1, Salvatorgasse 12

Underground stations
1, 2

First mentioned in documents in 1158, the Church of Maria am Gestade (Mary on the Strand) is popularly called the "Maria-Stiegen-Kirche" (Mary on the Steps). As its name suggests, it once stood on the banks of the old arm of the Danube. It is the Czech national church, and its entrancing pierced Gothic cupola is one of the characteristic sights of the northern Old City.

Maria am Gestade, originally a wooden oratory dating from the 9th c., used to stand on the steep slope up from the Danube. The present building, with its Gothic stained glass, was erected mainly between 1394 and 1414. The tower was badly damaged during the Turkish sieges and was renewed in the 16th c., while extensive restoration work was carried out in the 19th and 20th c.
  The west front of the church is only some 10m/30ft wide but nearly 33m/105ft high. The building looms above the old, narrow lanes like the prow of a ship.
  Inside, two Gothic sandstone figures (near the second pillar on the east side of the nave) date from the 14th c., while two Gothic paintings in the chapel dedicated to Clemens Maria Hofbauer, the patron saint of the city of Vienna, are 15th c. The organ-gallery and a stone Renaissance altar in the Johann Perger Chapel are 16th c.; the other church furnishings are 19th c. work.

Maria Hilf (church)   C 3

Location
6, Mariahilfer
Strasse 55

Underground station
Neubaugasse (U3)

Bus 57A

In the Maria Hilf pilgrimage church there are numerous sacred objects venerated by pilgrims. The "Gnadenbild" (Portrayal of Mercy) is a copy of the original on the Mariahilfberg at Passau.
  After the destruction of the original church by the Turks, it was rebuilt in 1683, probably by Sebastiano Carlone. It subsequently underwent considerable alterations and was not dedicated until 1730.
  In a chapel built on to the church stands a monumental figure of Christ on the Cross; it comes from the "Malefizspitzbubenhaus", an ancient prison which used to stand in Rauhensteingasse and from where criminals were conveyed to the Hoher Markt (see entry) for execution.

Pierced Gothic cupola: Maria am Gestade   *Haydn Memorial in front of Maria Hilf church*

In front of the church stands a memorial to the composer Joseph Haydn which was unveiled in 1887.

Haydn Memorial

★Maria-Theresien-Platz and Memorial

C 4

The monument to Empress Maria Theresa is one of the most impressive in all Vienna. It dominates the square of the same name which is flanked by the Kunsthistorisches Museum and the Naturhistorisches Museum (see entries). The square itself is laid out as a formal Baroque garden.

It was Franz Joseph I who commissioned the sculptor Kaspar von Zumbusch to design the monument, and his work was unveiled in 1887. The Empress is seated on her throne, holding the Pragmatic Sanction of 1713 in her left hand. She is surrounded by major personages of her day: the standing figures are State Chancellor Kaunitz, Prince Liechtenstein, Count Haugwitz and her physician, van Swieten, while Generals Daun, Laudon, Traun and Khevenhüller are on horseback. The high-reliefs depict illustrious figures from the fields of politics, economics and the arts, including Haydyn, Gluck and the child prodigy, Mozart. On the south-west side of the lawned square the Messeplatz (Exhibition Square) leads to the Museum Quarter (see entry).

Location
1, near the Burgring

Underground stations
Babenberger Strasse (U2)
Volkstheater (U2, U3)

Trams
1, 2, D, J

Mechitharist Congregation

C 3

Between Neustiftgasse and Lerchenfelder Strasse, behind the formerly unprepossessing walls of the monastery of the Mechitharist Congregation, lie valuable treasures of Armenian art and culture. The order was founded

Location
7, Mechitharistengasse 4

113

Mechitharist Congregation

Underground station
Volkstheater
(U2, U3)

Bus
48A

Opening times
Visits by prior arrangement: tel. 93 64 17

by Mechithar von Sebaste in Constantinople in 1701; it was soon confirmed by Pope Clement XI and followed the rules of St Benedict – it therefore became known as the "Armenian Order of St Benedict". Fleeing from the forces of Napoleon, a group of brothers of the order came to Vienna from Trieste in 1810 and were granted asylum by Emperor Franz I together with a deserted monastery in what later became called Mechitharistengasse. Here, true to the order's principles of religion, education and science, the fathers produced a great number of spiritual and scientific publications in their own printing-works and soon made the monastery an important seat of Armenian culture.

The church which formed part of the monastery complex was designed in 1874 by Camillo Sitte, while the altar dedicated to St Gregory was the work of Theophil Hansen, builder of the Viennese Parliament. The history of Armenian literature is illustrated in the library and museum by means of 2600 manuscripts, the oldest of which dates from the 9th c., some 170,000 volumes, an extensive coin collection as well as rare items of religious and popular art.

Very popular with visitors is "Mechitharine", a liqueur produced here in the monastery since 1889 to an old recipe dating back to 1680.

★ Michaelerplatz   B 4

Location
District 1

Underground station
Herrengasse
(U3)

Archaeological excavations

A start was made in constructing Michaelerplatz in accordance with plans drawn up by J. B. Fischer von Erlach, but Adolf Loos was responsible for completing it. In the course of archaeological digs carried out by the city authorities in 1990–91 when the square was being re-designed, the foundations of a Roman settlement and remains of the walls of the "Paradiesgartls" (Garden of Paradise) were unearthed. The Viennese architect and designer Hans Hollen described the excavations in 1991 as "a display window of Vienna's history" and built a stone wall around them which, while protecting the historic remains, does detract somewhat from the elegance of the square.

Michaelerkirche

The Redemptorist Church of St Michael, now also a cultural centre, used to be the parish church of the Imperial Court, and it was also favoured for the interment of prominent Austrians. It stands directly opposite the Michaeler wing of the Hofburg (see entry) on the east side of the Michaelerplatz.

It is not known for sure who was the founder of the church. It may have been the crusader Archduke Leopold IV or else perhaps Ottokar Přemsyl. The three-aisled arcaded Late Romanesque basilica was built in the first half of the 13th c., in the same period as the "Alte Burg" (see Hofburg). The architects were connected with St Stephen's Cathedral. The basilica was enlarged in the 14th c. and restored in the Gothic style in the 16th c. The Baroque narthex with its portal was added in 1724–25. The west portal with the sculpture of the Fall of the Angels by Lorenzo Mattielli dates from 1792, as does the Classical façade.

Among the oldest treasures of the church are the remains of the once-famed Late Romanesque frescoes in the tower, the "Man of Sorrows" (1430) in the Baptistery and the stone figures of 1350 in the Chapel of St Nicholas. Jean Baptiste d'Avrange designed the High Altar in 1781. The Chapel of St Nicholas, to the right of the choir, was founded by a ducal cook in about 1350 as a thanks-offering when he was acquitted in a poisoning case.

Crypt

The crypt was a burial place: the floors and walls are covered with bones and there are some 250 coffins of wood, metal and stone (guided tours: daily 11am, also at 3pm Mon.–Sat.).

Adolf Loos House

On the west side of the square stands a piece of scandalous Viennese architectural history, namely, the six-storey "Loos-Haus", carefully re-

Café Griensteidl steeped in legend

Adolf Loos House – plain and elegant

stored in 1989, which now houses the Raiffeisenbank. Adolf Loss designed the linear building in 1910 for the firm of master tailors Goldmann & Salatsch, and in doing so incurred the displeasure of Emperor Franz Joseph, who regarded the "house without eyebrows" – the windows appear to have no frames – as an absolute monstrosity. Loos used this plain form of construction as a protesting contrast to the grandiose style of the Hofburg. Simple elegance is expressed in well-proportioned marble on the façade of the lower double-storey, while the interior is decorated in expensive mahogany and contains a self-winding brass clock.

Re-opened in 1992, the Café Griensteidl at No. 2 is one of the legendary symbols of the coffee-house culture of old Vienna. From 1847 to 1897 the former Heinrich Griensteidl ran a coffee-house here in the Palais Dietrichstein which was patronised by such well-known writers and artists as Hermann Bahr, Hugo von Hofmannsthal, Arthur Schnitzler, Karl Kraus, Hugo Wolf and Arnold Schönberg. After Griensteidl's death the café had to move to the Palais Herbertstein, but Karl Kraus ensured it a place of honour in literary history by describing it in his satirical polemic "Literature Vandalised".

Café Griensteidl

Minoritenkirche (the Snow Madonna Italian National Church)   B 4

The former Minorites' church has officially been named the Snow Madonna Italian National Church since 1786. It has been a Franciscan church since 1957.

The first church of the "Frates Minores" in Vienna dates from 1230. It was a little chapel dedicated to the Holy Rood which twice burnt down. To replace it Duke Albrecht the Wise had the present Gothic aisle-less church built in the 14th c. In the course of rebuilding in the Baroque period between

Location
1, Minoritenplatz

Underground station
Herrengasse (U3)

115

1784 and 1789 Ferdinand von Hohenberg restored its Gothic appearance. Of particular architectural interest is the Gothic main portal, designed by Duke Albrecht's confessor, Father Jacobus in 1340–45.

Inside can be seen Giacomo Raffaelli's copy in mosaic of Leonardo da Vinci's famous "Last Supper". It was commissioned by Napoleon I, who wanted to take the Milan original to Paris and replace it with the the Vienna copy. After Napoleon's fall the Austrian court agreed to purchase the copy at a cost of 400,000 guilders. In 1845 it finally returned to the Minoritenkirche.

The picture above the High Altar by Chr. Unterberger is also a copy; the original "Snow Madonna" is an object of veneration in the Esquiline in Rome.

Museum für Völkerkunde (Museum of Ethnology)   C 4

Location
1, Neue Burg,
Heldenplatz
(entrance on
Burgring)

Underground station
Babenbergerstrasse
(U2)
Volkstheater (U2,
U3)

Trams
1, 2, D, J

Opening times
Mon., Wed.–Sun.
10am–4pm

This museum developed from the Ethnographical Department of the Naturhistorisches Museum (see entry).

The collection is housed in the former "corps de logis" of the Neue Burg (see Hofburg). it comprises more than 150,000 objects pertaining to races that have not used a written language. Because of lack of space most of the collections can only be displayed in temporary exhibitions.

The permanent exhibitions include, on the ground floor, Benin bronzes with royal portrait busts dating back to the 15th c., and the Mexican Collection which belonged to the Emperor Maximilian. It includes the notable head-dress and feather shield of an Aztec sacrificial priest. In the mezzanine can be seen the collections made by the British seafarer James Cook, which were purchased in London in 1806 on instructions from the Emperor. There are also valuable exhibits from Polynesia, African sculptures and pottery, Indian playing cards and cult-objects owned by North American and Brasilian Indians.

★Museum Moderner Kunst Stiftung Ludwig Wien (Museum of Modern Art)

Note

The Museum Moderner Kunst Stiftung Ludwig Wien consists of two exhibition halls – the Museum des 20. Jahrhunderts, which has been in existence since 1962, and the Palais Liechtenstein, which has been used since 1979. When the Museumquartier (Museum Quarter – see entry) is completed, probably in 1998, the museum will acquire new premises there.

Museum des 20. Jahrhunderts (Museum of the 20th century)   D 5

Location
3, Schweizer-
garten

Underground station
Südtiroler Platz
(U1)

Trams
18, D, O

Opening times
Tue.–Sun.
10am–6pm

The Austrian Pavilion at the 1958 Brussels World Fair was dismantled and rebuilt by Karl Schwanzer in the Schweizergarten in Vienna in 1960–62. The Museum of Modern Art (Museum Moderner Kunst) was housed here until it moved to the Palais Liechtenstein (see below). The Museum of the 20th Century ("Zwanzigerhaus") serves as a venue for large temporary exhibitions on the ground floor, while a collection newly formed in 1991 is displayed on the first floor. Highlights of the international art collections are those covering "conceptual art", "minimal art" and "land art", from 1960 to the present day. Artists represented include Joseph Beuys, Peter Halley ("Soul Control", 1953), Mario Merz, Richard Serra, Sol Le Witt, Jannis Kounellis, Donald Judd, Lawrence Weiner, Hanne Darboven, Bertrand Lavier ("Peugeot 103", 1949) and Günther Görg. Austrian avant-garde artists are represented by Franz West, Heimo Zobernig, Hartmut Skerbisch and Gerwald Rockenschaub.

Next to the museum is a sculpture garden with works by Moore, Arp, Rodin, Giacometti and Wotruba.

Bertrand Lavier's "Peugeot 103"   *"Soul Control" by Peter Halley*

Palais Liechtenstein (Gartenpalais; Museum of Modern Art)   **B 4**

This Summer Palace in Fürstengasse is accounted one of the most beauti-ful Baroque buildings in Vienna. Domenico Martinelli erected the building between 1691 and 1711 together with a town mansion for Johann Adam Andreas, Prince of Liechtenstein, whose family still owns it to this day. The rich sculptural decoration on the façade is by Giovanni Giuliani, the fres-coes in the vestibule by Johann Michael Rottmayr, the magnificent stair-cases and marble halls are the work of Andrea Pozzo and Antonio Bellucci, while Santino Bussi was responsible for the High Baroque stucco-work.

Until 1944 the Liechenstein Gallery was housed here; since 1979 it has been a permanent home for contemporary art following the acquisition on permanent loan of pictures from the Ludwig Collection (from Aachen) and the Hahn Collection (from Cologne), including works by the neo-Dadaists from the 1960s and 1970s.

The palais Liechenstein collections represent a cross-section of interna-tional 20th century art. Highlights are the "modern classicists", with works by Picasso, Kupka, Nolde, Schlemmer, Lipschitz, Kirchner, Klimt, Schiele and Kokoschka. Individual rooms are allotted to various art movements such as Expressionism (Schiele, Pechstein, Jawlensky), Cubism (Gleizes, Léger, Duchamp-Villon), Futurism (Balla), Constructivism (Pevsner, Albers), Surrealism (Magritte, Ernst), Nouveau Réalisme (Arman, Raysse), Viennese Fantastic Realism (Hausner, Lehmden, Fuchs, Hutter), Viennese Actionism (Muehl, Nitsch, Rainer), American Pop Art (Warhol, Rauschen-berg) and Photorealism. International artists of the 1980s and 1990s are also represented (Baselitz, Immendorff, Tatafiore).

In addition, temporary exhibitions are held every six to seven months, in which attempts are made to relate the Baroque ambience of the Palais Liechenstein to displays of contemporary art.

Buses
9, Fürstengasse 1

Underground station
Rossauer Lände (U4)

Bus
40A

Tram
D

Opening times
Tue.–Sun.
10am–6pm

Museum Quarter   C 4

Location
7, Messeplatz 1

Underground stations
Volkstheater
(U2, U3)
Babenberger
Strasse (U2)

Bus 48A

Tram 49

★★Leopold
Collection

On the south-west side of Maria-Theresien-Platz (see entry) lie the former Imperial Stables. Built in 1723–25 to plans by J. B. Fischer von Erlach and his son, and measuring 360m/1180ft in length, they formerly housed the carriages and horses belonging to the royal court. After being converted on several occasions the buildings finally served as exhibition halls for a number of years until 1994. At present a new Museum Quarter, designed by Ortner & Ortner, is being built behind the listed façade; it will be used for contemporary, inter-disciplinary art and cultural activities. On completion, which is planned for 1999, the new quarter will house the Museum Moderner Kunst/Stiftung Ludwig Wien (see entry), an Art and Events Hall run by the Vienna city council, a Children's Museum, a Gallery and Architectural Centre and the new Leopold Museum.

At a cost of almost £160 million/US$ 240 million the Austrian government purchased in 1994 the largest private art collection in the country from the Viennese eye specialist Prof. Dr Rudolf Leopold. Until now this collection, which includes examples of Austrian art from 1880 until the First World War, had been exhibited only in parts; it comprises some 600 oil paintings, more than 3000 water-colours, drawings and prints, about 300 items of furniture, including wotk by Wagner, Hoffmann, Loos and Moser, craftwork from Viennese studios, together with examples of Viennese Art Nouveau and Art Déco. The core of the collection is composed of works by pre-war Austrian modern artists such as Egger-Lienz, Boeckl, Faistauer and Walde, and those of the late 19th c. including Romako, Schindler, Jetl, Schuch, Pettenkofen and Gauermann. Leopold's Schiele Collection is known worldwide and includes 47 works by Early Expressionists, including "Dead Mother I" (1910), "The Hermits" (1912; portrait of Klimt and Schiele in monk's habits) and expressive nude self-portrayals. Klimt is represented with 10 paintings, including "Death and Life", and some 100 drawings; other highlights are works by Gerstl such as "Self-portrayal half-nude against a blue background" (1910) and several masterpieces by Kokoschka, including "Self-portrait, with the hand placed on the face" (1918/19) and "Dolomite landscape with the Cima Tre Croci" (1913). There are also nearly 160 canvases by Kubin. Among foreign modern classical works are "Three nudes in a studio" (1912) by Kirchner, a late portrait by Corinth and early drawings by Beckmann.

Netsuke and Japanese wood-carvings, porcelain by Rainer, medieval sculptures and African objects complete the collection. So that the collec-

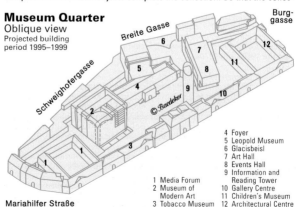

Museum Quarter
Oblique view
Projected building period 1995–1999

Breite Gasse

Schweighofergasse

© Baedeker

Burg-gasse

Mariahilfer Straße

1 Media Forum
2 Museum of Modern Art
3 Tobacco Museum
4 Foyer
5 Leopold Museum
6 Glacisbeisl
7 Art Hall
8 Events Hall
9 Information and Reading Tower
10 Gallery Centre
11 Children's Museum
12 Architectural Centre

tion can be kept together there are plans to provide it with its own building within the Museum Quarter, which will be managed by the patron himself.

The Tobacco Museum (Tabakmuseum) is housed in a side-wing (entrance Mariahilferstrasse 2; open: Tue.–Fri. 10am–5pm, Sat., Sun. 10am–2pm); when the Museum Quarter is completed it will be moved to the front (see plan). The collection belonging to Austria Tabak (the state monopoly which has been in existence since 1784) contains some 2500 exhibits pertaining to smoking and tobacco world-wide. On display are smoking utensils used by emperors, kings and statesmen, magnificent meerschaum pipes made in Vienna – at the turn of the century there were still more than 400 skilled workers employed in carving these pipes – South American clay pipes, *kif* pipes from Morocco, yellow-glazed pipes from the Cameroons and the Upper Volta, silver pipes from Thailand as well as opium pipes from China and Vietnam, to mention only a few.

Tobacco Museum

★Musikvereinsgebäude (concert hall)   C 4

The Gesellschaft der Musikfreunde (Music Lovers' Society) was founded in 1812. In 1867 it commissioned Theophil Hansen – who later designed the Parlament building (see entry) – to draw up plans for this building. The terracotta statues on the sienna-red Neo-Renaissance edifice are mainly by Franz Melnizki.

Many prominent musicians perform in the "Golden Hall", and it is the home of the Viennese Philharmonic, which was formed in 1842 and whose legendary New Year Concert is televised from here all over the world. Gustav Mahler and Hugo Wolf once taught here, and such famous conductors as Furtwängler, Böhm, Karajan, Bernstein and Claudio Abbado have held their audiences entranced in these surroundings.

The Golden Hall is decorated with 36 golden caryatids and boasts a magnificent coffered ceiling. It is 51·2m/165ft long, 18·9m/63ft wide and 17·6m/55ft high, and can seat an audience of 2000. There is room for 400 musicians and is reckoned to be one of the world's best concert halls for acoustics. The organ which was installed in 1968 has 100 registers and 7500 pipes. The "Music Lovers" also possess a comprehensive collection of items relating to the history of music and a vast store of over 300,000 musical scores.

Location
1, Dumbastrasse 3

Underground station
Karlsplatz
(U1, U2, U4)

Buses
4A, 59A

Trams
1, 2, D, J

★Naschmarkt (market)   C 4

The Naschmarkt is by far the largest and most interesting of the markets in Vienna, with an enormous amount of produce on sale (open: Mon.–Fri. 6am–6.30pm, Sat. 6am–1pm).

At the southern end of the Naschmarkt lies the Flea Market (open: Sat. 8am–6pm). Curios, valuable antiques, new articles and bric-à-brac are all offered for sale, and the dealers are usually prepared to haggle.

In nearby Linke Wienzeile there are two interesting Art Nouveau buildings by Otto Wagner. In 1973 the entire façade of No. 38 was regilded. The medallions between the windows are the work of Kolo Moser; the doorway in Köstlergasse was designed by Josef Plečnik. The oval stairway and decorative lift-cage are also of interest.

In 1899 Otto Wagner covered the façade of No. 40 entirely with majolica tiles decorated with plant motifs; on the frieze are sculpted lions' heads in bronze. This house, too, has an interesting stairway.

The Theater an der Wien (No. 6; tel. 5 88 30–0, fax 58 84 30–33) opened in 1801 and has been converted several times since. Its "Papagentor"

Location
6, Wienzeile

Underground stations
Karlsplatz (U1, U2, U4), Ketten-brückengasse (U4)

Linke Wienzeile

★Majolikahaus

★Theater an der Wien

Naschmarkt: a taste of the Mediterranean

Majolikahaus with Art Nouveau motifs

(Papageno Gate) in Millöckergasse shows the first manager of the theatre and librettist of the "Magic Flute", Emanuel Schikaneder, in the role of Papageno. It was in the Theater an der Wien that Beethoven's "Fidelio" had its première in 1805, and dramas by Grillparzer, Nestroy and Raimund as well as numerous operettas by Strauss, Lehár and von Suppé were also first performed here. Between 1945 and 1955 the Staatsoper (see entry) made this their temporary home, and in the early 1960s it was completely modernised. In the years 1983–92, under the leadership of Peter Weck, it developed into a first-rate musical theatre; in 1992 the successful musical "Elisabeth", put to music by the Grammy prizewinner Sylvester Levay and produced by Harry Kupfer, had its première here.

(Tickets in advance from Vienna Ticket Service, A-1043 Wien, Postfach 160; tel. 5 87 98 43, fax. 5 87 98 44.)

★★Naturhistorisches Museum (Natural History Museum)   C 4

Location
1, Burgring 7
(Entrance on
Maria-Theresien-
Platz

**Underground
station**
Volkstheater
(U2, U3)

Trams
1, 2, D, J, 52, 58

The Natural History Museum is the counterpart of the Kunsthistorisches Museum (see entry), which lies directly opposite. It was designed, like the latter, by G. Semper and K. Hasenauer and was completed in 1881.

The exhibits are displayed in 39 galleries and a domed hall, and now form one of the major European natural history collections. The collection was founded by Francis I, the consort of Maria Theresa who opened it to the public in 1765. The exhibits have been on show in the present building since 1889, and the lay-outs have been constantly extended and modernised.

Mineralogical and Petrographical Department (Upper Ground Floor)
Rooms 1 to 5: The nucleus is the collection of minerals, with many examples from Austria, and materials used in many Viennese buildings, such

as the limestone blocks and liassic pillars employed in the construction of the Burgtheater (see entry). Minerals from all over the world include a 1m/3ft 4in. long rock crystal from Madagascar.

In the Precious Stone Room (Room 4) can be found some beautiful pieces, including Maria Theresa's posy of precious stones, graduated emeralds, an 82-carat uncut diamond and a giant topaz weighing 117kg/258lb.

The highlights of the Meteorite Collection include an iron meteorite from Australia weighing 900kg/18cwt and moonstone which Apollo 17 brought back from the moon in 1972.

Geological and Palaeontological Department (Upper Ground Floor)
Rooms 6 to 10 (6 to 9 closed at present for conversion work): Fossils and petrified skeletons, including many finds from the Alps. The Dinosaur Room (Room 10) is particularly popular; finds from the mesozoic period include a 27m/89ft long impression of a skeleton from California and a pterosaur (archaeopteryx).

Prehistory Department (Upper Ground Floor)
Rooms 11 to 15: Finds from excavations in Austria are displayed, dating from the Stone Age to the Early Middle Ages. In Room 9 can be seen the oldest exhibit, the world-famous chalk figure of the "Willendorf Venus"; measuring barely 11cm/4½in. in height, it is a fertility statue dating from c. 25,000 B.C. Hallstatt finds (800–400 B.C.), which were discovered near Hallstatt in Upper Austria in the 19th and 20th c. and thus gave a phase of the Early Iron Age its name of "Hallstatt Period", include bronzes, grave-gifts and remains of Illyrian wooden houses.

Anthropological Department (Upper Ground Floor)
Rooms 16 and 17: The Osteological Collection includes a great number of human skulls from the Neo-Palaeolithic period to the present day. There is also a Somatological Collection.

Children's Room (Upper Ground Floor)
Room 18: Children can enjoy coloured picture-books, play with micro-scopes and video recorders and carry out their own natural history research.

Domed Hall (First Floor)
Skeleton of an extinct species of sea-cow (manatee), etc.

Botanical Exhibition Gallery (First Floor)
Room 21 (closed at present): Models of fungi and forms of spores.

Zoological Department (First Floor)
Rooms 22 to 39: The collection illustrates in impressive fashion the long evolution from the single-cell to anthropoid apes, and provides detailed information on various species of vertebrates, insects and invertebrates.

Opening times
Mon., Wed.–Sun.
9am–6pm
(in winter, 1st floor only, 9am–3pm)

Neuer Markt

From 1220 onwards the "New Viennese Market-place" served as a corn and vegetable market, as the site for jousting, as an arena for mountebanks such as Hans Wurst, and as a place where the Court and nobility could come to skate. Today it is a large car park and a feeder for the Kärnterstrasse (see entry) pedestrian zone. The oldest remaining houses date from the 18th c. No. 14 is a Baroque bourgeois house, No. 25 was formerly the residence of the piano virtuoso Mayseder, and No. 27 is known as the "Herrn-huter House". From 1795 to 1796 Joseph Haydn lived where No. 2 now stands, and it was there that he wrote the Austrian national anthem. The Kapuzinerkirche (see entry) dominates the west side of the square.

Location
1, Kärnterstrasse

Underground station
Stephansplatz
(U1, U3)

Donner Fountain on the Neuer Markt

★Donner Fountain
(Providentia
Fountain)

In 1737–39 Georg Raphael Donner was commissioned by the city to construct the Providentia Fountain, which is better known in Vienna as the Donner Fountain (Donner-Brunnen).

The city fathers desired that the central figure of Providentia should reflect the concept of the caring and wise government of the city. Donner decorated its plinth with four graceful naked cherubs. The figures on the edge of the fountain's basin symbolise the Rivers Enns (an old man), Traun (a youth), Ybbs and March (both in female form). Empress Maria Theresa objected to so much nakedness and had the figures removed, and it was 1801, during the reign of Francis II, before they were replaced. In 1873 the lead figures were so decayed that they had to be replaced by bronze replicas. Donner's originals are now on show in the Baroque Museum at the Belvedere Palaces (see entry).

Niederösterreichisches Landesmuseum
(Museum of the State of Lower Austria)

B 4

Location
1, Herrengasse 9

The former Mollard-Clary palace and its Rococo apartments are the setting for the Museum of the State of Lower Austria.

Underground station
Herrengasse (U3)

Opening times
Tue.–Fri.
9am–5pm
Sat. noon–5pm
Sun. 9.30am–1pm

On the second floor will be found the Department of Cultural History, the most important department of the museum. Here a series of pictures lead the visitor back into the past, from Kokoschka via Gauermann, Waldmüller, Kupelweiser, Schnorr von Carolsfeld, Röttmayr, Maulbertsch, Altomonte and Kremser-Schmidt right back to 15th and 16th c. altar-pieces and woodcarvings (e.g., the "Flachau Madonna" of 1500). There is also detailed information on the settlement, landscape, flora and fauna, life and customs of Lower Austria.

Oberlaa Health Centre   south beyond D 6

Vienna is renowned not only for its theatres, museums and as an international congress centre, but also as a health spa.

On the southern edge of the city lies the "Kurzentrum Oberlaa", the Oberlaa Health Centre, part of the old wine-producing village of the same name.

The sulphurous thermal spring was originally discovered when boring for oil in 1934; it comes from 418m/1260ft below ground at a temperature of 54°C/129°F, and produces 32 litres/7 gallons every second. In 1969 the spa building was completed and the new health centre, with the Ludwig Boltzmann Institute for Rheumatism and Balneology, opened in 1974 to coincide with the International Garden Show. The spa offers treatment for rheumatism, sciatica, slipped discs and circulatory disorders, as well as aftercare for fractures and sports injuries.

The indoor and outdoor thermal baths are equipped with four swimming pools, a children's pool, a sauna, a eucalyptus treatment room for respiratory disorders and a jacuzzi on the edge of the magnificent spa park which covers an area of 1sq.km/250 acres. Between the beautifully laid out walkways there are restaurants, children's playgrounds, tennis courts and a hall for cultural events.

Location
10, Kurbadstrasse
(Oberlaa)

Underground station
Reumannplatz
(U1); then Tram 67
or Bus 68A

★★Österreichische Nationalbibliothek (Austrian National Library)   C 4

The Austrian National Library is housed in the commanding Baroque building on Josefsplatz (see entry). It was built during the reign of Charles VI to plans by Fischer von Erlach, father and son, between 1723 and 1726. Nikolaus Pacassi made some changes in 1763–69.

The Baroque building was originally free-standing, but it was linked by the Redouten range (seriously damaged by fire in 1992 and now being rebuilt) to the Hofburg (see entry) in 1760. The huge central section is crowned by a group of statues depicting the goddess Minerva with her chariot, drawn by four steeds; it is by L. Mattielli and dates from 1725. The National Library, formerly the Court Library, came into the possession of the state in 1920 and is now one of the world's major libraries. Its extensive collection goes back to the 14th c. The first Imperial Library Director was appointed in the 16th c., and in the 17th c. the collections were kept in the upper storey of the Reitschule (see Hofburg). By the 18th c. there was no longer enough space available in the "Burg" and it was obvious that a new building would have to be provided.

The total collection of the National Library amounts at present to some 2½ million books. In addition, there are the following special collections: prints, manuscripts and incunabula, maps and globes, papyri, portraits and photographic archives, music and theatrical collections and an Esperanto museum. The "New" building long ago became too small, and it was necessary to expand into the south wing on Josefsplatz and into the Neue Burg (see Hofburg).

Location
1, Josefsplatz 1

Underground station
Herrengasse (U3)

Trams
1, 2, D, J

Opening times
For details
Tel. 5 34 10 397

The Hall of Honour is one of the most splendid of Baroque rooms. Designed by Fischer von Erlach, father and son, it measures 77·7m/250ft long, 14·3m/46ft wide and 19·6m/65ft high. The ceiling frescoes in the massive dome were painted in honour of Charles VI by Daniel Gran in 1730 and restored by Maulpertsch in 1769; the life-size marble statues are by Paul and Peter von Strudel (c. 1700). In the middle stand 15,000 gold-stamped books from what was once Prince Eugene of Savoy's library. The Hall of Honour is used for temporary exhibitions.

Hall of Honour

The historic Augustine Reading Room (Augustiner Lesesaal) was decorated by Johann Bergl in 1773 with beautiful frescoes depicting the Four Faculties.

Old Reading Room

Austrian National Library on Josefsplatz

Manuscript Collection

This collection on the second floor contains nearly 43,000 6th c. manuscripts, 8000 incunabula and some 24,000 autographs. Among the most impressive manuscripts held are the "Vienna Dioskurides", a Byzantine herbalist's treatise, written and illustrated *c.* 512; the 6th c. "Vienna Genesis"; St Peter's Antiphonary (*c.* 1160); the "Wenzel Bible" from Prague (1390/95); the beautifully illustrated "Livre du cuer d'amour espris" by Count René d'Anjou (*c.* 1465); the "Black Prayer Book" of Duke Galeazzo Maria Sforza (*c.* 1470), one of the most valuable examples of Flemish illuminated manuscripts; the Ambras Book of Heroes (16th c.) and a 15th c. Gutenberg Bible from Mainz.

Map and Globe Collection

The Map Collection on the third floor currently comprises about 240,000 sheets of maps and 280,000 geographical views. The most valuable items are the copy of a 4th c. Roman map for travellers, the 46-volume Blaeu Atlas, dating from the second half of the 17th c., and a map of the world made for Charles V in 1551.

The Globe Museum contains almost 150 exhibits; particularly impressive are two Mercator globes (*c.* 1550), four Coronelli globes (17th c.) and a magnificently coloured celestial globe by Eimmart dating from 1705 (open: Mon.–Fri. 11am–noon, Thur. 2–3pm).

Print Collection

About 2½ million volumes of the prints housed in the Neue Burg have been catalogued. There is also an open-shelf collection of about 56,000 volumes for ready reference.

Picture Archive

The Picture Archive and Portrait Collection (entrance Heldenplatz, Corps de Logis) comprises over 1½ million items and 120,000 volumes of specialist literature. It is the largest and most important institution for the specialist collection of pictorial documentation in Austria, and contains negatives, graphics and photographs of every variety and produced by every known technique.

The Esperanto Museum is also housed in the Neue Burg (entrance behind the Prince Eugene Memorial). The basis of the collection consists of the works and stock of the International Esperanto Museum of Vienna, founded in 1927 and taken over by the National Library in 1928. Today the special collection is made up of more than 17,000 volumes; 260 periodicals are being authenticated and put into the archives, including gazettes from China and Korea.

Esperanto Museum

As well as text books, autographs, posters and articles written in Esperanto, the museum also exhibits translations of the Bible, Dante's "Divine Comedy", works by Goethe, Heine, Raimund and Vicki Baum (open: Mon., Wed.–Sun. 10am–6pm).

The Papyrus Collection, one of the largest in the world, is housed in the buildings of the Albertina (see entry). Because of building work it will probably remain closed until 1998; for information regarding special exhibitions during this period tel. 5 34 83. Most of the 100,000 papyri come from Egypt and date from the 15th c. B.C. to the 14th c. A.D. The most precious possessions are three Egyptian Books of the Dead (the oldest dating from the 15th c. B.C.) and one of the oldest Greek papyri (4th c. B.C.).

Papyrus Collection

The Music Collection is also housed in the Albertina (see entry; currently closed – tel. 5 34 83 for details of special exhibitions during the period of closure).

Music Collection

Among the holdings are precious manuscripts and original scores, including Mozart's Requiem, Beethoven's Violin Concerto, Haydn's National Anthem, Franz Schubert's autograph, some of the papers left by Anton Bruckner and the score of Richard Strauss's "Rosenkavalier".

★★ Österreichisches Museum für Angewandte Kunst B 5
Austrian Museum of Applied Art

The commercial and industrial development of Austria is in no small measure attributable to the Museum of Applied Art. The buildings were erected when the former fortifications on Ringstrasse were being converted. The museum building, designed by Heinrich von Ferstel in 1871 in Italian Renaissance style, was completed by an extension in Weisskirchnerstrasse in 1909. Between 1989 and 1993 an expensive restructuring scheme was carried out.

Location
1, Stubenring 5

Underground station
Stubentor (U3)

Bus
74A

Trams
1, 2

Modelled on the South Kensington Museum (now the Victoria and Albert) in London, the Museum of Applied Art was founded in 1864 as the Austrian Museum of Art and Industry, with the object of promoting and documenting the development of contemporary arts and crafts through the study of old works of art. In 1868 a School of Arts and Crafts was added – now an independent College of Applied Art – offering a systematic training in these skills. Around the turn of the century the museum was reorganised, and the collections now comprise historical and contemporary items in equal proportions. Today it is one of the most important museums of applied art on the Continent of Europe. Incorporating the most modern ideas of climatic control and archive storage, the rebuilding and restructuring programme completed in 1993 has further widened its sphere of activities.

Opening times
Tue.–Sun.
10am–6pm
Thur. 10am–9pm

In May 1993 the new displays covered eleven rooms, and the Study Collection was opened at the end of 1993. In the same year the restored Library and an additional new Reading Room were handed over. Finally, in 1994, the new MAK Book Shop opened.

Painted in ultramarine blue by G. Förg, this room is devoted to the Romanesque vestments (c. 1260) from the Benedictine monastery of Göss in Styria, the only preserved collection of liturgical robes from such an early date, with costly silk embroidery. Boldly coloured Renaissance majolica and a range of medieval furniture are also on display.

Ground Floor
Romanesque,
Gothic,
Renaissance

Österreichisches Museum für angewandte Kunst

FIRST FLOOR

FIRST FLOOR

1 Art Nouveau, Art Deco
2 Viennese workshops
3 20th c. architecture and design
4 Exhibition hall, Weisskirchnerstrasse (temporary exhibitions)
5 Lecture hall
6 Library
7 Temporary exhibitions

GROUND FLOOR

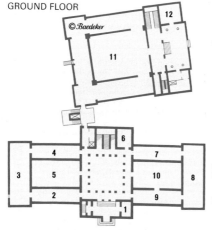

GROUND FLOOR

1 Bookshop
2 MAK Gallery (temporary exhibitions)
3 Café
4 Romanesque, Gothic, Renaissance
5 Baroque, Rococo, Classicism
6 Media room
7 Renaissance, Baroque, Rococo
8 Empire, Biedermeier
9 Historicism, Art Nouveau
10 Oriental
11 Exhibition hall, Weisskirchnerstrasse (temporary exhibitions)
12 Design shop

LOWER GROUND FLOOR

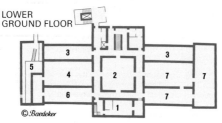

LOWER GROUND FLOOR

1 Bookshop
2 East Asia
3 Furniture
4 Textiles
5 Café
6 Metalwork
7 Ceramics, glass

"Porcelain Room" from the Dubsky Palace in Brünn

In the middle of this department a furnished room dated *c.* 1740 from the Dubsky Palace in Brünn has been reconstructed. Further examples of 18th c. furniture-making include Austrian cabinets and small tables, commodes from Paris and tabernacle cupboards from south Germany with artistic inlay-work and gilded bronze mounts.

Baroque, Rococo, Classicism

The Viennese centrepiece consisting of 60 groups of porcelain figures and vases was commissioned in 1768 for the golden jubilee of Abbott Rayner I, for which Joseph Haydn composed his "Applause"; the female singers can be seen represented as allegorical figures in the centrepiece.

Examples of applied art techniques of the 16th–18th c. include needlework and lace-work from Venice and Brussels and beautiful Bohemian and Venetian glass (room designed by Franz Graf).

Renaissance, Baroque, Rococo

The effects of the Industrial Revolution in the first half of the 19th c. were reflected in the increasing number of consumer goods produced, ranging from luxury items to cheaper, mass-produced goods. The vast variations in form are seen from the many different types of furniture and crockery (room designed by Jenny Holzer).

Empire, Biedermeier

The late 19th c. is represented by the aesthetic work in wood, innovatively economic in its method of construction, by the successful furniture designer Michael Thonet. Beechwood furniture designed by the Thonet brothers won international acclaim and became a familiar sight in many coffee houses in Vienna (room designed by Barbara Bloom).

Historicism, Art Nouveau

The highlights of the valuable collection of oriental carpets are the 16th and 17th c. knotted carpets (room designed by Gang Art).

Orient

Biedermeier vase

Bureau chair by the Thonet brothers

First Floor
Art Nouveau
Art Déco

The star exhibit is G. Klimt's cartoons for the dining-room frieze in the Palais Stoclet in Brussels (1911). When the museum was being re-designed the builders uncovered the frieze designed in Glasgow in 1911 by Margaret Macdonald, the wife of Charles Rennie Mackintosh of Glasgow, for Fritz Waerndorfer's villa. Also of note are the writing desk by K. Moser, decorative vases by J. Hoffmann and a rose-water sprinkler by Louis Comfort Tiffany (room designed by Eichinger and Knecht).

Vienna Studio

The exhibits are inherited from the Vienna Studio, formed in 1903 by Hoffman, Moser and Waerndorfer in order to create functional as well as decorative objects in line with changing tastes. Initially strictly geometric in design, ornamental fantasy subsequently plays an increasingly important part in the forms of the furniture, vases and tableware produced (room designed by Heimo Zobernig).

20th century
architecture
and design

The Architectural Department documents new constructional ideas and idealistic concepts, including plans and models by the Austrians Himmelblau, Domenig, Pruscha and Richter and the Americans Frank Gehry and Lebeus Woods. There are exemplary furniture designs by Pichler, Eichinger, Starck and Morrison (room design by Manfred Wakolbinger).

Library

The museum's specialised library has grown out of a private library owned by its first director, Rudolf von Eitelberger (1817–85), which was expanded following generous gifts from the nobility, the Court and major manufacturing firms. Today the library boasts some 150,000 volumes, including valuable manuscripts, incunabula and tracts from the Renaissance to the 19th c., as well as literature on all aspects of applied art dating from the 18th to the 20th c.

Art print
collection

This collection includes more than 500,000 prints, including some magnificent ornamental specimens from the 15th to the 18th c., pattern books from the Vienna Porcelain Factory, Japanese painted wood-carvings and the famous "Hamza Nama" – a 16th c. Mongolian romance and a unique example of Indo-Persian book-illumination.

The new reading-room offers an open-shelf reference library, magazines and publications relating to contemporary architecture.

Reading-room

Designed by Peter Noever, this bright room on the second floor (not included in the plan) houses the collection of contemporary art commenced in 1986. It includes works by Brus, Eichinger, Gironcoli, Frank, Donald Judd, Jürgennsen, Knizak, Kowanz, Kupelwieser, Leitner, Mark, Rainer, Schlegel, Schwarzkogler, Turrell, Weigand and Wurm, as well as architectural designs by Himmelblau, Domenig, Gehry and Woods.

Second Floor
Contemporary art

Examples illustrating the study and interpretation of chair design are on display, as well as select examples of candlesticks, drinking vessels and tea-pots in metal. The Glass and Porcelain Study Collection, broken down into historical periods, provides an insight into the history of hollow glass-ware and glass-painting from the Middle Ages to more recent times, with the Augarten Porcelain Factory (see Augarten) providing the highlights. The Textile Collection includes liturgical vestments and explains the stylistic and technical developments in textile production from the 13th to the 20th c. The East Asian Collection comprises Kangxi porcelain from the collection of Augustus the Strong, 14th c. Chinese porcelain and burial objects from the Han dynasty (A.D. 25–220).

Basement

Österreichisches Museum für Volkskunde (Austrian Museum of Folk Art) **B 3**

The Folk Museum, founded in 1895 by the Austrian Folklore Society, has been housed since 1917 in the former Schönborn Palais. The palace was built by J. L. von Hildebrandt and F. Jänggl between 1706 and 1711, and the Classical façade added in 1770, probably by Isidor Canevale.

The display rooms were restored in 1992–94 and portray the lives and traditions of the inhabitants of the Alpine and Danubian regions from Lake Constance to the Neusiedler See near the Austro-Hungarian border. There are models, pictures and plans illustrating different types of houses and farms, traditional interiors with country furniture and utensils, farming and craftwork, costumes, as well as jewellery and musical instruments from the 16th to the 19th c. Also explained are marriage customs, religious life in the Middle Ages and the Baroque period, popular art in Vorarlberg and the Tyrol, the guild system, puppets, religious life and pilgrimages and the making of masks, gingerbread men and Christmas cribs.

Location
8, Laudongasse
15–19

Underground station
Rathaus (U2)

Trams
5, 43, 44

Opening times
Tue.–Fri.
9am–5pm
Sat. 9am–noon
Sun. 9am–1pm

★Österreichisches Theatermuseum (Austrian Theatre Museum) **C 4**

The impressive Palais Lobkowitz was built in 1685–87 by Pietro Tencal for Count Sigismund Dietrichstein. In 1709–11 J. B. Fischer von Erlach added a portal and columns in High Baroque style. In the "Eroica Room", with its beautiful ceiling-frescoes by J. van Schuppen, Beethoven conducted the first performance of his Third Symphony in 1804 and that of his Fourth three years later.

Until 1991 the Austrian Theatre Museum had exhibited its extensive collections in a subsidiary building at Hanuschgasse 3. In that year, following nine years of renovation work, the new museum here at Lobkowitzplatz opened its doors to the public. With more than 1,500,000 exhibits it is the largest museum of its kind. In addition to excellent temporary exhibitions on various epochs and famous personalities in the theatrical world, the permanent exhibition – with its 1000 stage models, 600 costumes and props, almost 100,000 sketches, autographs and posters and about 700,000 photographs – forms a part of theatrical history.

Location
1, Lobkowitzplatz 2

Underground station
Stephansplatz
(U1, U3)

Trams
1, 2, D, J

Opening times
Tue.–Sun.
10am–5pm

Guided tours
by arrangement
Tel. 5 12 88 00–0

Theatre Museum: "Visitors' Throne"   *. . . and scenery decoration*

In 1938 Stephan Zweig bequeathed to the museum his valuable collection of manuscripts before he was forced into exile by the Nazis and finally committed suicide in Brazil in 1942. At the beginning of the tour of the museum visitors may sit on the imposing "Visitors' Throne".

Children's Theatrical Museum

In the adjoining Children's Theatrical Museum there is a slide leading to a puppet show, Punch and Judy and computer games, all aimed at making the young visitors interested in the stage. Children can also pretend to be producers and stage-technicians (under supervision only).

Memorial Rooms

Theatre buffs will also wish to visit the Memorial Rooms in the nearby branch of the museum at Hanuschgasse. The ground floor is taken up with the collection of the actor Hugo Thimig (1854–1944), and there are also rooms in memory of the director Max Reinhardt (1873–1943), the actor Josef Kainz (1858–1901), the set-designer Caspar Neher (1897–1962), the writer Hermann Bahr (1863–1934) and his wife, the renowned actress Anna Bahr-Mildenburg, the operetta composers Emmerick Kálmán (1882–1953) and Carl Michael Ziehrer (1843–1922) and the theatre work of Wotruba and Kokoschka (open: Tue.–Fri. 10am–noon, 1pm–4pm; Sat., Sun. 1–4pm. Tel. 5 12 24 27).

Palais Ferstel

See Freyung

Palais Liechenstein (Gartenpalais)

See Museum Moderner Kunst Stiftung Ludwig Wien

Palais Liechenstein (Stadtpalais)   B 4

Counts Kaunitz and Khevenhüller were previous owners of this four-winged urban mansion before, completely rebuilt, it came into the possession of the wealthy Princes of Liechtenstein in 1694. The architect of this impressive house as well as of the "Gartenpalais" (summer palace) of the same name (see entry) was Domenico Martinelli. The richly ornamented side doorway was probably the work of J. B. Fischer von Erlach and dates from c. 1700. The monumental main doorway is decorated with statues by Giuliani, who also designed the cherubs in the stairwell. In the courtyard stands an imposing Triton fountain (1695).

Because of its suspect construction, with subsidence in the walls and floors requiring constant repairs, the locals have nicknamed the Palais the "Künstlerversorgungshaus" or "welfare home for artisans".

Location
1, Minoritenplatz
4/Bankgasse 9

Palais Pálffy   C 4

With its interior modernised and adapted the former Palais Pálffy is now available, under the title "Österreich-Haus", for cultural events. The Emperors' Austrian Chancellery stood on this site c. 1500. It was converted into a nobleman's palace at the end of the 16th c. The buildings were damaged by fire in the 18th c. and partially restored.

Mozart produced his "Marriage of Figaro" for the first time before an audience of his friends in the room now called the "Figarosaal".

Location
1, Josefsplatz 6

Underground station
Stephansplatz
(U1, U3)

Palais Schwarzenberg   C 5

Palais Schwarzenberg, now a luxury hotel, was one of the first summer residences to be constructed outside the city walls. Its interior is particularly fine.

Prince Schwarzenberg settled in his own way the rivalry between the two great Baroque architects, J. B. Fischer von Erlach and J. L. von Hildebrandt. The first sketches were the work of Hildebrandt, in 1720 alterations were undertaken by Fischer von Erlach, and the magnificent Baroque gardens were laid out by the latter's son.

After the end of the war the damaged palace was meticulously restored. However, it proved impossible to save completely the frescoes by Daniel Gran.

Location
3, Rennweg 2

★Parlament (Parliament Building)   B 4

Since 1918 the meetings of the National and Federal Parliament have been held in these impressive buildings. Measuring 137m/450ft wide and 145m/475ft long, they had been built between 1873 and 1883 by Theophil Hansen for the Imperial and Provincial delegacies which had been called into being by the 1861 Declaration and survived until 1918. It was in allusion to Greece, the birthplace of democracy, that he chose Greek forms for the building, with Corinthian columns and rich decoration on the metopes and pediments. The carvings in the pediment above the portico depict the granting of the Constitution by Franz Joseph I to the 17 peoples of Austria, while the attica is decorated with 76 marble statues and 66 reliefs.

Mon.–Fri. 11am (except when Parliament is in session), mid-July–Aug. 9, 10 and 11am, 1, 2 and 3pm.

Location
1, Dr-Karl-Renner-Ring 3

Underground station
Lerchenfelder
Strasse (U2)

Trams
1, 2, D, J

Guided tours

Palais Schwarzenberg, once a summer residence, now a luxury hotel (see page 131)

The "Horse-tamer" stands guard . . .   *. . . near the Pallas Athene Fountain*

Josef Lax's bronze "Horse-tamer" stands guard over the flight of steps; on the left can be seen the seated marble figures of Herodotus, Polybius, Thukydides and Xenophon, and to the right those of Sallust, Caesar, Tacitus and Livy.

The Pallas Athene Fountain was erected in front of the main portal in 1902. The 4m/13ft high figure of Pallas Athene with gilded helmet and armed with a lance is the work of the sculptor Kundmann. The recumbent figures symbolise the Rivers Danube, Inn, Elbe and Moldau.

Pallas Athene Fountain

To the left of the building stand memorials to the Social Democrats Jakob Reumann (mayor of Vienna 1919–23), Viktor Adler (in 1918 founder and first Foreign Minister of the First Republic) and Ferdinand Hanusch (Minister of Social Affairs, 1918–20).

Republican Memorial

On the right stands a memorial to Dr Karl Renner, who led Austria when the Republics were founded in 1918 and 1945 and who held the office of Federal President until 1950.

Dr Karl Renner Memorial

Pasqualatihaus (Beethoven and Stifter Museum) **B 4**

Beethoven came to reside here several times in the period between 1804 and 1815. The house was owned by Beethoven's life-long friend Johann Baptist von Pasqualati. Tradition has it that whenever Beethoven moved out Pasqualati stated publicly "The house is not for rent; Beethoven will be back". It was here that the composer wrote his Fourth, Fifth and Sixth Symphonies, his Fourth Piano Concerto, the "Leonora" overtures and the opera "Fidelio".

Although the memorial rooms are not exactly those which Beethoven occupied they are in close proximity. On display are furniture and articles used by the composer, pictures such as Mähler's portrait of Beethoven painted in 1801, drawings, lithographs and music.

The Adalbert Stifter Museum has also been housed here since 1979. On show are manuscripts and first editions by the author as well more than half the surviving pictures and landscapes which he painted.

Location
1, Mölkerbastei 8

Underground station
Schottentor (U2)

Trams 1, 2, D

Opening times
Tue.–Sun.
9am–12.15pm,
1–4.30pm

Paulanerkirche (church) **C 4**

The Paulanites were summoned to Vienna by Emperor Ferdinand II, who gave them their vineyards on the "Wieden" (meadows). Dedicated to the "Guardian Angels", the monastery church was built between 1627 and 1651.

It was rebuilt following its destruction in the Turkish siege of 1668 and was restored in 1817. After the dissolution of the monastic order it was made a parish church in 1784. Inside will be found some important oil-paintings, including a "Crucifixion" (second altar) by J. M. Rottmayr. The ceiling fresco is attributed to Carlo Carlone.

Location
4, Wiedner Hauptstrasse 6

Underground station
Karlsplatz
(U1, U2, U4)

Trams 62, 65

Pestsäule (Plague Pillar)

See Graben

★Peterskirche (church) **B 4**

The Collegial and Parish Church of St Peter is modelled on St Peter's, Rome.

Location
1, Petersplatz

133

Peterskirche

Underground station
Stephansplatz
(U1, U3)

According to tradition, the site was originally occupied by a late Roman church, and then by one founded by Charlemagne in 792. The first documentary evidence for a church here, however, dates from 1137. That building was restored several times, to be replaced early in the 18th c. by the present edifice which was commenced by Gabriel Montani and probably completed by Lucas von Hildebrandt.

The church, oval in plan, is roofed with a massive dome, with a fresco by J. M. Rottmayr. There are many artistic treasures to be seen.

Left-hand side

Going round the church in a clockwise direction, visitors pass through Andreas Altomonte's magnificent portal and come to the St Barbara Chapel, in which Franz Karl Remp's "Decollation of St Barbara" is especially noteworthy. The side-altar on the left has a reredos by Anton Schoonjans depicting the Martyrdom of St Sebastian. There is a painting by Altomonte in the Chapel of the Holy Family.

Choir

The choir lies just beyond the richly carved Baroque pulpit. Beneath Antonio Bibiena's false dome stands the High Altar, the work of Santino Bussi, with a reredos by Altomonte and a painting of the Immaculate Conception

Peterskirche – Baroque architecture at its best

by Kupelwieser. The entrance to the crypt is also in the choir. Every Christmas the crib which is set up here attracts many to the church.

The right-hand side of the church contains the Johann von Nepomuk Altar, with a "Madonna in Glory" ascribed to Matthias Steinl. The St Michael Chapel is adorned with a "Fall of the Angels" by Altomonte. In a glass coffin can be seen Benedict, the Saint of the Catacombs. The reredos on the side-altar is also by Rottmayr, while the St Anthony Chapel contains works by Altomonte ("St Anthony with the Virgin") and Kupelwieser ("Heart of the Madonna").

Right-hand side

Petronell (Carnuntum)

Excursion

The little market town of Petronell (Carnuntum), with a population of 1250, on the right bank of the Danube, can look back on a long history spanning almost two thousand years. Although the earliest finds made in the region date from the Late Stone Age, it was A.D. 9 when the Romans founded the legionary fortress of Carnuntum about 2km/1¼ miles east of the present town. The name "Carnuntum" is of Illyrian origin and means "stone" or "fortified place". Between A.D. 69 and 79, under Emperor Vespasian, it grew into a a fortified military base with a harbour. During its heyday under the Emperors Hadrian and Marc Aurel Carnuntum had a population of more than 60,000, was an important trade and traffic centre and formed the east–west route along the river as well as being on the "amber road" running north to south along the eastern Alps.

The Roman civilian settlement which has been uncovered to the west of present-day Petronell boasted some magnificent villas, large functional and welfare buildings and sophisticated plumbing and drainage systems. Carnuntum was the capital of the Roman province of Upper Pannonia, and it was here that Septimus Severus was appointed Emperor and Diocletian called an imperial conference. The camp lasted until A.D. 375 before being razed by the invading hordes.

The excavated Roman town has been made into an open-air museum. Visitors can see foundations of dwellings, the ruins of a palace built in the first half of the 2nd c., and owned by the Roman governor, with remains of the central heating systems, cellars, bathrooms and marble cladding, the 4th c. Heidentor ("Pagans' Gate"), over 20m/65ft high, and the 2nd c. amphitheatre, discovered in 1922, which would have seated 15,000 spectators in seats only 4m/13ft above the arena. Finds relating to the plumbing system in the auxiliary castle and to the burial ground can be viewed in the new Petronell-Carnuntum Museum on the eastern edge of the town.

Location
42km/26 miles
east of Vienna

★**Open-air**
museum
of the Roman
legionary camp
and civilian
settlement

Opening times
Apr.–Oct.
daily 9am–5pm

Originally an 11th c. moated castle, Schloss Petronell was converted to the Baroque in the 17th c. It is now owned by the Abensperg-Traun family. A feature is the Knights' Hall decorated with frescoes.

The Romano-Gothic parish church is dedicated to St Petronilla, after whom the town is named.

The massive Round Chapel dates from the first half of the 12th c.; it was initially used as a baptismal chapel and then from the 18th c. as a burial-chamber, while the simple Chapel of St Anna was built in 1744, in accordance with the final wishes of Katharina Gabriele, Countess of Abensperg-Traun.

Other sights

Piaristenkirche Maria Treu (church)

B 3

The Piaristenkirche is a parish church and a church of the Order of the Piarists (Patres Scholarum Piarum).

When the Piarists came to Vienna in the 17th c. they first built themselves a little chapel. The present church is based on plans drawn up by Lucas von

Location
8, Jodok-
Fink-Platz

135

Piaristenkirche Maria Treu

Underground
station
Rathaus (U2)

Bus
13A

Hildebrandt in 1716. A number of changes were introduced, and the building was not completed until the middle of the 18th c., probably by Kilian Ignaz Dietzenhofer. It was consecrated in 1771, but the towers were not completed until 1858–60. It is decorated with particularly beautiful frescoes by F. A. Maulbertsch; dating 1752–53, they are his first major frescoes. The church has eight chapels; the oldest, the Chapel of Sorrows, is in fact the foundation-chapel, dating from 1699. The historic votive painting of "Our Lady of Malta" dates from the first half of the 15th c.

Of the other chapels, the most important by far is the Chapel of the Holy Cross, to the left of the choir. The picture of Christ on the Cross is also by Maulbertsch and dates from 1722.

The votive picture of the Virgin above the High Altar is only a copy. The original is in Rome.

Porzellanmanufaktur

See Augarten

★Prater   B 6

Location
2nd District

Underground/S-
Bahn station
Praterstern (U1, S7)

Bus
80A

Trams
N, O

The Prater, the large natural park between the Danube and the right-hand Danube Canal, is almost like another world. It is lively and exciting by day and something of a twilight zone by night. The park covers an area of some 1287ha/3200 acres, stretching south-eastwards almost 10km/6½ miles from the Prater crossroads through the former "Augebiet" to the end of the Prater. In the first section lies the so-called "Wurstel" or "Volk" Prater, with eating-houses, dance-halls, a giant wheel, roundabouts, switchback, dinosaur park and many other attractions.

Nearly every kind of sport is catered for in the Prater. There is riding in the Freudenau, trotting in the Krieau, swimming in the stadium pool, football in the Ernst Happel stadium built in 1931 and roofed over in 1986, cycling in the Ferry-Dusika stadium, tennis and bowls at the WAC courts.

History

The Prater was first documented in 1403. Maximilian II had the area fenced off in the 16th c. so that he could use it as a personal hunting reserve, and it was not opened to the general public until 1766. The first Punch and Judy shows date from 1767, and the first firework displays from 1771. In 1791 Blanchard's first hot-air balloon rose into the sky; in 1840 Calafati began to operate a big roundabout here; since 1854 it has been guarded by "the Great Chinaman".

Prater Museum
and Planetarium

The Prater Museum, situated at the beginning of the main avenue, documents the history of the Prater from a hunting reserve to the leisure park of today. The emphasis is on the history of clowns and the great period of puppet theatres, ventriloquists, Aunt Sallys and the legendary "Praterfesten".

The adjoining Planetarium, a gift from the Zeiss family in 1927, was one of the first of its kind in Europe (open: Tue.–Fri. 9am–12.15pm and 1–4.30pm, Sat., Sun. 2–6.30pm; guided tours for children on Sun. at 9.30am).

Volksprater/
Wurstelprater

"The trees are in bloom again in the Prater . . ."; when these words of the popular song by Robert Stolz become fact the "Volksprater" (People's Park) emerges from its winter sleep and the Giant Wheel starts to turn again, the tunnel of love opens and the roundabouts and other attractions spring into life. Family days, children's parties and the traditional "Praterfest" on May

The Third Man

Vienna after the Second World War: much of the city has been destroyed in bombing raids, and hunger and squalor prevail among the sombre ruins. Each of the four Allied Powers has several districts under its control; only the 1st District, the heart of the city lying between the Ringstrasse and the Danube Canal, is administered jointly by all of them. This is the background to Graham Greene's thriller about the author Holly Martins who is looking for his boyhood friend by the name of Harry Lime. "Hard luck, I'm afraid, there is nobody there. He is dead". Martins simply cannot believe that Lime has apparently been the victim of a mysterious accident. At the funeral in the Vienna Central Cemetery Martins learns from a police officer that Harry Lime had been accused of being the head of an infamous band of drug-pushers. Martins refuses to accept this or to believe that Lime's death was an accident. The only witness who can confirm his suspicions is found murdered a day later, but not before Martins had been able to learn from him that not two but three men had been at the scene of the crime, and he now sets out to track down the supposed murderer of his school pal, the Third Man. He finds him in Harry Lime himself, an almost likeable villain who had faked his own death in order to escape from the police. In the grand finale to their friendship the two men meet on the Great Wheel at the Prater fairground, before Martins – after a wild chase through the Viennese sewers – shoots the fugitive, who then is really buried in the Central Cemetery.

Following the success of the black-and-white film of 1949, with Joseph Cotten as Holly Martins and Orson Welles as Harry Lime in the starring roles, the "Third Man" became a worldwide hit, and its haunting melody by Anton Karas played on the zither remains one of the masterpieces of cinema history. The author himself wrote the film script, while Carol Reed was the director.

Even though nothing now remains of the depressing conditions of those days, keen readers and cinema enthusiasts can still follow in Harry Lime's footsteps. In place of the Hotel Sacher, which was destroyed at that time, the filming was done in the "smoky night-club" of the Hotel Orient on Tiefer Graben, which at one time included among its guests such illustrious personages as the actress Katharina Schrad and the well-loved Emperor Franz Josef, and still reflects the genteelness of the early years of this century. In Bäckerstrasse Martins met a close friend of Harry Lime in "Old Vienna", which was probably modelled on the Café Alt-Wien. Full of symbolism, the friendship between the two men ends in a car at the top of the Giant Wheel on the Prater fairground – "Martin thought to himself: Just one hefty blow and he will fly out through the glass". That is the beginning of the end for Harry Lime, and the story moves to the Viennese underworld and the network of sewers under the city, now blocked off for safety reasons. In his despairing attempt to escape Lime leaps into the sewer shaft under Girardiplatz and is able to avoid his pursuers as far as Friedrichstrasse; finally, however, under a drain-cover opposite the Café Museum, Martin's bullet finds its target and Lime's life of crime comes to an end.

Since then most of the large cities of the world have been the scene for numerous crime novels, but it is only recently that Vienna has again become the backdrop to the activities of resourceful fictional detectives and police officers such as Helmut Zenker's Major Adolf Kottan. Those who are interested in the real legal history of Vienna, in its spectacular murder cases and legendary villains during the last three hundred years should visit the Criminal Museum at Grosse Sperlgasse 24; as well as a large number of historical documents some truly gruesome curiosities from its "dark" past await the visitor.

Prater: fun for young and old alike

1st all add to the colour. Although modern technology now plays a large part, the fairground owners try to retain the old-fashioned atmosphere, and there are still numerous roundabouts, dodgem cars, race-tracks, swings and helter-skelters and shooting galleries. Visitors can also watch stilt-walkers, organ-grinders, sword-swallowers, ventriloquists and ponies.

★Giant Wheel

The Giant Wheel is an important Viennese landmark, providing a fine view over the city and awakening memories of the "Third Man" and the James Bond film "The Living Daylights". The wheel was the brain-child of Gabor Steiner (1858–1944) and was built in 1896 by the English engineer Walter B. Basset, who produced similar designs in London and Paris. It was erected in the record time of eight months and was operated for the first time on June 21st 1897.

It was destroyed during the last war, but was rebuilt and has been constantly in operation since 1946, although with fewer red coaches. The giant wheel is 61m/200ft in diameter. The weight supported by eight pylons is 165·2 tonnes/160 tons; the total weight of the whole construction is 430·05 tonnes/425 tons. It revolves at a speed of 0·75m/3ft per second. On the occasion of its 90th jubilee one of the coaches was luxuriously fitted out, and it can now be hired for a party of up to 12 people at a cost of some £200/US$ 300. The wheel is in operation Apr.–Sept. 9am–11pm, Mar. and Oct. 10am–10pm.

Ziehrer Monument

This larger than life statue of the composer C. M. Ziehrer (1843–1922) in Deutschmeister uniform was made by Robert Ullmann in 1960.

Constantin Hill

This hill is man-made from the soil dug out when the buildings for the 1873 Vienna Exhibition were erected, and was named after Franz Joseph's Chief Chamberlain, Constantin of Hohenlohe-Schillingsfürst.

Miniature Railway

The "Liliputbahn" miniature railway is driven partly by steam and partly by diesel, and covers a 4km/2½ mile stretch of line near the main avenue. It runs to the Stadium swimming-pool and the Exhibition Ground.

A Giant Wheel on the Prater   *The Prater's miniature railway*

The café-restaurant at the end of the main avenue was a summer retreat out in the country 400 years ago. Emperor Joseph II had it rebuilt by Isidor Carnevale in 1783. Its greatest moment came in 1814 when, during the Congress of Vienna, the allied monarchs and their generals celebrated here the anniversary of the Battle of Leipzig when Napoleon was crushingly defeated. 18,000 soldiers were treated to a meal on tables erected around the building.

Summer House

This little pilgrimage church stands on the site once occupied by a forest shrine. The "Maria-Grün" (Madonna in Green) picture above the High Altar is an object of veneration. A "Hubert" Mass for hunters is celebrated here each November.

Maria-Grün Chapel

Built in 1993, the "Dinopark", with its electronically-operated dinosaurs in prehistoric surroundings provides a half an hour of fun for young and old alike (approach road No. 140; open: Mon.–Sat. 2–10pm; Sun. 10am–10pm).

Dinosaur Park

East of the People's Park (Volksprater) lies the Exhibition Ground of the City of Vienna, with exhibition halls, pavilions and the 150m/492ft high Mannesmann Tower (information: Wiener Messen & Congress GmbH, Südportalstrasse, A-1020 Wien; tel. 2 17 20–0, fax 2 17 20 307).

Exhibition Ground

Praterstrasse

B 5

Praterstrasse no longer enjoys the importance it used to have in the great days of the Prater. It lives on its memories now.
Josef Lanner and his band used to give concerts in No. 28 "Zum Grünen Jäger" (Green Huntsman's House). The office building at No. 31 occupies

Location
2nd District

the site where once stood the famous Carl Theatre which made the figure of Kasperl immortal and had Johann Nestroy as its manager.

No. 54, the house in which Johann Strauss wrote "The Blue Danube" in 1867, has become a museum. Documents relating to the Waltz King's life are on display as well as personal mementoes (open: Tue.–Sun. 9am–12.15pm and 1–4.30pm).

★Rathaus (Town Hall)   B 4

Location
1, Rathausplatz

**Underground
station**
Rathaus (U2)

Trams
1, 2, D, J

Tours
Mon.–Fri. 1pm
(except when the
Assembly is in
session)

The Town Hall is just over one hundred years old. The impressive Neo-Gothic building is the seat of the Vienna City and Provincial Assembly and is the administrative centre of the city. The huge building, occupying nearly 14,000sq.m/17,000sq.yds of the former Parade Ground, was erected in 1872–83 during Franz Joseph's reign by Friedrich von Schmidt, who was also responsible for the decoration and furnishings.

The symbol of the Town Hall is the "Rathausmann" on the top of the 98m/320ft high tower. This banner-carrying iron figure is 3·40m/11ft tall (6m/20ft including the raised banner) and weighs 1800kg/4000lb; it was the work of Alexander Nehr and was a gift from the master locksmith, Wilhelm Ludwig.

The arcaded courtyard in the centre of the building is the largest of the seven courtyards. Originally intended for assemblies, it is now the scene of the popular summer concerts (see Practical Information, Festivals).

The tour of the Rathaus interior begins in the Schmidthalle, the former "Community Vestibule" into which carriages could once drive. Today it houses the Civic Information Office (Stadtinformation; see Practical Information, Information). The two Grand Staircases lead to the official rooms: the Assembly Hall (71m/233ft long, 20m/66ft wide and 17m/56ft high), two Heraldic Rooms, the City Senate Chamber and the "Roter Salon", the Mayor's reception room.

The Neo-Gothic Town Hall (Rathaus)

The council chamber of the Vienna City and Provincial Assembly extends over two floors. Since 1922 Vienna, as the country's capital, has also enjoyed the status of a province and so the City Council is also a provincial body. Notable features of the chamber include the coffered ceiling decorated with gold-leaf and the Art Nouveau candelabra, weighing 3·2 tonnes and lit by 260 lamps, also the work of Friedrich Schmidt.

★★Ringstrasse

B/C 4/5

The handsome Ringstrasse is a thoroughfare encircling the city centre of Vienna. Going in a clockwise direction, it consists of the following sections: Stubenring, Parkring, Schubertring, Kärnterring, Opernring, Burgring, Dr-Karl-Renner-Ring, Dr-Karl-Lueger-Ring and Schottenring. The circle of the Ringstrasse is completed by the Fanz-Josef-Kai (quay) along the Danube Canal.

The razing of the fortifications during Emperor Franz Joseph's reign made possible the laying-out between 1858 and 1865 of a tree-lined ceremonial way. Many large buildings were erected here in the second half of the 19th c., in the grandiose style that became known as the "Ringstrasse style".

The Ringstrasse is 4km/2½ miles long and 57m/185ft wide. The ceremonial inauguration took place on May 1st 1865. Its finest hour, however, was in 1879 when the artist Hans Makart mounted a parade with 10,000 participants in honour of the Imperial couple on the occasion of their Silver Wedding.

The following buildings and parks are situated along the Ringstrase, going from Stubenring towards Schottenring: the Post Office Savings Bank by Otto Wagner; the Museum für Angewandte Kunst; the Stadpark; the Staatsoper; the Hofburg; the Kunsthistorisches Museum and the Naturhistorisches Museum; the Volksgarten; the Parlament; the Rathaus; the Burgtheater; the University and the Votivkirche (see entries).

Location
1st District

Underground stations
Karlsplatz (U1, U2. U4), Schottentor (U2), Schottenring (U2, U4) Schwedenplatz ((U1, U4) Stubentor (U3)

Trams
1, 2, D, J

Rohrau

Excursion

Rohrau is Joseph Haydn's birthplace (house No. 60; the room in which he was born and mementoes; open: Apr.–Oct. Tue.–Thur. 10am–5pm). Here, too, stands Count von Harrach's castle. The last great Viennese nobleman's picture collection was brought here from the family mansion at Freyung in 1970.

The gallery possesses some 200 paintings, including works by Rubens, Brueghel, Van Dyck, Jordaens and Ruysdael.

Location
47km/30 miles east, near Petronell (Carnuntum)

★Ronacher (theatre)

B 5

Built by Ferdinand Feliner the Elder in 1871/2, the "Vienna City Theatre" was badly damaged by fire in 1884, only the façade remaining. In 1886–88 Anton Ronacher built a magnificent variety theatre and coffee house in its place. When, in 1890, Ronacher was forced to withdraw from the enterprise for financial reasons, the building was being used for theatrical performances, operettas and concerts. After the First World War it served as a broadcasting centre, and after the Second World War until 1955 it provided alternative premises for the Burgtheater (see entry), and after that as television studios for Austrian Radio. Finally, between 1991 and 1993, the building was extensively restored and redesigned at considerable expense by the architectural firm of Coop Himmelblau. It now provides a wide and varied programme of entertainment (tickets can be ordered from Ticket Express, A-1040 Wien, Waltergasse 14; tel. 50 52 55 05, fax 5 04 55 50).

Location
1, Sellerstätte 9

Underground station
Stephansplatz (U1, U3)

Trams
1, 2

Information
Tel. 5 13 85 65

The Ronacher variety theatre

Ruprechtskirche (church)   B 5

Location
1, Ruprechtsplatz

Underground station
Schwedenplatz
(U1, U4)

Trams
1, 2

Opening times
From Easter to
end of Sept.
10am–1pm

St Ruprecht's (Rupert's) Church is the oldest church in Vienna. It stands high up on the eastern edge of the old Roman military settlement. It is said to have been built by Bishop Virgil of Salzburg on the site of the subterranean Oratory of Cunard and Gisalrich, two apostles of the faith. The church is first mentioned in documents in 1161.

There is evidence that the nave and the lower floors of the tower were built in the 11th c. The tower was twice made higher, in the 12th and 13th c. A choir was added in the 13th c., as was a south side aisle in the 15th c. The church was thoroughly restored between 1934 and 1936 and between 1946 and 1948.

Its treasures include the oldest stained glass in Vienna (13th c.) in the central window in the choir, and the Altar of Our Lady of Loretto, the so-called "Black Madonna", whose aid was invoked when there was danger from the Turks or the plague.

Salvatorkapelle (Salvator Chapel)   B 4

Location
1, Salvatorgasse 5
(Entrance through
Altes Rathaus)

Underground station
Stephansplatz
(U1, U3)

The Salvator Chapel was founded in 1301 by Otto Haymo (Heimo), a famous conspirator. It formed part of the house which the authorities took over after the failure of the rebellion against Frederick the Fair and converted into the Altes Rathaus (see entry).

On October 10th 1871 the church passed into the possession of the Old Catholics. After sustaining severe damage in the Second World War it was fully restored in 1972–73.

The magnificent Renaissance door, dating from 1520 and one of the few Renaissance works in Vienna, is especially noteworthy. The statues of knights are copies; the originals are in the Historisches Museum der Stadt Wien (see entry).

★★Sammlung Alter Musikinstrumente   C 4
(Collection of Old Musical Instruments)

The Collection of Old Musical Instruments is housed in the middle section of the Neue Burg (see Hofburg). To form the collection the resources of Archduke Ferdinand of Tyrol and the Union of Viennese Music Lovers were pooled.

After several years of restoration work the magnificent collection of musical instruments owned by the Kunsthistorisches Museum (see entry) was re-opened to the public at the end of 1993. This valuable collection contains some unique Renaissance pieces and an extensive collection of keyboard instruments, from clavichords and cembaloes of the 16th c. down to modern pianos.

At the start of the tour visitors will be given headphones on which is played the music relevant to the individual rooms and to the historical instruments displayed therein. As the music is received by means of a sensor in each room visitors can chose which particular music they wish to concentrate on, and can miss out certain epochs if they wish or enjoy others in more detail.

Illustrious personalities in the history of music act as "guides" to the various musical eras: Emperor Leopold I, no mean composer and musician himself, is the main character in the reports on Austrian Baroque, while Viennese Classical music centres on Beethoven and Mozart. The waltz composer Joseph Lanner can be heard playing on his own fiddle, while the Strauss family and the Schrammel brothers present the many faces of Viennese dance music. Gustav Mahler, Richard Strauss and Hugo Wolf, whose pianos can be seen and admired, cover the turn of the century.

The most valuable instruments include a cembalo and a table piano which belonged to Joseph Haydn, a grand piano which Erard Frères of Paris presented to Beethoven, and a Viennese table piano at which Schubert composed his music.

Among the brass wind instruments are a richly ornamented trumpet made for Duke Ferdinand of Tyrol in 1581 and silver trumpets from Maria Theresa's Court Band, The woodwind collection includes "Zinken" (lit. cornets) used by the town pipers.

Location
1, Neue Burg, Heldenplatz

Underground station
Babenberger Strasse (U2)

Trams
1, 2, D, J

Opening times
Wed.–Mon.
10am–6pm
(closed Tue.)

Sammlung Religiöser Volkskunst (Collection of Popular Religious Art)   C 4

Th Collection of Popular Religious Art is housed in the former Ursuline Convent. It is an offshoot of the Museum für Volkskunde (see entry). In its four rooms are exhibited examples of religious popular art from the 17th to the 19th c.

Room I: Domestic altars, pictures on glass, wooden sculpture and wax figurines.

Room II: The old convent pharmacy, with original furniture and equipment. A painting depicts Christ as the Apothecary.

Room III: This room is devoted to the cult of the Virgin. All the Marian pilgrimage centres are marked on maps.

Room IV: Material concerned with popular saints.

Location
1, Johannesgasse 8

Underground station
Stephansplatz (U1, U3)

Opening times
Wed. 9am–4pm
Sun. 9am–1pm

Schillerdenkmal (memorial)

See Akademie der Bildendenkünste

Schloss Belvedere

See Belvedere-Schlösser

★★Schönbrunn (palace and park)   D 1

Location
13, Schönbrunner
Schlossstrasse

**Underground
stations**
Schönbrunn,
Hietzing (U4)

Bus
15A

Trams
10, 58

**Information and
bookings**
Tel. 8 11 13
Fax 8 11 13 333

In 1559 Emperor Maximilian II acquired a small summer palace in a converted mill on this site. After the glorious defeat of the Turks in 1683 Emperor Leopold I commissioned J. B. Fischer von Erlach to design an Imperial palace on the site of the little Palace of Klatterburg which had been destroyed. For the Glorietta Hill Fischer planned a castle larger and more magnificent than the Palace of Versailles, but the project never came to fruition.

The "more modest" Baroque Palace of Schönbrunn with 1441 rooms and apartments was built between 1696 and 1730. In 1744–49 Nikolaus Pacassi converted the palace into a residence for Maria Theresa. There were further alterations between 1816 and 1819, and following severe damage in the Second World War reconstruction was completed in 1952.

After the time of Maria Theresa the most brilliant period for the castle was during the Congress of Vienna, which met here in 1814/15. Other important dates associated with the palace are 1805 and 1809 when Napoleon I, whose troops had occupied Vienna, took up residence in Maria Theresa's favourite rooms. In 1918 Charles I relinquished the throne here, and in 1945 the British High Commissioner set up his headquarters in part

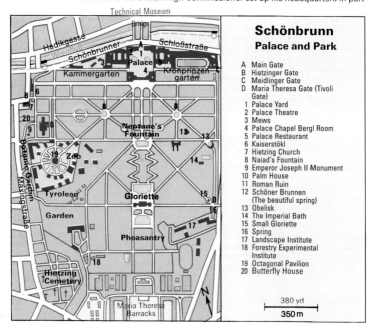

Schönbrunn
Palace and Park

A Main Gate
B Hietzinger Gate
C Meidlinger Gate
D Maria Theresa Gate (Tivoli Gate)
1 Palace Yard
2 Palace Theatre
3 Mews
4 Palace Chapel Bergl Room
5 Palace Restaurant
6 Kaiserstökl
7 Hietzing Church
8 Naiad's Fountain
9 Emperor Joseph II Monument
10 Palm House
11 Roman Ruin
12 Schöner Brunnen (The beautiful spring)
13 Obelisk
14 The Imperial Bath
15 Small Gloriette
16 Spring
17 Landscape Institute
18 Forestry Experimental Institute
19 Octagonal Pavilion
20 Butterfly House

380 yd
350 m

of the building. Today the palace is used for state receptions given by the President of Austria.

Rooms open to the public

Of the 1441 rooms in the palace 39 on the first floor can be seen by visitors participating in guided tours (open: Apr.–Oct. daily 8.30am–5pm, Nov.–Mar. daily 8.30am–4.30pm).

Opening times

The Palace Chapel to the left of the entrance hall dates from c. 1700. The ceiling painting "Apotheosis of Mary Magdalene" is by Daniel Gran (1744), and that above the High Altar, "The Marriage of Mary", is by Paul Troger. The altar itself is the work of Franz Kohl.

Palace Chapel

Also to the left of the entrance hall lie the garden apartments which were furnished to Maria Theresa's taste. They were originally known as the "Indian Rooms" on account of their Romantic and exotic decoration, the work of the Bohemian artist Johann Bergl between 1769 and 1777 (guided tours by prior arrangement on the hour every hour on Sat., Sun. and public holidays).

Bergl Rooms

Emperor Franz Joseph's audience chamber takes its name from the walnut panelling dating from 1766. The candelabra carved out of wood is covered in real gold.

Walnut Room

It was in this simple soldier's bed that the Emperor died on November 21st 1916 after a reign of nearly 68 years.

Franz Joseph's Bedroom

On the walls of this reception-room hang pastel portraits by Jean-Etienne Liotard of Maria Theresa's children.

Empress Elisabeth's Salon

On the left hangs F. Amerling's celebrated portrait of Francis I with the insignia of the Order of the Golden Fleece. A peculiarity of this picture is that the Emperor's eyes seem to follow the spectator wherever he or she may go in the room.

Marie Antionette's Room

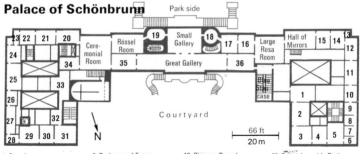

Palace of Schönbrunn

1 Guard room
2 Franz Joseph's Antechamber (Billiard Room)
3 Walnut Room
4 Franz Joseph's Writing-room
5 Franz Joseph's Bedroom
6 W Terrace Cabinet
7 Stair Cabinet
8 Dressing-room
9 Bedroom of Franz Joseph and Elisabeth
10 Empress Elisabeth's Salon
11 Marie-Antoinette Room
12 Nursery
13 Breakfast-room
14 Yellow Salon
15 Balcony Room
16 Small Rosa Room
17 Small Rosa Room
18 Chinese Round Cabinet
19 Oval Chinese Room
20 Blue Chinese Salon
21 Vieux Laque Room
22 Napoleon's Room
23 Porcelain Room
24 Million Room
25 Tapestry Room
26 Memento Room
27 Red Drawing-room
28 E Terrace Cabinet
29 Franz Joseph's Birth-room
30 Writing-room
31 Archduke Francis Charles's Drawing-room
32 Wild Boar Room
33 Passage Chamber
34 Machine Room
35 Lamp Room (Anteroom)
36 Lamp Room

Schönbrunn

Nursery	The Louis XVI *bonheur du jour* in this panelled room belonged to Marie Antoinette, the future Queen of France. Her portrait is to be seen on the left-hand side.
Breakfast-room	Maria Theresa used to take her breakfast in this room. The pictures of flowers are thought to be the work of the Empress' daughters.
Yellow Salon	The white marble clock which stands on the left-hand side was a gift from Napoleon III to Franz Joseph I. The salon takes its name from the yellow damask used for covering the chairs.
Hall of Mirrors	It was in this room, the walls of which are covered with crystal mirrors in gilded Rococo frames, that Maria Theresa's ministers used to swear their allegiance to her. Mozart performed here as a six-year-old prodigy.
Rosa Room	Joseph I's private apartments take their name from the Late Rococo-style landscape paintings (1760–69) by the artist Josef Rosa.
Chinese Round Cabinet	It was here that Maria Theresa set up her "conspiracy headquarters" amid the East Asian lacquered screen panels under the dome with its stucco decoration. At that time State Chancellor Kaunitz was allowed to enter by way of a secret staircase.
Small Gallery	It was in this 18m/60ft long gallery that the Imperial Household held its more intimate dinners. The painted ceiling (1761) is by Gregorio Guglielmi and takes as its theme the glorification of the House of Habsburg.
Ceremonial Room	Major weddings, baptisms and investitures were held here under the Habsburgs. The gold-framed paintings – School of van Meytens – depict the marriage of Joseph II to Isabella of Bourbon-Parma in 1760.

The Great Gallery – scene of many glittering banquets

Hand-painted Far Eastern wallpaper, blue and white Japanese vases and light blue silks form the setting in which the monarchy came to an end. It was in this room that Charles abdicated in 1918 and Austria became a Republic.

Blue Salon

In the private apartment of the elderly Empress Maria Theresa East Asian art is combined with Viennese Rococo.

Vieux Laque Room

Napoleon I lived in Maria Theresa's former bedroom in 1805 and 1809. It was here, too, that his son, the Duke of Reichstadt, who had grown up in Schönbrunn, died in 1832.

Napoleon's Room

Blue and white wooden garlands look deceptively like genuine porcelain. Some of the 213 blue Indian ink sketches are by Maria Theresa's children who were artistically gifted.

Porcelain Room

Maria Theresa's former private salon is panelled with precious rosewood, ornamented with gilt carvings. Set under glass in the panelling are 260 precious Indian and Persian miniatures which Maria Theresa had brought to Vienna from Constantinople.

Million Room

The walls and furniture are covered with Brussels tapestries depicting Dutch folk scenes, including "Port and Fish Market", which is 26sq.m/280sq.ft in area.

Tapestry Room

Glittering Imperial banquets used to be held in the Great Gallery under Gregorio Guglielmi's ceiling-paintings, and it was here that dances were held during the Congress of Vienna in 1814/15. Now the Republic holds its greatest receptions here.

Great Gallery

The wrought-iron gate to the former parade ground (24,000sq.m/25,000sq.yd), a magnificent example of Baroque layout, is flanked by two obelisks.

Palace Yard

The sole remaining Baroque theatre in Vienna was built in 1747 by Nikolaus Pacassi, Maria Theresa's favourite architect, and the Rococo decoration added by Hetzendorf in 1767. Here in the "Habsburg private theatre" the Empress herself acted in plays, and later Haydn and Mozart gave concerts on the Baroque stage which was restored in 1979–80. Today it is used for the Max Reinhard seminars, and is open to the public only in July and August when the Viennese Chamber Opera gives performances.

Palace Theatre

More than 60 historical state coaches, sledges and sedan-chairs as well as harness and Court livery from the period 1690–1918 are on display in the former Winter Riding School. The highlight of the collection is the richly decorated Imperial Coach which, drawn by eight greys, was used at royal weddings and coronations from 1745 onwards. The black-painted Funerary Coach, also drawn by a team of eight, was used to take the Habsburgs to their final resting place in the Imperial vault in the Kapuzinerkirche (see entry). It was last used in 1989 for Empress Zita's funeral. Also on display are Napoleon's coach from Paris which was used for the coronation in Milan, the baby carriage made in Paris for the Duke of Reichstadt (son of Napoleon I and Marie Louise), the Empress Caroline's Coronation Landauer, Emperor Franz Josef's State Coach, the simple coach in which the Empress Elisabeth drove to Geneva, never to return, and Empress Zita's plain coach (open: Apr.–Oct. daily 9am–6pm, Nov.–Mar. Tue.–Sun. 9am–4pm).

Wagenburg (Carriage Museum)

Palace Park

The park around the palace covers an area of about 2sq.km/500 acres. Laid out by Jean Trehet in 1805 to a design by Fischer it is one of the most

Palace of Schönbrunn – summer residence of the Habsburgs

important Baroque gardens in the French style. Between 1765 and 1780 Adrian von Steckhoven and J. F. Hetzendorf von Hohenberg gave it its present appearance. By the paths on each side of the flower-beds stand 44 mythological marble sculptures from the period *c.* 1773 (open: daily 6am–dusk).

Neptune's Fountain

Neptune's Fountain, designed by Hetzendorf, forms the southern boundary of the garden area. About 1780 F. A Zauner sculpted the beautiful decoration based on themes from Greek mythology, including "Thetis implores Neptune's aid when her son Achilles sets out on a sea-voyage".

Schöner Brunnen (Beautiful Fountain)

The "Kaiserbrunnl" (Emperor's Spring) is the old spring which gave the palace its name. Legend has it that whoever drinks from it will become or remain handsome. Emperor Matthias (1557–1619) discovered it while out hunting and Emperor Joseph I had his drinking water drawn from it. In 1799 it was turned into a grotto-like pavilion in which the nymph Egeria (designed by J. C. Beyer) pours out the water,

Roman ruins

The so-called Roman ruins are a Romantic folly with the appearance of a half-buried palace with Corinthian columns dating from 1778. J. F. Hetzendorf von Hohenberg who designed it wanted to symbolise the fall of Greece before the might of the Roman Empire. Recent archaeological research suggests that the Roman ruins may have come from the Neugebäude ("new building"), an Imperial palace which once stood in the present-day suburb of Simmering and which Emperor Maximilian II (d. 1576) had built for his recreation activities and court festivities. By the time of Maria Theresa the palace had been relegated to a powder-store. The Empress ordered the palace to be dismantled and brought to Schönbrunn.

Obelisk

This, too, was designed by Hetzendorf von Hohenberg and dates from 1777. The turtles on which it stands were at one time gilded. The carved scenes depict the family history of the Habsburgs.

Once the Empress Maria Theresa used to take her breakfast in this little pavilion decorated with frescoes. | Small Gloriette

Winding paths lead up to the Clasical Gloriette Arcade on the top of the hill. J. F. Hetzendorf von Hohenberg built it in 1775 to crown the prospect at the end of the park. Here too, as with the Roman ruins, parts of the Neugebäude have been discovered. The Gloriette commemorates the Battle of Kolin (1757) in which Maria Theresa's troops defeated the Prussian army of Frederick the Great. There is a superb view of the city from the roof (open: May–Oct. daily 9am–5pm). | Gloriette

Archduke Johann introduced an Alpine note into the Schönbrunn park by having these two Tyrolean timber houses built and an Alpine garden laid out here c. 1800. In 1865 the Alpine garden was moved to the Belvedere, where it is now the oldest of its kind in Europe. In the place of the old Tyrolean timber houses a farmhouse, built in 1722 and also from the Tyrol, was re-erected here. | Tyrolean Garden

The origins of the Schönbrunn Zoo (access to which is via the Hetzinger Gate) go back to Francis I's menagerie which he founded in 1752, and it is thus the oldest zoo in the world. At present some 750 species of animals live here in special houses or running free in paddocks. In the middle of the zoo stands an octagonal pavilion dating from 1759 which is now a café and restaurant; originally the Imperial family used to go there to watch their "pets" (open: Nov.–Jan. daily 9am–4.30pm, Feb. daily 9am–5pm, Mar. daily 9am–5.30pm, Apr. daily 9am–6pm, May–Sept. daily 9am–6.30pm, Oct. daily 9am–5pm). | Zoo

This was the largest glasshouse in Europe; it was built by Segenschmid in 1883 and fully renovated in 1990. There are three sections in which numerous exotic plants are kept at various temperatures (open: May–Sept. daily 9.30am–6pm, Oct.–Apr. daily 9.30am–5pm). | Palm House

Opposite the Palm House stands the Sundial House with a butterfly garden (open: May–Sept. daily 10am–5pm, Oct.–Apr. daily 10am–3.30pm). | Butterfly House

Schönlaterngasse **B 5**

Schönlaterngasse, the winding lane in the oldest district of the inner city, takes its name from "The House with the Fine Lantern", which was built here in 1680. The original "fine lantern" is now on display in the Historisches Museum (see entry), a copy having been placed on No. 6 Schönlaterngasse in 1971. In this street the houses of the bourgeoisie and merchants are basically medieval with Baroque façades. | **Location** 1, Sonnenfelsgasse/Postgasse **Underground stations** Stephansplatz (U1, U3), Schwedenplatz (U1, U4)

The Heiligkreuzhof and the Basilikenhaus (see entries) and the old Jesuit House (No. 11), where the painter Kupelweiser lived, should be noted.

The Alte Schmiede (Old Smithy) at No. 11 was, until 1974, the workshop of Meister Schmirler who created the present "Schöne Laterne" and gave it to the city. His workshop is open to visitors Mon.–Fri. 10am–5pm and by appointment; in addition, it serves as a cultural centre with an art gallery, café and a literary rendezvous where readings and lectures are given. | Alte Schmiede

Schottenkirche and Schottenstift (church and picture gallery) **B 4**

In the 12th c. Irish monks were invited to come to Vienna fom Regensburg. At that time Ireland was known as "New Scotland" and this is why the church dedicated to our Our Lady which was built for Irish Benedictines | **Location** 1, Freyung

149

Schottenkirche and Schottenstift

Underground station
Herrengasse (U3)

came to be called the "Scots Church". It has been in the possession of the German Benedictines since 1418.

The Scots Monastery was founded by the Babenberg Duke Heinrich Jasomirgott in 1155, and work on construction of the buildings began in 1177. The church was rebuilt in the Gothic style in the 14th and 15th c. It was altered and given a Baroque appearance by Andrea Allio and Silvestro Carlone in the mid-17th c, and restored again in the 19th c. There is a memorial to its founder on the façade.

In the interior there are altar-pieces by Tobias Pock (1651–55), Joachim Sandrant (1652–54) and August Eisenmanger (1887–88). The finest is the "Apostles' Departure" (near the Imperial Oratory). The Baroque memorial on the right behind the Penitents' Chapel was designed by J. E. Fischer von Erlach and is dedicated to Count von Starhemberg, who defended Vienna against the Turks.

The High Altar, dating from 1883, was the last work by Heinrich Ferstel. The altar-piece in the Lady Chapel has the oldest votive painting of the Virgin in Vienna. In the Crypt Chapel, which was converted into vaults in 1960, lie the founder of the church, Heinrich II Jasomirgott, his consort Theodora and his daughter Agnes, Count Rüdiger von Starhemberg (d. 1701) and the Baroque artist Paul Troger (d. 1762).

★ Schottenstift

Visits by appointment
Tel. 5 34 98–0

The Schottenstift (Scots Foundation) at Freyung 6 is linked to the Schottenkirche by the Schottenhof. It boasts a famous secondary school and an important picture gallery. The Foundation Bull dates from 1161, and the abbey was ceded to the German Benedictines in 1418.

The buildings date from the 12th c. but were extensively renovated in the 17th c. and enlarged in the 18th c. In 1832 they were rebuilt by Josef Kornhäusl in simple Classical style.

Pupils of the school included the writers Bauernfeld, Nestroy, von Saar and Hamerling. the "Waltz King" Johann Strauss and the painter Moritz

The Scots Church

The Basiliskenhaus in Schönlaterngasse

von Schwind. Austria's last Emperor, Charles I, also attended this school, as did the founder of Austrian Social Democracy, Viktor Adler.

The collection of pictures here has been in existence for more than 250 years. As well as works from the 16th to the 19th c. there are in the chapter-house 19 pictures from the famous Late Gothic winged altar of 1469–75, which was painted by two "Scottish Masters" and originally stood in the Schottenkirche. The oldest surviving views of Vienna can be seen in the backgrounds to these pictures.

Schubert Museum   A 3

On January 31st 1797 Franz Schubert was born in this little one-storey house – "Zum roten Krebs" (The Red Crab) – in the Himmelpfort district. The city of Vienna owns this house and has been able to preserve Schubert's birthplace virtually unaltered. A Schubert Museum has been installed here, with musical scores, manuscripts, pictures and everyday objects used by the composer (open: Tue.–Sun. 9am–12.15pm and 1–4.30pm). Not everything is entirely authentic, however, for when he was only four years old Schubert moved to a nearby house at Säulengasse 3, where he lived for the next 17 years.

The house in which Schubert died is at Kettenbrückengasse 5, where there is also a memorial room (see Practical Information, Museums and Memorial Locations).

Location
9, Nussdorferstr. 54

Trams
37, 38

Schubert Park   A 3

A few gravestones and a Late Baroque cemetery cross indicate that the Schubert Park was laid out on what used to be the Währinger Cemetery. On the east wall of the park can be seen the original graves of Schubert and Beethoven. Both composers were exhumed in 1888 and re-interred in the Zentralfriedhof (see entry). It was in the Währinger Cemetery that Franz Grillparzer pronounced his funeral oration over Beethoven. He said: "Beethoven withdrew from human society after he had given men all that he had and received nothing in return".

Location
18, Währinger Strasse

Trams
40, 41

★ Secession (art gallery)   C 4

The exhibition gallery of the Artists' Union is easily recognised on account of its remarkable cupola in the form of a bronze laurel bush, popularly known as "the golden cabbage". The building was designed by Josef Olbrich, a disciple of Otto Wagner, in 1898, and was the first and epoch-making example of Viennese Art Nouveau (called "Wiener Jugendstil" or sometimes "Secessionstil"). It was damaged during the war and robbed of its treasures in 1945, but was restored and opened again in 1964. Reconstruction since 1986 has made it possible to put on musical and theatrical performances and video displays.

The need for the building arose after 1892 when the Union of Young Artists under the leadership of the painter Gustav Klimt "seceded from" the more conservative Künstlerhaus (see entry) group. In 1897 the still surviving Artists' Union, called "Secession", came into being under the motto "To the time its art – to art its freedom" and created the artistic style that bears the same name.

The huge Mark Anthony bronze group by Arthur Strasser on the east side of the building is especially noteworthy. The Roman statesman's lion-drawn chariot was displayed at the 1900 World Exhibition in Paris.

Location
1, Friedrichstr. 12

Underground station
Karlsplatz
(U1, U2, U4)

Trams
1, 2, D, J

Opening times
Tue.–Fri.
10am–6pm;
Sat., Sun.
10am–4pm

The Secession building with its "laurel bush" cupola

★Beethoven Frieze by Gustav Klimt

Today in the Secession building visitors can see Gustav Klimt's masterpiece, the Beethoven Frieze. This huge mural measuring some 70sq.m/270sq.ft in area on the theme of Beethoven's Ninth Symphony was painted for the 14th exhibition of the Vienna Secession in 1902. The State purchased it for nearly £1,000,000/US$ 1,500,000 in 1973 and had it restored in 1977 at a cost of £400,000/US$ 600,000. It is now once more "at home" in a newly-built room in the basement where it can be viewed.

Servitenkirche (church)   B 4

Location
9, Servitengasse 9

Underground station
Rossauer Lände (U4)

Tram
D

The Servites' (or "Servants of Our Lady") Church, dedicated to the Annunciation, was founded by Field-Marshal Octavio Piccolomini, one of the leaders of the Wallenstein Conspiracy. It was built by Carlo Carnevale between 1651 and 1677; Piccolomoni died in 1656 and so did not live to see the work completed. The Servites' Church is the earliest building in Vienna based on a central oval form with its main nave elliptical in shape. The transept houses wide, rectangular chapels and in the diagonal corners there are small, semicircular altar-niches. In the narthex can be seen two large 17th c. Baroque figures and a magnificent wrought-iron trellised screen dating from c. 1670. The rich stucco decoration is by Giovanni Battista Barbarino (1669) and Giovanni Battista Bussi (1723–24). Near the 19th c. High Altar can be found a late 15th c. wooden crucifix from the "Raven Stone", the site of executions in days gone by. The carved figures of the Four Evangelists and the Three Virtues on the pulpit of 1739 are by Balthasar Moll. Field-Marshal Octavio Piccolomini (d. 1656) lies buried in front of the altar in the middle chapel on the left-hand side; there is no gravestone.

The Peregrini Chapel was built on to the middle chapel on the right in the 18th c.; its fine Rococo ironwork and the frescoes in the dome are the work of Josef Mölk (1766).

The Tower Chapel on the right leads through to the little Chapel of the Poor; its altar-painting is attributed to Martin J. Schmidt. The Tower Chapel on the left leads to the Lourdes Grotto.

★★Spanish Riding School   B 4

The Spanish Riding School is the last living survivor of the Baroque era and the Viennese monarchy. The institution dates back to the time of Emperor Maximilian II who introduced the breeding of Spanish horses into Austria in 1562. The name "Spanish Riding School" is first documented in 1572. This is the only place where the Classical style of riding, once popular at every Court in Europe, is still practised. The famous equestrian displays have been held in the Baroque Winter Riding School (see Hofburg) since the time of Charles VI. The magnificent hall, built in 1735 to plans by J. E. Fischer von Erlach, was designed for the nobility to show their ability in riding skills and to compete together, It was later used for a variety of other purposes, but since 1894 has been reserved exclusively for the training of the Lippizaner horses and their displays.

Location
1, Josefsplatz

Underground station
Stephansplatz (U1, U3), Herrengasse (U3)

Information
Tel. 5 33 90 31–0
Fax 5 35 01 86

The horses are a cross of Berber and Arabian stock with Spanish and Italian horses. The horses were bred in Lipizza until 1918 when the stud was transferred to Piber in Styria. The stud, part of which was moved to Czechoslovakia during the Second World War, was saved from destruction in 1945 by Colonel Podhajsky, who was then head of the riding school (until 1956), as well as by the horse-loving American General Patton. The spectacular "Flight of the White Stallions" to Bavaria was made into a film by Walt Disney.

Lippizaner performances

The foals are born any shade between brown and mouse-grey; their coats turn white when they are between four and ten years old. Lippizaners

Performance by the Lippizaners

153

are more suited than any other breed of horses to the difficult courtly dressage. Their compact build makes grouping easier, their long, strong necks provide the required upright posture, while the powerful hindquarters assist in performing difficult piaffes, pirouettes, etc. The high knee action enables them to demonstrate the special "Spanish step" in which the legs appear to bend effortlessly as if in slow motion.

There still survive today six lines of stallions which can be traced back to their forefathers, Pluto (1765), Conversano (1767), Maestoso (1773), Neapolitano (1790), Favory (1799) and Siglavy (1810). The stallions do not begin their training until they are four years old. At the age of about seven they learn the so-called ground exercises, including high-speed gait changes, piaffes, passage and pirouettes. They then graduate to the "aerial exercises", with pesades, levades, courbettes and caprioles. In the levade the horse lowers its hindquarters and elegantly raises its body with the front legs bent, in the courbette the horse leaps forwards several times, and in the capriole it leaps in the air and kicks out backwards with lightning speed. The finale, in which eight snow-white Lippizaners elegantly dance the "Spanish step", demonstrates perfection in the art of courtly riding.

The impressive displays of the Spanish Riding School have always been performed in historical costume. The riders wear white buckskin breeches with high black boots, a brown riding-jacket and a bicorn hat trimmed with gold. Deerskin saddles cover the gold-trimmed red and blue saddle-cloths. At the beginning and end of each display the riders silently salute the portrait of Charles VI who commissioned the building.

Admission tickets

Tickets for the performances are very sought after and should therefore be booked as early as possible in advance by writing to the Spanish Riding School. Performances are put on from March to June and in September, on Wednesdays at 7pm and Sundays at 10.45am, in November and December on Sundays only at 10.45am – the exact dates and times can be obtained from the Spanish Riding School and from the Vienna Tourist Board. Visitors can watch the horses at their morning practice to music from April to June and in September, on Saturdays at 10am (tickets can be ordered from ticket and travel agencies in Vienna); normal morning practice takes place from mid-March to the end of June and August to mid-December, Tuesday to Friday 10am–noon (tickets on the day of the event at the entrance in Josefsplatz, Gate 2).

Spinnerin am Kreuz   D 4

Location
10, Triester
Strasse 52

Tram
65

The Spinnerin am Kreuz is a 16m/52ft high Gothic stone pillar in the shape of a phial-shaped tabernacle. One of the landmarks of Old Vienna, it was designed by Hans Puschbaum, the architect of St Stephen's Cathedral, and erected in 1452 to replace an older one which had been donated by Leopold III. According to legend a faithful wife sat here at her spinning-wheel, awaiting her husband's return from a Crusade.

From 1311 to 1747 and again from 1804 to 1868 the "gallows by the Spinnerin" was the site of public executions. Severin von Jaroszynski was hanged here in front of 30,000 spectators in 1827. He was a Polish aristocrat who had robbed and murdered a man in order to be able to satisfy the excessive financial demands of the popular actress Therese Krone.

Spittelberg   C 3/4

Location
7, Spittelberg-
gasse and
surroundings

A densely built but architecturally pretty community grew up during the Baroque era on the Spittelberg, a hill which once belonged to a hospital. It was from this hill that Turkish cannon were directed at the city during the second siege of Vienna (1693) and Napoleon's troops also positioned their artillery here. With time the district deteriorated into a low-class but nevertheless very lively quarter. The Spittelberg was the haunt not only of "lieber Augustin", the wandering piper, but also of many traditional artists and actors, ballad singers and the strolling players who created the "Spittelberg Songs", some of which are still known today.

The Emperor Joseph was thrown out of a local inn, the "Sonnenfels-Waberl", run by a notorious landlady, when he visited it anonymously in 1787. The event is commemorated by an inscription in the entrance of the house at Gutenbergstrasse 13.

The charm of this district was rediscovered in the present century and the city authorities began renovation work in the 1970s. Nowadays it is an attractive district offering many cultural and social facilities. The Spittelberg Cultural Centre in the Amerlinghaus at Stiftgasse 8 provides a venue for musical events, poetry readings, exhibitions, children's activities and dances for senior citizens, appealing to both old and new residents. In the "Werkhaus" on Stiftgasse young people have created a collective workshop where pottery, dressmaking, furniture restoration, ceramics, bookbinding and a goldsmith have come together under one roof. There is a gallery in the centre of the building. The renovated old houses are now occupied by speciality shops, boutiques, pubs and galleries. A market for arts and handicrafts has also been opened; all of which make Spittelberg an attractive and popular district.

Underground station
Volkstheater
(U2, U3)

Bus
48A

Tram
49

★★Staatsoper (State Opera)   C 4

The Vienna State Opera House is one of the world's largest and most splendid theatres, where numerous prominent composers and conductors, international soloists and dancers have performed. After Franz Schalk, the first director, there have been 30 others including Gustav Mahler, Richard Strauss, Herbert von Karajan, Egon Hilbert and Karl Böhm. Under the law, the Austrian Republic is required to ensure that full use is made of its famous opera house, and so there is a different opera or ballet on the programme on 300 evenings in the year.

The Viennese obsession with music goes far back into Habsburg history. The first recorded Viennese Court opera was performed in 1625, on the occasion of the birthday of Ferdinand II, on the Hradschin or Prager Burg, where the Emperor resided for six months. In 1660 Leopold II, probably the greatest music-lover and theatrical devotee of the Baroque period, had a smart theatre built on the square in front of the Court Riding School in 1660–62. After 1668 numerous operas were performed, first on the site of the present Österreichische Nationalbibliothek (see entry), then in the Redoutensälen and in the old Burgtheater on Michaelerplatz, where Mozart's "Il Seraglio", "Marriage of Figaro" and "Cosi fan tutte" were first performed, and subsequently in the Kärntnertor Theatre, where Weber's "Euryanthe" had its unhappy première and Beethoven's "Fidelio" began its series of triumphs in 1814. A few years later the first performances in Vienna of works by Rossini and Verdi ushered in a period of euphoria for Italian opera. After the destruction by fire of the Ringtheater the opera moved to its new home on the Ringstrasse in 1869.

Location
1, Opernring 2

Underground station
Kalsplatz
(U1, U2, U4)

Trams
1, 2, D, J

Tours
July, Aug. daily
10 and 11am,
1, 2 and 3pm
Sept.–June
on demand
Tel. 5 14 44–26 13

The vast Opera House with its clearly defined structure is in the French Early Renaissance style. It was built between 1861 and 1869 to plans by August von Siccardsburg and Eduard van der Nüll. It opened on May 25th 1869 with Mozart's "Don Giovanni" and a prologue spoken by the popular actress Charlotte Wolter. Neither architect lived to see the day. The criticisms and cruel jibes of the local populace while building was in progress drove van der Nüll to suicide, and Siccardsburg died just two months later, in 1868, from a heart attack. The Opera House was hit by bombs on March 12th 1945 and gutted by fire. Reconstruction was not completed until 1955. The second inauguration of the "Opera House on the Ringstrasse" took place on November 5th 1955, when Beethoven's "Fidelio" was performed.

History of
the building

The magnificent Vienna State Opera House

The Opera House can accommodate an audience of 2211, with 110 musicians; the Vienna Philharmonic has been the resident orchestra since 1842. The buildings cover an area of 9000sq.m/10,760sq.yd and a permanent staff of more than 1000 is required to ensure the efficient running of the enterprise. The main façade with its two-storey foyer opens onto the Ringstrasse. The tripartite stage covers an area of 1500sq.m/1800sq.yd and is 45m/148ft high.

Inside a grand staircase leads up to the first floor. Immediately opposite lies the "Schwind Foyer" which takes its name from the pictures by Martin Schwind of scenes from operas. The staircase, the foyer and the tea-room with its valuable tapestries were the only parts of the building left undamaged after the fire in 1945. The restored former Imperial Box, on the left of the proscenium, is now reserved for the Federal President, while the Archduke Box opposite is used by the Federal Chancellor for social functions.

Tickets

Information: tel. 5 14 44 26 13; Tickets can also be booked in writing from : Österreichischer Bundestheaterverband, A-1010 Wien, Hanuschgasse 3; fax 5 14 44 29 69 (up to 10 days prior to the performance), Bookings by credit card: tel. 5 13 15 13 (from 6 days prior to the performance); Vienna Ticket Service, A-1043 Wien, Postfach 160; tel. 5 87 98 43, fax 5 87 98 44.

★★Opera Ball

Every year on the Thursday before Carnival (Fasching) the Opera Ball is held here. It is one of the most elegant and famous balls in the world. The stage and the rows of seats in the auditorium, which is decorated in cream, red and gold, are brought up to the same level by means of a specially fitted floor. Thousands of carnations are flown in from the Riviera to decorate the boxes just for the one night. (Tickets: Opernball-Büro, A-1010 Wien, Goethegasse 1; tel. 5 14 44 26 06.)

Franz Lehár Memorial . . .   *. . . in the Stadtpark*

Stadtpark (City Park)   C 5

The two parts of the City Park are linked by bridges over the Danube. It covers an area of 11·4ha/28 acres.

In 1857 Franz Joseph I instigated the creation of a garden where the old fortifications went down to the water's edge, judging the site to be "well suited to embellishment". The landscape-gardener Dr Siebeck carried through the plans drawn up by the landscape artist Josef Szelleny. The gardens were opened in 1862, and the Spa Pavilion – where waltz concerts are now held from Easter to the end of October – in 1867.

In the part of the park nearest to the city centre stand monuments to the painters Hans Canon, Emil Schundler, Hans Makart and Friedrich von Amerling, to the composers Johann Strauss the Younger, Franz Schubert and Anton Bruckner, as well as to Anton Zelinka, the founding mayor. The "Donauweibchenbrunnen" (The Spring with the Sprite of the Danube) is a copy; the original stands in the Historisches Museum (see entry).

Location
1, Parkring

Underground stations
Stubentor (U3)
Stadtpark (U4)

Trams
1, 2

Stanislaus-Kostka-Kapelle (chapel)   B 4

This chapel in the courtyard of the Jesuit presbytery is decorated in gold and silver.

Until 1582 the chapel was a single room in the house called "Zur goldenen Schlange" (The Golden Snake), where the Polish Jesuit Stanislaus Kostka lived between 1564 and 1567. After the occurence of two miracles the room was converted into a chapel and given rich stucco ornamentation in 1742 in memory of Stanislaus Kostka who was canonised in 1726. The altar-piece "St Stanislaus Kostka taking Communion with the Angels" was painted by Franz Anton Stecher c. 1840.

Location
1, Steindlgasse 6/
Kurrentgasse 2

Underground station
Stephansplatz
(U1, U3)

★★Stephansdom (St Stephen's Cathedral)   B 4/5

Location
1, Stephansplatz

Underground station
Stephansplatz
(U1, U3)

Tours
Mon.–Sat.
10.30am and 3pm
Sun. and public
holidays 3pm
June–Sept.
also Sat. 7pm

St Stephen's Cathedral, with its 137m/450ft high spire, is not only the major sight and symbol of Vienna; it is also the city's most important Gothic edifice and has been the cathedral church of the archbishopric since 1722.

The cathedral reflects the never-ending labours of generations since the 12th c. and represents eight centuries of architectural history. The original Romanesque church was replaced by a Late Romanesque one in the 13th c. All that remains of it are the massive gate and the "Heidentürme" (Heathen Towers). Next came reconstruction in the Gothic style in the 14th c. by Duke Rudolf IV of Habsburg – known as "The Donor".

The choir, and the Chapels of St Eligius, St Tirna and St Catherine were completed in that same century, while the south tower, the nave and the Chapel of St Barbara belong to the 15th c. The uncompleted north tower was roofed over in the 16th c. Improvements and further construction followed in the 17th, 18th and 19th c.

The roof was destroyed by fire in the final days of the Second World War in 1945. The vaulting of the middle and the right-hand side choirs collapsed and the towers were gutted. Reconstruction and restoration went on from 1948 to 1962. It was a communal effort, involving the whole of Austria. The new bell was paid for by Upper Austria, the new floor by Lower Austria, the pews by Vorarlberg, the windows by Tyrol, the candelabra by Carinthia, the communion rail by Burgenland, the tabernacle by Salzburg, the roof by Vienna and the portal by Styria. Today atmospheric pollution is the chief danger, especially the effects of sulphur dioxide. The exterior is being painstakingly cleaned with soft brushes and pure water: chemical cleaners

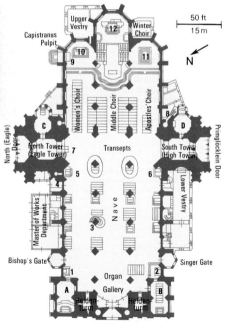

St Stephen's Cathedral

A Tirna Chapel (Holy Cross Chapel), burial-place of Prince Eugene (d. 1736); above it the Treasury Chapel
B Eligius Chapel
C Barbara Chapel
D Catherine Chapel

1 H. Prachatitz's altar canopy.
2 Canopy with Pötscher Madonna
3 A. Pilgram's pulpit with Peeping Tom on the plinth. On the pillar, the Servant's Madonna
4 Lift to Pummerin Bell
5 Organ-case by A. Pilgram (with Pilgram's self-portrait)
6 H. Puchsbaum's canopy
7 Entrance to catacombs
8 Tower stairs (313 steps)
9 Donor's gravestone
10 Wiener-Neustadt Altar (Frederick's reredos)
11 Emperor Frederick III's (d. 1493) raised sarcophagus
12 T. and J. J. Pock's High Altar

Dimensions: length, outside 350 ft (107 m), inside 300 ft (92 m). Width across transepts 230 ft (70 m) outside. Width across nave, inside, 130 ft (39 m). Height of nave, inside, 92 ft (28 m). Height of Heiden towers 215 ft (66 m), of N tower 200 ft (61 m), of S tower 450 ft (137 m).
Largest Bell: Pummerin – 20 tons (21 t); the original bell, dating from 1711, was recast in 1945

and sand-blasting are out of the question, as they would do more harm than good.

The cathedral buildings cover an area of 3500sq.m/4186sq.yd. They are 107m/350ft long and 39m/128ft across. The nave is 28m/92ft high. The Heathen Towers are 66m/217ft high, the south tower 137m/450ft and the uncompleted north tower 61m/200ft. The roof, the apex of which is 60m/200ft above ground-level, is roofed with 230,000 glazed tiles.

Buildings

The Late Romanesque Giant Gateway dates from 1230 and has uncommonly rich ornamentation. In earlier times it was opened only on festive occasions. In 1805 Napoleon's farewell proclamation hung down from the frieze with its dragons, birds, lions, monks and demons. To the left of the vestibule two iron measuring rulers have been let into the wall: the longer one represents a normal Viennese cubit length, while the shorter one is the Viennese cubit length used when measuring cloth. It is also probable that passion plays were performed in front of this gate, the stage being erected on the cemetery area (see Stephansplatz).

Giant Gateway

The Heathen Towers (Heidentürme) are part of the Romanesque church which was first mentioned in documents in 1295. The name recalls the heathen shrine which is thought to have occupied this site formerly. The towers are 66m/215ft high and from the third storey upwards their shape alters from rectangular to octagonal.

Heathen Towers

Prince Eugene is buried in the Tirna Chapel, which dates from c. 1359. The conqueror of the Turks is commemorated in a gravestone set in the floor. The Crucifix above the altar is 15th c. work. The beard of Christ is made of human hair and according to legend it is still growing!

Tirna Chapel

It is likely that the pierced stone Gothic canopy dating from c. 1437 is the work of Hans von Prachatiz; the painting of the Sacred Heart beneath it, however, is 18th c.

Stone canopy

The gate – a counterpart to the Singer Gate – was the entry reserved for female visitors to the cathedral. Its figurative sculptures, dating from c. 1370, are examples of High Gothic art. Among coats-of-arms can be seen the figures of Duke Albrecht III and his consort.

Bishop's Gate

This is the most important work of art in the nave, a masterpiece of Late Gothic sculpture in sandstone. It was carved by Master Pilgram c. 1515 and is decorated with the figures of the Four Fathers of the Church. On the plinth Pilgram carved a representation of himself in the pose of a "peeping Tom".
   The so-called Servants' Madonna, on the pillar by the pulpit, dates from 1340. According to legend, a maid employed by a Count turned to the Virgin for help when she was wrongly suspected of theft. The true miscreant was discovered, and the Count's lady paid for this figure in St Stephens's to commemorate the event.

Pulpit

The spacious three-aisled interior is divided up by clustered pillars which support the stellar and reticulated vaulting. On the pillars are life-size statues in stone and clay, the most valuable of which is that of St Christopher on the left-hand pillar in the choir; dating from 1470, it was probably a gift from Emperor Frederick III.

Nave

The original organ disappeared in 1720, and only the magnificent Late Gothic organ-case by Pilgram remains; the monogram suggest that it was made in 1513. The man with the compass and set-square, again in the pose of a "peeping Tom", is Pilgram himself. The new organ, installed in 1960, has 10,000 pipes.

Organ-case

The "Eagle" Tower was never completed; the reason, according to legend, is as follows: Hans Puschbaum, who was in charge of construction, made a

North (Eagle) Tower

Nave of St Stephen's Cathedral

pact with the Devil to assist him in completing the work quickly, but was cast down into the abyss because he ventured to pronounce a holy name. The new Pummerin bell, cast in 1951 from the remains of its 1711 predecessor which was smashed in the air-raids of 1945, has hung in the Tower since 1957. It weighs 21tonnes/20 tons and its diameter 3·14m/10ft. It is rung only on special occasions such as New Year's Eve. Visitors can travel up to the "Pummerin" in a fast lift (Apr.–Sept. daily 9am–6pm, Oct.–Mar. 8am–5pm).

Catacombs

The entrance to the catacombs is through the chamber under the North Tower; however, they can be visited only as part of a guided tour (daily 10, 11 and 11.30am, 2, 2.30, 3.30, 4 and 4.30pm). They extend from under the cathedral choir out under Stephansplatz (see entry), and the bones of thousands of Viennese citizens are piled up in tiers (but this part is not open to the public). This section has a connection with the cemetery which once surrounded the cathedral. As the dead were buried there in a very negligent manner – often the vaults were not properly closed or the graves not dug deep enough – and bodies were often prematurely exhumed because the space was needed for fresh interments, there was a general smell of putrefied corpses. So, in about 1470, it was decided to build a new charnel-house, and the catacombs were constructed and were large enough to supplant the cemetery, which was closed down in 1735. By 1783, when Emperor Joseph II prohibited any more burials in the catacombs, more than 10,000 bodies had been interred there. The major attraction of the catacombs is the Ducal Vault which Rudolf IV had constructed for members of the Houise of Habsburg in 1363. After the construction of the Imperial Vault in the Kapuzinerkirche (see entry) it became the custom to place here only copper urns containing the intestines of the members of the Ruling House, while their bodies were laid to rest in the Imperial Vault and their hearts in the Augustinerkirche (see entry). Since 1953 there has also been a vault in the catacombs reserved for the Archbishops of Vienna.

The master builder Puchsbaum is thought to be the builder of this part of the cathedral. The upper row of figures on the 19th c. canopy include Frederick III, Maximilian I, Franz Joseph I, Elisabeth and Maria of Burgundy. The iron cylinder on the pillar to the left may be a medieval sanctuary knocker.

Galilee/Eagle Gate

The plan of the Barbara Chapel is similar to that of the Catherine Chapel (see below); it was also designed by Puchsbaum.

Barbara Chapel

Among the Early Gothic stone figures dating from before 1340 there is an especially fine Angel of the Annunciation and a statue of Our Lady the Protectress. They serve as ornamentation to the "Women's Choir", as it is known. Among the most important graves is the donor grave of Rudolf IV (which is, in fact, empty).

Donor Memorial

Frederick II was the donor of this winged reredos of 1447. It was only in 1884 that it was brought to Vienna from Wiener-Neustadt.

The Wiener-Neustadt Altar

This was constructed from black marble between 1640 and 1660 by Tobias and Johann Jakob Pock. The statues around it represent the patron saints of the province, Leopold and Florian, and St Roch and St Sebastian, who were invoked in time of plague. Gothic stained glass has been preserved to the left and right of the High Altar.

High Altar

The south choir is dominated by the huge raised sepulchre of Frederick III. It is made of red marble and has a larger than life-size statue of the Emperor which is surrounded by coats of arms. The design is by the Dutch artist Niclas Gerhaert van Leyden (1467–1513), who himself made the top of this Gothic grave.

Frederick III's raised sepulchre

The marble font dates from 1481. The reliefs on the 14-sided basin depict Christ, John the Baptist and the Twelve Apostles. On its plinth can be seen the Four Evangelists. The carved wooden font cover is particularly fine.

Catherine Chapel

The famous "Steffl", as the Viennese call it, was begun in 1356. It is 137m/450ft high and is considered to rival the tower of Freiburg Minster as the most beautiful German Gothic tower. The statues below the richly-ornamented canopies on the second floor are of those who endowed the church (copies; the 14th c. originals are in the Historisches Museum der Stadt Wien (see entry)). It is possible to climb the tower as far as the watch room (daily 9am–5.30pm), but there are 343 stairs to negotiate.

South Tower

The porch between the two buttresses of the tower is 14th c., as are the seated figures of the Evangelists.

Primglöcklein Door and Galilee

The Late Gothic canopy over the Leopold Altar is believed to be the work of Hans Puchsbaum. It was donated in 1448.

Canopy

This was the entry for male visitors to the cathedral. The donor figures, the nine Apostles and the legend of St Paul in the tympanum date from 1378.

Singer Gate

The Pötscher Madonna under its Late Gothic canopy has been an object of veneration in Austria and Hungary since the Battle of Zenta in 1697. According to legend, tears streamed from the eyes of the Madonna for a fortnight at the time of the battle against the Turks.

The Pötscher Madonna

This chapel is also known as the Dukes' Chapel, and its statues count among the most important of the second half of the 14th c. The "Hausmut-tergottes" (the Protective Mother of God) from the former Himmelpfort Monastery was revered by the Empress Maria Theresa.

Eligius Chapel

Stephansplatz (square)   B 4

Location
1, Stock-im-Eisen-Platz/Rotenturmstrasse

Underground station
Stephansplatz (U1, U3)

The square in front of St Stephen's Cathedral (see Stephansdom) forms the centre of the inner city of Vienna and is now a bustling pedestrian precinct surrounded by shops and cafés. After war damage and the building of an underground station the entire open space was newly laid out. Of interest are houses No. 2, "Zur Weltkugel" (The Globe), No. 3, Das Churhaus (Election House), No. 5, Domherrenhof (Prebendary's Court), No. 6, Zwettlerhof (Zwettler Court) and No. 7, the Archbishop's Palace.

Until 1732 Stephansplatz was a cemetery, as is indicated by the tombstones incorporated in the external walls of the cathedral and the Late Gothic column in which the eternal light burned for the dead. A copy can be seen at the west end of the south cathedral wall. To the right of the cathedral coloured stones mark the outline of the Chapel of Mary Magdalene, in which burial services were once held. It was first documented in 1378 and burned down in 1781. When Stephansplatz underground station was being constructed the Virgilkapelle (Virgilian Chapel) was discovered beneath the crypt of Mary Magdalene.

★ **Virgilian Chapel**

Opening times
Tue.–Sun.
9am–12.15pm,
1–4.30pm

This extraordinary relic of Vienna's medieval past, which also houses a collection of historic Viennese ceramics, is open to the public.

A comparison of architectural features – for example, the zig-zag motif on the rounded cross directly below the niche-vaulting is similar to that on the Giant Gate of St Stephen's Cathedral – has enabled experts to date the chapel as 13th c. This subterranean room of niches was probably planned as a mausoleum and belonged to the Chrannest family from the early 14th c. It was their family vault in which they erected altars, the most important of which was dedicated to St Virgil. The fact that such a monumental vault belonged to a family without rank is somewhat puzzling. It is possible that the chapel was built by Duke Frederick the Quarrelsome (who wished to have Vienna created a bishopric) as a crypt for the bishop of the new diocese. The Duke died before his plan was realised – it was 1469 before

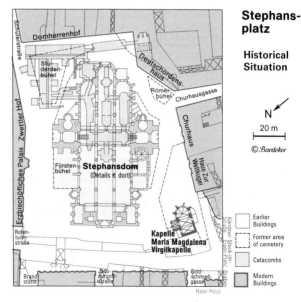

Stephans-platz

Historical Situation

N

20 m

© Baedeker

Stephansdom (Details s. dort)

Domherrenhof

Deutschordens-haus

Stu-denten-bühel

Römer-bühel

Churhausgasse

Churhaus

Haus zur Weltkugel

Fürsten-bühel

Kapelle Maria Magdalena Virgilkapelle

Roten-turm-straße

Jaso-margott-straße

Goldschmied-gasse

Brand-stätte

Schulerstraße

Zwettler Hof

Erzbischöfliches Palais

Kärntner Straße   Stock-im-Eisen-Platz   Graben

Earlier Buildings

Former area of cemetery

Catacombs

Modern Buildings

Haas-Haus

Vienna became an independent diocese – and so the Chrannest family were able to buy the vault. After the last of the family had died the chapel became the seat of newly-formed religious brethren (the Gottleichnams-bruderschaft and the Kaufmannsbruderschaft) in the early 16th c. In the 16th and 17th c. it again became a place of burial. The subterranean vault was abandoned when the remains of the Chapel of Mary Magdalene were cleared away in 1781.

The Virgilian Chapel is rectangular, 10·5m/35ft long and 6m/20ft wide. It was 13.5 /45ft high; today its clay floor lies 12m/40ft below street level. The entrance was probably via a trap-door in the floor of the chapel above.

Stock-im-Eisen-Platz (square)　　　　　　　　　　B 4

Stock-im-Eisen-Platz is a square next to Stephansplatz and leading directly into Kärnter Strasse (see entries). It takes its curious name from a tree-trunk into which many nails have been hammered and which stands in a niche of house No. 3/4, at the corner of Graben and Kärnter Strasse. There is evidence that the tree-trunk has been here since 1533. According to legend,

Location
1, Stephansplatz/
Graben

Haas-Haus – Hollein's ultra-modern shopping mall

Underground station
Stephansplatz
(U1, U3)

every locksmith's apprentice who came to Vienna in the course of his wanderings had to hammer a nail into the tree-trunk.

Visitors are recommended to view the charming stairway and beautiful inner courtyard of the "Equitable" house at No. 3.

Haas-Haus

On the site of No. 6, directly opposite the west door of the cathedral, can be seen an ultra-modern, futuristic building by the Viennese architct Hans Hollein. It is a shopping mall modelled on that of Horton Plaza in San Diego, USA. Behind the cool and elegant façades of shimmering green quarzite and marble with a round oriel window can be found five floors of exclusive designer boutiques and specialist shops, Vienna's largest hi-fi and video shop, offices and banks and a "Gourmet Storey" owned by Do & Co, and aimed at a discerning clientele. From the roof terrace of the café restaurant a view of Stephansdom, Graben and Kärnter Strasse (see entries) can be enjoyed.

Strassenbahnmuseum (Tram Museum) C 6

Location
3, Erdbergstrasse 109

Underground station
Schlachthaus-gasse (U3)

Buses
77A, 79A

The Vienna Tram Museum was opened in 1986 and enlarged in 1990–92. More than 80 historical vehicles are displayed on 1·8km/1 mile of track. The collection begins with horse-drawn carriages used in 1871 and then ranges over the first articulated vehicles and old buses of the 1950s to more modern suburban railway coaches (open: May–early Oct. Sat., Sun, public holidays 9am–4pm).

Those who enjoy such nostalgic trips may like to go on a tour of the city on the Oldtimer Tram (May–early Oct. Sat. 1.30pm and Wed., Sun., public holidays 10am and 1.30pm, departing from Karlsplatz; tickets from the Karlsplatzpassage underground station; information; tel. 5 87 31 86).

Technisches Museum für Industrie und Gewerbe (Technical Museum) D 1

Location
4, Mariahilfer Str. 212

Closed for renovation until 1996

Emperor Franz Joseph laid the foundation-stone of the new three-storey museum in 1908, but it did not open until 1918, after his death.

The Imperial "physical collection" evolved into an "industrial collection", which itself later became a "production collection". Finally this gave rise to the Technical Museum together with the Railway and Postal/Tele-graph Museum. The collections provide a cross-section of the development of technology, commerce and industry with special reference to the contribution made by Austria. As the museum is at present undergoing complete renovation it will remain closed to visitors until this is completed.

Theresianum (academy) C 4

Location
4, Favoritenstr. 15

Underground station
Taubstummen-gasse (U1)

The Diplomatic College and the endowed Theresian Academy are housed in the Favorita, formerly an Imperial summer palace.

The Favorita was built between 1616 and 1625 and refurnished in the Baroque style in 1690. It was the favourite residence of Leopold I, Joseph I and Charles VI, who died here. His daughter Maria Theresa, however, preferred Schönbrunn (see entry) and handed the Favorita over to the Jesuits, enjoining them to provide a "Collegium Theresianum" where the sons of aristocrats could be trained as public officials, as well as the Oriental Academy for the education of officials and diplomats.

In the large park of the Theresianum (Argentinierstrasse) stands Radio House, built by Clemens Holkmeister between 1936 and 1938. It is a building with a simple façade and a beautiful entrance hall.

Technical Museum

★Uhrenmuseum der Stadt Wien (City of Vienna Clock Museum)   B 4

The City of Vienna Clock Museum has been housed since 1921 in the "Harfenhaus" (Harpist's House), one of the oldest houses in Vienna. The collection is on three floors and illustrates the development of clocks from the 15th c. to the present day. The 1200 or so exhibits include very basic clocks, tower and table clocks, pocket watches, Austrian lantern timepieces of the Biedermeier period, clocks with illustrated faces, wrist-watches, and a 1992 computer clock.

Following the rebuilding of the second and third floors more Empire and Biedermeier clocks are exhibited. One room on the second floor contains only clocks with illustrated faces, and on the third floor are electrical wall-clocks with regualtors. The development of the wrist-watch is illustrated by means of more than 170 items, beginning with some superb jewelled watches from *c.* 1850, followed by First World War trench timepieces, gentlemen's self-winding watches from the 1930s, together with unusual and novelty items from the present day.

Room 1: Mainly tower clocks, among one from St Stephen's Cathedral dated 1699 (Cat. No. 3043) and the oldest item in the collection, a 15th c. tower clock.

Room 2: Hand-made, weight-driven wall clocks. The *pièce de résistance* is an astronomical clock of 1663 (No. 794).

Room 3: Travelling, table and wall clocks. The four-poster bed clock (No. 2472) was made in the 17th c.

Room 4: Pedestal clocks. One of the most valuable is a pendulum clock by Louis Monet of Paris, dated 1752 (No. 50).

Location
1, Schulhof 2

Underground station
Stephansplatz
(U1, U3)

Opening times
Tue.–Sun.
9am–4.30pm

Tours
1st and 3rd Sun.
of each month
10 and 11am

Room 5: Part of Marie von Ebner-Eschenbach's collection, including a Swiss gold pendant watch c. 1800 (Nos. 1490–1492). Also other valuable gold-enamelled timepieces.

Room 6: Commode, pedestal and travelling clocks. The astronomical pedestal clock (No. 232) is dated 1810 and comes from a Viennese workshop.

Room 7: Rare Japanese clocks, including unusual 18th c. pillar clocks (Nos. 799–802).

Room 8: Desk clocks and clocks in the form of figures. The "Rider's Clock" (No. 3064) is of Austrian manufacture and dates from c. 1802.

Room 9: Empire grandfather clocks.

Room 10: Seven clocks with illustrated faces.

Room 11: Biedermeier time-pieces in veneered wooden cases.

Room 12: Wall clocks and a remarkable astronomical clock of 1863 (No. 326).

Room 13: Clocks from the turn of the century; one in the form of a bicycle.

Room 14: Clocks from the Black Forest and also a particularly fine Austrian carved cuckoo-clock (No. 3065).

Room 15: Novelties, such as a night-light clock (No. 250), probably Swiss.

Room 16: About 270 pocket watches and more than 170 wrist-watches dating from 1850 to the present day.

Room 17: Toy clocks and automata movements.

Room 18: Clocks in the form of flutes, organs and harps.

Universität (university)   B 4

Location
1, Dr-Karl-Lueger-Ring 1

Underground station
Schottentor (U2)

Trams
1, 2, D

The University buildings were erected during the period when the Ring-strasse was being developed. The plans were by Heinrich Ferstel, who took inspiration from the Italian Renaissance style, the era which ushered in the "Golden Age" of European science. The buildings were opened in 1884 and renovated in 1953 and 1965. In the arcaded central courtyard will be found monuments to famous university lecturers, including Anton Bruckner, Gerhard von Swieten, Theodor von Billroth, Marie von Ebner-Eschenbach, Ludwig Boltzmann, Anton von Eselsberg, Philipp Semmelweiss, Sigmund Freud and the Nobel prize-winners Karl Landsteiner and Julius Wagner-Jauregg.

★UNO-City (Vienna International Centre)   north-east beyond A 6

Location
2, Wagramer Strasse

Following measures taken in the early 1970s to construct the Danube Relief Channel, UNO-City and an international conference centre, the Austria Center Vienna, were created at the end of the Danube Bridge which lies opposite the Altstadt. In years to come it is planned to develop a second ultra-modern city centre around UNO-City, to be known as Danube City (see entry).

UNO-City is leased by the State on a 99-year agreement for a peppercorn rent of one schilling a year to the United Nations, several of whose organisations are housed here. These include the United Nations Industrial Development Organisation (UNIDO), the Department of the UN for International Commercial Law (UNCITRAL), the International Atomic Energy Authority (IAEA) and the High Commission for Refugees (UNHCR). Since August 27th 1979 the complex has officially been extra-territorial.

The idiosyncratic office-blocks, standing between 54m/177ft and 120m/395ft high, were built between 1973 and 1976 to plans by Johann Staber. The architectural embellishments and the interiors are mainly the work of renowned Austrian artists; on the UNO Plaza stands "Polis", a bronze casting by Joannis Avramidis, while inside can be seen pictures by Wolfgang Hollegha, Georg Eisler, Karl Korab, Kurt Regschek, Peter Pongratz and Friedensreich Hundertwasser, with reliefs by Alfred Hrdlicka and Giselbert Hocke.

Underground station
Kaisermühlen/
Vienna
International Centre
(U1)

Buses
90A, 91A, 92A

The Austria Center Vienna adjoining UNO-City was opened in 1987. It is an ultra-modern centre for events and conferences and can seat anything between 50 and 4000 delegates.

Austria Center Vienna

Fourteen rooms of various sizes are available for concerts, dances, banquets, exhibitions and theatrical and TV shows. The accommodation is on four floors and each room has its own foyer so that different events can be held at the same time. The floor space of the foyers, totalling over 9390sq.m/1,000,000sq.ft, can also be used for exhibitions. All the public rooms have the necessary technical provisions for TV, film and slide projections as well as for simultaneous translation in up to nine languages.

In addition there are offices and rooms for 10 to 70 people available for meetings. In the main centre conferences of UN size can be held (there are direct links to the HQ of the United Nations). When laid out in parliamentary style it can accommodate 2100 delegates; in rows, twice as many can be seated. In addition there are a press centre and a radio station, a post office, bank, travel bureaux, restaurants, coffee-shops and a cocktail lounge.

Austria Center Vienna

Temple of Theseus in the Volksgarten

Virgilian Chapel

See Stephansplatz

Volksgarten (park)   B 4

Location
1, Dr-Karl-
Renner-Ring

**Underground
station**
Herrengasse (U3)

Trams
1, 2, D, J

The Volksgarten lies between the Hofburg and the Burgtheater (see entries). This, the second largest park in the city centre, was opened in 1820 on the site of the fortifications which had been blown up by the French in 1809, and soon became a favourite spot with Viennese citizens out for a Sunday afternoon stroll.

In the centre of the gardens stands the Temple of Theseus, built in 1823 by Peter Nobile for Antonio Canova's statue of Theseus and modelled on the Theseion in Athens. The order for this had originally been given by Napoleon I while he was in Vienna, but nothing came of it, for obvious political reasons, until Francis I stepped into the breach. Later, in 1890, the statue was removed from the Temple and placed in the staircase of the Kunsthistorisches Museum (see entry).

Notable monuments in the park include the Grillparzer Memorial with reliefs portraying scenes from six of his plays, and the memorial to the Empress Elisabeth.

Votivkirche (church)   B 4

Location
9, Rooseveltplatz

The prebendal church Zum Göttlichen Heiland (The Divine Saviour) was built as a votive offering after the abortive attempt in 1853 to assassinate

Franz Joseph I. Archduke Ferdinand Maximilian, Franz Joseph's brother, who was later to become Emperor of Mexico, led the way in raising the necessary finance. Heinrich Ferstel chose the Neo-Gothic style, in imitation of the French Gothic cathedrals, and the chancel is one of the best examples of 19th c. historically-inspired architecture.

The church possesses several important works of art. In the baptistery in the south transept can be seen Count Niklas Salm's Renaissance sepulchre (1530–33) surmounted by a recumbent figure of the Count (commander during the first Turkish siege in 1529) and with twelve superb reliefs on the sides; it is a product of Loy Hering's workshops. In the side-chapel in the south transept the important 15th c. Antwerp Altar is beautifully carved and contains scenes from the Passion. In a niche in the north transept is a copy of Our Lady of Guadeloupe which serves as a reminder of Emperor Maximilian of Mexico, the church's first protector (see above).

Underground station
Schottentor (U2)

Trams
1, 2, 37, 38, 40, 41, 42, 44, D

★Waffensammlung (Weapons Collection)   C 4

The first collectors of the armour and weapons displayed here were Archduke Ernst of Styria (15th c.) and Archduke Ferdinand of Tyrol (16th c.) It eventually became the major collection of its type when in 1889 all the Habsburg armouries were combined. The collection was transferred from the Kunsthistorisches Museum (see entry) to the Neue Burg (see Hofburg) in 1935–36, and extensive restoration work went on until 1994 in the Hunt and Armour Rooms.

The valuable exhibits include medieval helmets, the armour of Frederick I of the Palatinate and a ceremonial sword belonging to Frederick III, Late Gothic suits of armour and swords and Louis XII's crossbow, tournament armour, Maximilian I's jousting equipment, mainly from the Innsbruck Court workshops, High Renaissance armour and ceremonial swords, with

Location
1, Neue Burg, Heldenplatz

Underground station
Babenberger Strasse (U2)

Trams
1, 2, D, J

Staircase leading up to the Arms Museum in the Neue Burg

Opening times
Mon., Wed.–Sat.
10am–6pm

two suits of boy's armour made for Charles V, parade armour for Charles V, Philipp II, King Ferdinand I and Francis I, early firearms, the "Adlergarnitur" (Eagle Armour), some of the finest 16th c. armour, numerous examples of the armour worn by Archduke Ferdinand of Tyrol, 16th c. costumes, ceremonial weapons belonging to Maximilian II, including his golden dagger, richly ornamented shields and helmets and some superb 16th c. Ottoman weapons.

Also on display are weapons for hunting and target practice, Maximilian II's "Rose Petal" armour and the "braided" armour of his sons, Papal gifts to Ferdinand II of Tyrol and Tyrolean armour belonging to his sons, Baroque armour and richly inlaid 17th c. sporting weapons including Archduke Leopold V's silver gun by Hans Scmidt, Turkish weapons seized as booty in the time of Leopold I as well as a large quantity of Imperial hunting weapons and equipment from the 18th and 19th c.

Winterpalais des Prinzen Eugen (palace)   C 4

Location
1, Himmelpfort-
gasse 3

**Underground
station**
Stephansplatz
(U1, U3)

Prince Eugene's town mansion has been occupied by the Ministry of Finance since 1848. There was almost an architectural tragedy when the conqueror of the Turks decided to change architects while construction was in progress. J. B. Fischer von Erlach was in charge from 1695 to 1698, but he was replaced by J. L. von Hildebrandt from 1702 to 1724.

Prince Eugene died here in 1736 without receiving the final respects to which he was entitled. Emperor Charles VI was not present at his funeral, having gone to Laxenburg (see entry) the day before "to pass the time". Prince Eugene's heiress, Anna Victoria of Savoy-Soissons, squandered the inheritance in a short while. In the end Maria Theresa purchased the palace for the State in 1752.

Visitors are allowed only into the vestibule with the Hercules Fountain and the famous ceremonial staircase.

Wotruba Kirche (Church of the Most Holy Trinity)   beyond D 1/2

Location
23, Mauer, corner
of Georgsgasse/
Rysergasse

Bus
60A (from S-/R-
rail station
Liesing)

Opening times
Mar.–Oct.
Mon.–Fri. 2pm–
5pm, Sat. 2pm–
8pm, Sun. and
public hols. 9am–
6pm; Nov.–Feb.
Tue.–Fri. 2pm–
4pm, Sat. 2pm–
8pm, Sun. and
public hols. 9am–
5pm

Guided tours
by arrangement;
tel. 8 81 61 85

This church stands on St Georgenberg. It has no tower, no dome, no pillars and no gables; it obtains its powerful effect by being constructed of 152 cast concrete cubic blocks piled above one another in an asymmetrical pattern. Designed by Fritz Wotruba (1907–75), one of the most famous modern Austrian sculptors, the church was dedicated in 1976. Wotruba, who was not a practising Catholic, nevertheless made a statement of faith in his church:

"The form of this church is unconventional because it acknowledges the principle of asymmetry, a style of building which has been used only rarely in the past. If this building works it will be very dynamic and dramatic. The apparent chaos of the asymmetrical blocks is really intended to create a harmonious whole: a unit of many elements which differ in form and size. The aim is to show order – law – harmony: prerequisites of faith. A community is made up of individuals; a happy community is a harmonious community. This is a problem not only of our time but also of the church. This building is intended to demonstrate that chaos can be only overcome by law and order. It is the law of survival . . .

It is a fact that harmony can be achieved only by overcoming many opposing forces; this church aims to demonstrate this fact."

Holy Trinity Church is a religious centre for the local community and also acts as a State school, an institute for home education and a school for the physically handicapped.

In the basement of the building, which is 15·5m/50ft high, 30m/98ft long and 22m/72ft wide, are meeting-rooms, an archive, a sacristy and a room for servers. The church itself can accommodate a congregation of 250. The altar consists of a block of marble with a cross which is a replica of one which Wotruba made for the castle chapel of Bruchsal.

★Zentralfriedhof (cemetery)   south-east beyond D 6

Vienna's Central Cemetery was opened in 1874. It is the largest cemetery in Austria, with an area of 2·5sq.km/1sq.mile. The massive Main Gate was designed in 1905 by Max Hegele (1873–1945), with reliefs by Georg Leisek and Anselm Zinsler. Hegele also built in 1907–10 the Karl-Lueger-Kirche, the Art Nouveau-style church in the centre of the cemetery. From the Main Gate an avenue leads to the "graves of honour" reserved for famous personalities and to the vault of the Austrian Federal Presidents.

Location
11, Simmeringer Hauptstrasse 234

S-Bahn station
Zentralfriedhof (S7)

Trams
71, 72

A detailed plan of the cemetery and of the "graves of honour" can be obtained at Gate 2.

Among the many notable persons laid to rest here are the following musicians: Beethoven, Brahms, Gluck, Mozart (commemorative grave; he is actually buried in St Marx Cemetery), Schubert, Johann Strauss (the Elder and the Younger), von Suppé and Wolf.

On the other side of Simmeringer Hauptstrasse, opposite the Main Gate, lies the crematorium designed in 1922 by Clemens Holzmeister. It is situated where Emperor Maximilian's summer palace used to stand (see Schönbrunn, Roman ruins and Gloriette).

Crematorium

Central Cemetery: tombs of Beethoven . . .   . . . and Theophil von Hansen

171

Zentralfriedhof

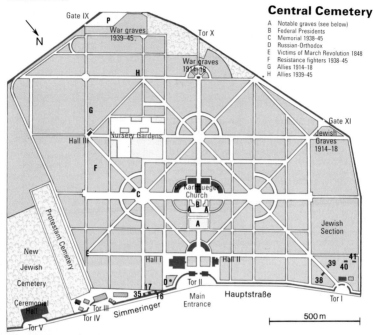

Central Cemetery

A Notable graves (see below)
B Federal Presidents
C Memorial 1938–45
D Russian-Orthodox
E Victims of March Revolution 1848
F Resistance fighters 1938–45
G Allies 1914–18
H Allies 1939–45

(Map labels: Gate IX, P, War graves 1939–45, Tor X, War graves 1914–18, H, G, Gate XI, Jewish Graves 1914–18, Hall III, Nursery Gardens, F, C, Dr Karl Lueger Church, A B A, A, Jewish Section, E, Hall I, Hall II, 39 40 41, 38, Protestant Cemetery, New Jewish Cemetery, Ceremonial Hall, Tor V, Tor IV, Tor III, 35, 17, 16, Q, Tor II, Main Entrance, Hauptstraße, Simmeringer, Tor I, 500 m, N)

Notable Graves (selection)

COMPOSERS
1 L. v. Beethoven († 1827)
2 J. Brahms († 1897)
3 Ch. W. Gluck († 1827)
4 J. Lanner († 1843)
5 K. Millöker († 1899)
6 W. A. Mozart († 1791)
7 H. Pfitzner († 1949)
8 A. Schönberg († 1951)
9 F. Schubert († 1828)
10 R. Stolz († 1975)
11 J. Strauss, Father († 1849)
12 J. Strauss, Son († 1899)
13 F. v. Suppé († 1895)
14 H. Wolf († 1903)
15 C. M. Ziehrer († 1922)
16 K. Czerny († 1857)
17 A. Salieri († 1825)

ACTORS
18 P. Hörbiger († 1981)
19 W. Krauss († 1959)
20 Th. Lingen († 1978)
21 H. Moser († 1964)
22 A. Skoda († 1961)
23 A. Albach-Retty († 1980)
24 C. Jürgens († 1982)

WRITERS
25 L. Anzengruber († 1889)
26 E. v. Bauernfeld († 1890)
27 F. Th. Csokor († 1975)
28 E. v. Feuchtersleben († 1849)
29 F. K. Ginskey († 1963)
30 R. Hawel († 1923)
31 M. Mell († 1971)
32 J. Nestroy († 1862)
33 K. Schönherr († 1943)
34 J. Schreyvogel († 1832)
35 B. Viertel († 1953)
36 F. Welfel († 1945)
37 A. Wildgans († 1932)

Jewish Section
38 F. v. Dingelstedt († 1881)
39 K. Kraus († 1936)
40 A. Schnitzler († 1931)
41 F. Torberg († 1979)

PAINTERS
42 R. Alt († 1905)
43 F. v. Amerling († 1966)
44 H. Boeckl († 1966)
45 H. Makart († 1884)
46 A. v. Pettenkofen († 1889)

SCULPTORS
47 A. D. v. Fernkorn († 1878)
48 V. Tilgner († 1896)
49 F. Wortruba († 1975)

ARCHITECTS
50 Th. E. v. Hansen († 1891)
51 C. v. Hasenauer († 1894)
52 J. Hoffmann († 1956)
53 E. van der Nüll († 1868)

SCIENTISTS
54 Th. Billroth, Doctor († 1894)
55 L. Boltzmann, Physicist († 1906)
56 A. Negrelli, Engineer († 1858)
57 J. Wagner-Jauregg, Psychiatrist and Nobel Prize winner († 1940)

Notable Graves
(selection)

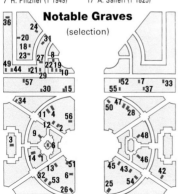

Graves of Helmut Qualtinger . . .   *. . . and Bruno Kreisky*

Zum grünen Anker (restaurant)   B/C 5

An Italian aroma hangs over the "Grünen Anker", for this restaurant, where the Viennese first came to enjoy a glass of wine and later on a glass of beer, has specialised in Italian cuisine since 1820. It was a favourite meeting-place of Schubert and his friends, and Grillparzer was also a regular customer.

Close by the Grüner Anker stands the "Kipfelhaus" (the Croissant House) at No. 8 Grünargergasse. It was here that this famous Viennese delicacy came into being, for the very first croissant was baked here in 1683, probably as a joke at the expense of the Turkish crescent moon symbol.

Location
1, Grünanger-gasse 10

Underground station
Stephansplatz
(U1, U3)

173

Practical Information

Note
The number preceeding a street name, etc., is the number of the district of Vienna. The number following the street name is the number of the building.

The telephone dialling code for international calls to Vienna is 1 while the domestic area code for Vienna is 0222.

Advance booking

Theatre tickets
The box-offices selling tickets in advance for the Staatsoper (State Opera), Burgtheater, Volksoper and Akademietheater are situated in Hanuschof; tel. 5 14 44–29 59/60 (for information only). Open: Mon.–Fri. 9am–6pm, Sat. 9am–2pm, Sun. 9am–noon.

Advance ticket sales always open seven days before the performance. For first nights or performances with celebrated guest artists theatre-lovers often begin to queue many hours – sometimes through the night – before tickets go on sale.

All other theatres have their own box-offices. It is advisable to check by telephone whether tickets are available.

Postal bookings from abroad
All postal applications for tickets must arrive at the box-office at least ten days (Staatsoper and Volksoper at least three weeks) before the performance. The address is:
Österreichischer Bundestheaterverband
Hanuschgasse 3
A-1010 Wien; tel (1) 5 14–29 69

Holders of the major credit cards can telephone requests for tickets for the Austrian State Theatres and Opera, beginning six days before the performance:
tel. (1) 5 13 15 13.
Vienna Ticket Service, Postfach 160, A-1043 Wien,
tel. (1) 5 87 98 43, fax 5 87 98 44; Mon.–Fri. 9am–6pm; also sells tickets for most venues.

Ticket agencies
Tickets for all performances in the theatres of Vienna can also be obtained from private agencies which normally charge a commission of up to 25% of the price of the tickets. Centrally located ticket agencies are:
Hoberg (in the Hotel de France), 1, Schottenberg 3; tel. 3 19 78 40
Kehlendorfer, 1, Krugerstr. 3; tel. 5 12 63 12
Lienerbrünn, 1, Augustinerstr. 7; tel. 5 33 09 61
Österreichisches Verkehrsbüro, 1, Opernpassage;
tel. 5 86 23 46/52, fax 5 87 71 42

Last Minute Ticket for Musicals
Reduced price tickets for evening performances of musicals can be purchased from 2pm on the day in the pavilion near the Staatsoper (State Opera) in Kärnter Strasse.

Spanish Riding School
See A–Z, Spanish Riding School

Vienna Boys' Choir
Seats for the Sunday concerts of the Vienna Boys' Choir (Wiener Sänger-knaben) in the Burgkapelle at 9.15am must be booked at least eight weeks

◀ *Café garden on the Graben*

in advance at the Verwaltung der Hofmusikkapelle, Hofburg, Schweizerhof, A-1010 Wien; tel. 5 33 99 27.

Tickets may be collected on payment at the Burgkapelle on Fridays preceeding the performance between 11am and noon or on Sundays by 9am at the latest. Tickets for any seats still available are on sale at the box-office of the Burgkapelle on Fridays from 5pm Only two tickets per person are allowed.

Airlines

Austrian Airlines	Head Office: Fontana Strasse 1; tel. 68 35–0, fax 68 55 05 Information and bookings: 3, Barichgasse; tel. 7 17 99, fax 7 15 52 79 1, Kärntner Ring 18 (city office); tel. 5 05 57 57–0, fax 5 05 14 34 Schwechat Airporrt: tel. 7 11 10–25 10, fax 7 11 10–27 29
Tyrolean Airways	1, Opernring 1/R/7; tel. 56 36 74
Lauda Air	1, Opernring 6; tel. 5 14 77–0
British Airways	1, Kärntner Ring 10; tel. 5 05 76 91–0
TWA	1, Opernring 1/R/742; tel. 5 87 68 68
Air Canada	1, Opernring 1/R/717; tel. 5 86 19 09

Air travel

Airport	Schwechat, Vienna International Airport, lies 19km/12 miles south-east of the city centre. Its facilities include banks, restaurants, a supermarket, newspaper and souvenir shops, a duty-free shop, car-rental desks and a tourist information office where hotel reservations can also be made (see Information).
Shuttle services	There is a bus shuttle service between the airport and the City Air Terminal (Central Rail Station/Wien Mitte) every 20–30 minutes from 5am to 0.30am (Apr.–Oct. 24-hour service). There are also shuttle bus services between the airport and the West and South Rail Stations (journey time: 20–30 mins.). Express trains run hourly between the underground station at the airport and the North and Central Rail Stations (Wien Nord and Wien Mitte).
Flight information	Tel. 7 11 10–22 33 (24 hours)
Inland flights	Austrian Air Services fly several times daily from Vienna to Graz, Klagenfurt and Salzburg, and twice daily to Linz.

Antique dealers

Shops	Antique dealers can be found in the narrow side-streets to the west of the Graben: Bräunerstrasse, Stallburggasse, Dorotheergasse, Plankengasse, Spiegelgasse and Seilergasse. A smaller "antique quarter" has become established to the south of the cathedral: Singerstrasse, Franzplatz, Himmelpfortgasse, Annagasse, Akademiestrasse, Walfischgasse and Mahlerstrasse. Goods on sale range from individual articles of medieval art to examples of Art-Nouveau and items from the Vienna workshops.

Antique shop in Stallburggasse   *D & S art dealers in Dorotheergasse*

An art and antique market takes place near the Schwedenplatz from May to September (Sat. 2–8pm and Sun. 10am–8pm).

Art and antique market

An art and handicraft exhibition is held in Spittelburg (District 7) every Saturday from April to November and every day in December, 10am–6pm.

Art and handiwork exhibition

An art and crafts market is held in the Heiligenkreuzer Hof in Schönlaterngasse (District 1) on the first week-end in the month from April to November and each week-end in December, 10am–6pm.

Art and crafts market

See A–Z, Naschmarkt

Flea market

See A–Z, Dorotheum and Auctions (below)

Auctions

Art galleries

Galerie Alte Kunst Neue Kunst
4, Prinz-Eugen-Str. 34; tel. 5 05 24 37

Selection

Galerie Ambiente
1, Lugeck 1 (Rotenturmstr. 8); tel. 5 13 11 30
Art Nouveau

Galerie and der Stiege
6, Gumpendorfer Str. 34; tel. 5 86 29 87
Art Nouveau interiors and decoration

Galerie Asboth
1, Spiegelgasse 19; tel. 5 12 51 37
Asian art, antique jewellery

177

Art galleries

Galerie at the Albertina
1, Lobkowitzplatz 1; tel. 5 13 14 16
Antiques

Galerie at the Belvedere
4, St-Elisabeth-Platz 3; tel. 5 05 07 46
Art Nouveau interiors; contemporary art, etc.

Galerie at the Burgtheater
1, Teinfaltstr. 3; tel. 5 35 80 29
Portrait painters and picture framing

Galerie Gabriel
1, Seilerstätte 19; tel. 5 12 78 02
Drawings, sculptures; tapestries by contemporary artists

Galerie Image
1, Ruprechtsplatz 4–5; tel. 5 35 42 84
Posters

Galerie Otto (13 branches)
Main gallery: 3, Lanzer Str. 53; tel. 8 77 75 00–0
Paintings, graphics, picture framing

Galerie Pabst
1, Habsburgerring 10; tel. 5 33 70 14
19th and 20th c. art

Galerie Sankt Lukas
1, Josefsplatz 5; tel. 5 12 82 37
Paintings by old masters

Galerie Slavik
1, Himmelpfortgasse 17; tel. 5 13 48 12
Antiques and contemporary applied art

Galerie Wickenburg
8, Wickenburggasse 4; tel. 4 08 18 26
Pottery and weaving studio

Galerie 7/45
1, Wildpretmarkt 2; tel. 5 33 93 72
English furniture

Galerie 10
1, Getreidemarkt 10; tel. 5 87 57 44
Portraits by contemporary Austrian artists

Galerie 33
7, Burggasse 88; tel. 9 36 97 73
Applied art

Glasgalerie Kute
1, Franziskanerplatz 6; tel. 5 13 53 22

Auctions

Whether out of interest or simply for the atmosphere it is worth paying a visit to an auction in one˙of the world's greatest salesrooms, the Dorotheum (see A–Z) at 1, Dorotheergasse 17; tel. 5 15 60–212.
    Auctions are held Mon.–Fri. about 2pm and Sat. about 10am
    Items are also on sale Mon.–Fri. 10am–6pm; viewing Mon.–Fri. 10am–6pm and Sat. 8.30am–noon.

At the auctions the emphasis is on furniture Mon., Wed., and Fri. 2pm; valuables Mon.–Fri. 2pm; decorative and practical items Mon.–Fri. 2pm and Sat. 10am

Emphasis

Bicycles

Vienna has some 460km/286 miles of signposted cycle tracks. The Association for the Environment (ARGUS; 4, Frankenberggasse 11; tel. 65 84 35 or 5 05 84 35 has published a very good plan of Vienna for cyclists, and this can also be obtained from bookshops.

Plan for cyclists

At road junctions not controlled by traffic lights where a cycle lane is marked in yellow, cyclists must give way to traffic going across.

Cycles can be transported in the Underground (ticket required) on Saturdays from 2pm and all day on Sundays and public holidays; from July–Aug. additionally Mon.–Fri. 9am–3pm and 6.30 until the last trains; Sat. from 9am; Sun. and public holidays as above.

Transport

Barl Cycle Rental, 1, Franz-Josef-kai; tel. 66 34 22
Hammermayer Cycle Rental, 19, Heiligenstädter Str. 180; tel. 37 45 98
Hochschaubahn Cycle Rental, 2, Prater 113; tel. 26 01 65
Intersport Luef, near the car park on Danube Island,
    21, Floridsdorfer Brücke; tel. 2 78 86 98
Prater Cycle Rental, 2, Praterstern, in the high-speed train building;
    tel. 26 85 57
Im Prater Cycle Rental, 2, Vivariumstr. 8; tel. 26 66 44
Safari Lodge Cycle Rental, 22, Steinspornbrücke, Neue Donau; tel. 22 33 78

Bicycle rental

Sightseeing by bicycle
See City Sightseeing

Vienna Bike

The leaflet "See Vienna by bike" is available from the Vienna Tourist Board.

Information

Business hours

See Opening times

Camping

Six large camp sites are situated between 6 and 15km/3¾ and 9 miles from the city centre.

Camp sites

Campingplatz Wien-Ost
22, Am Kleehäufl; tel./fax 2 20 93 10
Open: mid-May–mid-Sept. 3.3 ha; reservation not possible

Campingplatz Wien-West I
14, Hüttelbergstr. 40; tel. 94 14 49; fax 9 11 35 94
Open: May–Sept. 1.5 ha; reservation not possible

Campingplatz Wien-West II
14, Hüttelbergstr. 80; tel. 94 23 14; fax 9 11 35 94
Open: all year. 2 ha; reservation not possible

Campingplatz Wien-Süd
(Atzgersdorf)
23, Breitenfurter Str. 267; tel. 8 65 92 18; fax 9 11 35 94
Open: May–Sept. 2.5 ha; reservation not possible

Schwimmbad Camping Wien-Süd Rodaun
23, An der Au 2, Rodaun, on A2 motorway; tel. 88 41 54
Open: mid-March–mid-November
1.2 ha; reservation possible

Campingplatz Schloss Laxenburg
Münchendorfer Strasse, Laxenburg; tel. (0 22 36) 7 13 33;
  fax (0 22 36) 71 33 48
Open: beginning April–mid-October
2 ha; reservation possible

Caravans | Spending the night in a caravan or "motorhome" away from official camp sites is classed as "wild camping" in Vienna and offenders are liable to be fined. Outside the city it is tolerated for a maximum of three days.

Camping guide | Details of camp sites in and around Vienna, including size of site and plots, facilities, opening times, directions how to get there, etc. are published in the leaflet "Jugendherbergen Camping" by the Vienna Tourist Board.

Car rental

International firms | Avis
1, Opernring 1; tel. 5 87 62 41

Budget
3, Landstrasser Hauptstr. 2a; tel. 7 14 65 65

Hertz
1, Kärntner Ring 17 ; tel. 5 12 86 77

Europcar
1, Kärntner Ring 14; tel. 5 05 42 00–0

Electric cars | Electric cars for use within the city – they have a maximum range of 80km/50 miles on a single charge – can be hired from the ÖAMTC (Austrian Motor Car, Motor Cycle and Touring Club) at Schubertring 1–3, A-1010 Wien; tel. 74 16 21 17.

Casino

See Nightlife

Chemists

Business hours | Mon.–Fri. 8am–noon, 2–6pm; Sat. 8am–noon.
To ascertain which chemist is on duty; tel. 15 50. Details of chemists on duty at night can also be found in the daily newspapers.

International Pharmacy | Foreign medicaments can be obtained from the Internationale Apotheke, 1, Kärntner Ring 17; tel. 5 12 28 25.

Church services

Roman Catholic | In most of Vienna's Catholic churches some services begin at 6.30am; Saturdays at 6pm (including masses in several languages; see A–Z Votivkirche). High Mass is celebrated on Sundays and on church festivals at 9am (July and Aug.) and at 10am. Information: tel. 5 15 52–375).

St Salvator
1, Wipplingerstr. 6; tel. 63 71 33
Service on Sun. 10am
(see A–Z, Salvatorkapelle)

Old Catholic

Anglican church
3, Jaurésgasse 17–19
Service on Sun. at 10.30am

Protestant

Lutheran City Church
1, Dorotheergasse 18; tel. 5 12 83 92/0
Services (except July and Aug.) on Sun. 8 and 10am

Reformed City Church
1, Dorotheergasse 16; tel. 5 12 83 93/12
Service on Sun. at 10am

"City Temple" synagogue
1, Seitenstettengasse 4; tel. 5 31 04
Services daily, morning and evening

Jewish

Islamic Centre (mosque)
21, Am Hubertusdamm 17–19; tel. 30 13 89
Prayers at 5am and at 1, 5.05, 8.10, and 10pm
Visits (except Fridays) only outside hours of prayer

Islamic

Cinemas

Admiral, 7, Burggasse 119; tel. 93 37 59
Old films, cult films, screening at night

Cinemas with special programmes

Artis, 1, Schultergasse 5; tel. 5 35 65 70
Latest films shown in six modern cinemas

Bellaria Kino, 7, Museumstr. 3; tel. 93 75 91
Austro nostalgia (1930–60)

Breitenseer-Lichtspiele, 14, Breitenseer Str. 21; tel. 9 82 21 73
Old films, cult films, screening at night

Burg-Kino, 1, Opernring 19; tel. 5 87 84 06
Films in original version

De France, 1, Heßgasse 7; tel. 34 52 36
Latest English and French films in two suites of the Hôtel de France

Erika-Kino (oldest cinema in the world), 7, Kaiserstr. 44–46; tel. 93 13 83
Films shown here since 1900

Filmcasino, 5, Margaretenstr. 78; tel. 5 87 90 62
Films in the style of the 1950s; unusual

Filmhaus Stöbergasse, 5, Stöbergasse 11–15; tel. 5 46 66–30
Documentaries and alternative programmes

Filmmuseum (see A–Z; Albertina)

Gartenbau, 1, Parkring 12; tel. 5 12 23 54
Vienna's largest film theatre with super-wide screen

Imax Filmtheater, Mariahilfer Str. 212; tel. 8 94 01 23
Fascinating natural phenomena in 3-D on 400sq.m screen

Imperial, 1, Rotgasse 9; tel. 5 33 32 23
Mainly animated cartoons for children

Künstlerhaus-Kino, Akademiestr. 13; tel. 5 05 43 28
Discriminating

Metro, 1, Johannesgasse 4; tel. 5 12 18 03
Former theatre (boxes); discriminating

Movie, 5, Schönbrunner Str. 12; tel. 5 87 94 97
Old films, cult films, screening at night, original versions

Rendezvous mit Wien; see City Sightseeing

Cinema
programmes:
tel. 15 77

Schikaneder, 4, Margaretenstr. 24; tel. 5 87 02 62
Old films, cult films, screening at night

Recommended
films:
tel. 15 22

Star Kino, 7, Burggasse 71; tel. 93 46 83
Old films, cult films, screening at night

Stadtkino, 3, Schwarzenbergplatz 7–8; tel. 7 12 62 76
Avant-garde films (often in original version), programmes at night;
videothèque

Top Kino Center, 6, Rahlgasse 1; tel. 5 87 55 57
Cult films (sometimes in original version)

Urania, 1, Uraniastr. 1; tel. 7 15 82 06
Notable political film cycles and experimental films

Votiv, 9, Währinger Str. 12; tel. 34 35 71
Old films and good animated cartoons

City sightseeing

Suggestions for a
short stay

See Sightseeing Programme

By bus

Vienna Sightseeing Tours, 3, Stelzhammergasse 4/11;
tel. 7 12 46 83–0 and 7 15 11 42–0
Central departure point: Bus station, Vienna Central (Wien Mitte), also at
the Opera and other places.

Cityrama, 1, Börsegasse 1; tel. 5 34 13–0
Departure: Kursalon Stadtpark.

City Touring Vienna Raab Reisen
14, Penzingerstr. 46; tel. 8 94 14 17
Departure: Air Terminal, Hotel Hilton

Participants in all the above tours can be picked up at their hotels. Booking
can be made at hotel reservation desks or at travel bureaux.

On foot

Viennese tourist guides offer some 50 different walks with expert guides.
They lead through the Old Town to medieval Vienna above and below
ground, Habsburg highlights, Art Nouveau architecture and the Hundertwasser Haus, through old lanes and hidden courtyards, to legendary

coffee-houses, sumptuous palaces and the residences of great composers, follow in the footsteps of "Sissi" and the "Third Man", shed light on Viennese legends and criminal records, provide an insight into the life of Sigmund Freud and the Vienna of the Jews at the turn of the century, and much, much more. The walks last between 90 minutes and 2 hours, and details can be obtained from the leaflets "Walks in Vienna" and "Per Pedes", obtainable from the Tourist Information Offices (see Information), daily newspapers and the Viennese Monthly Programme.

Three-hour guided tours of Vienna's more unusual contemporary buildings. Alternative Sightseeing Tours, 9, Kollingasse 6; tel. 34 33 84.

Other round trips

There are guided bicycle tours of the Old Town lasting two hours on the first and third Mondays in the month from May to September, departing at 3.30pm, and also on the second and fourth Mondays at 10.30am in May, June and September. Meet near the cycle hire shop under Salztorbrücke (for details, tel. 3 19 12 58).

By bicycle

See Fiaker

By horse-cab

Early May–early Oct.: "Oldtimer Tramway", a 2½ hour ride in a 1929 tram through the city; every Sat. 1.30pm, Sun. and public holidays 10am and 1.30pm, from Otto Wagner Pavillion, 4, Karlsplatz; information and tickets: tel. 5 87 31 86. Foreign schoolchildren up to 15 years of age travel free Sun. and public holidays and during the Vienna school holidays.

By tram

Round trips (15–20 minutes) over Vienna; operated by VIENNAIR-Polsterer Jets, Hanger 3, A-1300 Vienna-Schwechat Airport; tel. 7 11 10–20 77.

By air

Boat trips on the Danube are run by the Erste Donau Dampfschifffahrts Gesellschaft (DDSG, see Information); landing stage: 1, Schwedenbrücke.
Round trips Vienna–Little and Great Danube: May–Sept. daily 10.30am, 1, 1.30, 2, 4, 4.30, 5 and 7.30pm (different departure times from the terminus at the Hotel Scandic Crown/Prater); there are additional "Evergreen" evening trips with dancing (8.30pm Fri. and Sat. from mid-May and Thur. also from mid-June). There is a three-hour round trip (daily 10.30am, 1, 2, 2.30, 4.30pm; includes bus from the Hotel Scandia Crown to KunstHausWien station), which goes from the famous buildings designed by the late 19th/early 20th c. architect Otto Wagner to the Hundertwasser project and the KunstHausWien.
Alternatively, visitors can hire a boat taxi (tel. 63 96 69, from 2pm) as a means of exploring the city; the landing stage is at the Riverside Bakery on the Old Town side of the Danube Canal Promenade/Salztorbrücke; guests can be collected by prior arrangement.

By boat

A four-hour city tour "rund um die Donau" (tour round the Danube) by limousine/minibus and yacht is offered by Jet-Car (A-1030 Vienna, Khunngasse 3; tel. 78 99 66, fax 78 99 664). It takes in Strauss' residence (where the "Blue Danube" waltz was written), the Giant Wheel and the Leopoldsberg mountain in the Viennese Forest, from where there is a superb view of the city. After a visit to the Klosterneuberg monastery the ship continues upstream to the Greifenstein ruins and finally returns to the Wiener Kahlenbergerdorf for a drink (departures: Apr.–Oct. daily 9am and 2pm).

Panorama Tour

7, Mariahilferstr. 2; tel. 5 23 68 42
Former residency cinema with 104 seats
A new form of city sightseeing and an introduction to the history and culture of Vienna is provided by the multilingual film presentation "Rendezvous mit Wien". The 35-minute film (daily 9am–5pm on the hour) covers a wide spectrum taking in the Romans, the Habsburgs, its world-famous musicians and coffee-house writers, Viennese Classical and Art Nouveau styles, the Spanish Riding School, Heuriger wine, the Third Man, opera ball and much more, right up to the present day.

Rendezvous mit Wien

Coffee houses (Kaffeehäuser)

Official guides for visitors

Charlotte Speiser, A-1220 Wien, Rennbahnweg 27/43/1; tel. 2 59 25 35, fax 2 59 32 23
Travel Point, A-1090 Wien, Boltzmanngasse 19/13; tel. 3 19 42 43, fax 3 10 38 75
Vienna Guide Service, A-1190 Wien, Sommerhaidenweg 124; tel. 4 43 09 40, fax 44 28 25
Approved guides must produce their authority and official badge.

Coffee houses (Kaffeehäuser)

Varieties of coffee

In a coffee house the customer does not simply order a coffee (pronounced *café* as in French) but chooses his favourite from among the many varieties. The basis of all coffee specialities is "mocca", and a glass of water is always served as well.

Einspänner: black in a glass with whipped cream
Fiaker: large black coffee in a glass
Original Fiaker: black with rum
Kaffee verkehrt ("reversed"): more milk than coffee
Kaisermelange: black with yolk of egg
Kapuziner: small bowl of black coffee with a drop of "Obers" (whipped cream), and sprinkled with cocoa or grated chocolate
Konsul: black with a small shot of whipped cream
Mélange: milky coffee in a cup or a glass, and a shot of cream
Mocca gespritzt: black with a shot of brandy or rum
Nussschwarzer: mocca
Pharisäer: coffee with rum, sugar and whipped cream
Piccolo: small black coffee in a piccolo bowl, with or without whipped cream

The Landtmann coffee house on the Ringstrasse

Schale Braun or Gold: black coffee which acquires a golden hue when whipped cream is added

Eiskaffee: A glass is half filled with vanilla ice-cream, topped up with cold strong black coffee, garnished with whipped cream and served with a straw and a long spoon

Mazagran: cold mocca with rum or maraschino and ice cubes, sprinkled with grated cloves and served in a glass with a straw

Türkischer: Turkish mocca served in a copper jug

★Alte Backstube
See A to Z, Alte Backstube

Coffee houses
(a selection)

Bräunerhof, 1, Stallburggasse 2; tel. 5 12 38 93 (rich in tradition; chamber music at weekends)

★Central im Palais Ferstel
See A to Z, Freyung

Diglas, 1, Wollzeile 10; tel. 5 12 57 65–0 (delicious home-made gâteaux)

Dom Café, 1, Stephansplatz 9; tel. 5 34 05–0 (with terrace, at the foot of the Stephansdom)

Dommayer, 13, Dommayergasse 1; tel. 8 77 54 65 (large garden with waiter service)

Europa, 1, Kärnterstrasse 18; tel. 5 15 94 (popular rendezvous after a long tour of the city)

Frauenhuber, 1, Himmelpfortgasse 6; tel. 5 12 43 23 (rich in tradition, with luxurious plush furnishings)

The Hawelka, a coffee house rich in tradition

Coffee, Communication, Culture

The Viennese coffee house has become more than just an institution. Like nowhere else in the world it has for hundreds of years been an intellectual home, an essential meeting-place for artists and writers and all those who – in the words of the feature writer Alfred Polgar – "want to be alone yet need company at the same time". It is here that literary schools have been born and discarded, political developments and scientific findings analysed, and new styles in painting, music and architecture have first seen the light of day.

It was in 1683 that Franz Georg Kolschitzky, a Pole, was granted the first Imperial licence to make the beverage. During the Turkish siege this resourceful messenger brought the then mayor of Vienna, Andreas von Liebenberg, the news of the arrival of the relief forces led by King Sobieski of Poland. Although it was the Turks who first introduced coffee into south-east Europe it was merchants from Armenia who opened the first coffee houses in Vienna. In 1685 Johannes Deodato, a secret agent of the Imperial war department with a flair for business, was granted a licence to open a coffee house, and in 1697 Isaak de Luca (or Sahal Lucasian) introduced coffee-making on a commercial basis.

In a coffee house a customer does not simply order "a coffee" (pronounced *café* as in French) but chooses his favourite as precisely as if he were purchasing a certain brand of cigarettes at a tobacconist's (which, incidentally, is usually called a *Trafik* in Austria). The fame of Viennese coffee is based on the huge range of special mixes and subtle differences in flavour. Names such as *Mélange, Einspänner, Kapuziner, Baruner* or *Schale Gold* are examples of the varying blends of coffee, milk and cream. A knowledge of these varieties is necessary in order to be able to be able to call oneself even a "semi-connoisseur", but is frequently beyond the ken even of visitors who are sufficiently sophisticated to know that espresso and capuccino are not the names of Bohemian villages! Moreover, a coffee in a café is "a means, not an objective" – people visit coffee houses not simply to have a meal but rather after having eaten, in order to satisfy their spiritual and intellectual rather than their physical appetites.

The regular clientele of the coffee houses has always been made up very largely of writers and the like. It was in the Biedermeier period (mid 19th century), in particular, that the Viennese "Kaffeehaus" became a salient feature of the city's cultural life, when in the "Silver Coffee House" owned by Ignaz Neuner such illustrious artists and writers as Franz Grillparzer, Moritz von Schwend and Ferdinand Raimund met, and the "waltz kings" Strauss and Lanner filled the concert cafés with their melodies. Before the end of the 19th century the history of Viennese literature was intrinsically linked to the culture of the coffee house. Around 1890 the Café Griensteidl (rebuilt in 1990) on Michaelerplatz was the haunt of the young Viennese poets Arthur Schnitzler, Richard Beer-Hofmann, Hermann Bahr and Hugo von Hofmannsthal, the eloquent critic Karl Kraus, the architect Adolf Loos and the revolutionary Leo Trotsky, before the mantle of leading coffee house fell, at the end of the First World War, on the now faithfully restored Café Central in Herrengasse, with Karl Kraus, Peter Altenberg, Egon Friedell and Alfred Polgar among its regular patrons. According to Alfred Polgar, the literary café of those days was synonomous with "a world philosophy, the innermost concern of which is not to philosophise upon the world". People lived parasitically "below the Viennese line of latitude on the meridian of loneliness", loved and set little store by other guests, discussed and brooded over social injustices, the masques of wit and stupidity, free and casual liaisons, and the enjoyment of a "devil-may-care approach to the moment". In the late 1920s and early 1930s the noble Herrenhof became the main rendezvous of writers and starry-eyed idealists, who found time to "think about what those outside are not able to experience" and developed a distinct "pleasure in talking clever nonsense". At the marble tables of the roomy café, which was closed in 1960, Hermann Broch, Robert Musil, Franz Werfel, Joseph Roth, the young Manès Sperber and Sigmund Freud drank their milky coffee and played chess. The Café Museum, which Adolf Loos had

Café Griensteidl on Michaelerplatz

designed in 1907 in the style of an American bar, was the haunt of the as yet unknown Franz Léhar, Oskar Kokoschka and Gustav Schütt, while the Café de l'Europe near Stephansplatz was crowded during the day with the local populace and at night with the colourful demimonde of the time; from the spring of 1933 onwards political refugees from Nazi Germany made it their nightly haunt, before most of them were obliged to seek exile in Paris, London or the USA.

Although they are no longer the creative institutions of those earlier days, the coffee houses of the late 20th century still retain something of the same ambience, although there is a considerable difference between the famous "in" cafés near the castle, such as the Central, Griensteidl and Landtmann, and those preferred by the locals, where one can still pass many a happy hour reading the newspapers, playing billiards or chess or having a good gossip. In the old-fashioned atmosphere of the Café Bräunerhof, where the grumbling Thomas Bernhard spent his mornings reading the newspapers, the spirit of the classical era still lingers. Other legendary oases of cosy comfort or *Gemütlichkeit* are: the Café Museum in Friedrichstrasse, where Vienna's Art Nouveau artists once discussed this new form of expression, the lovingly restored Sperl in Gumpendorfer Strasse frequented by artists and thespians since 1880, and the Hawelka in Dorotheergasse, famous for its jam-filled yeast dumplings; an artists' café in the 1950s and now a favourite rendezvous of rich young people, the formerly quiet Café Grillparzer, and the Altwiener Drechsler on Naschmarkt which has been owned by the same family for three generations. Some distance from the Bohemian quarter are the stuccoed suburban cafés and casinos such as the Ritter in Ottakring, popular with Viennese workers, where the muffled click of billiard balls mingles with the almost incomprehensible Viennese dialect. Which of the enormous variety of coffee houses to patronise must remain a matter of personal preference, but there is little doubt that the visitor will enjoy discovering the enigmatic phenomenon of the Viennese coffee house in the course of a leisurely stroll through the city.

Coffee houses (Kaffeehäuser)

Griensteidl, Michaelerplatz 2; tel. 5 35 26 92 (re-opened in 1990 – old Viennese ambience)

Haag, 1, Schottengasse 2; tel. 5 33 18 00 (a beautiful garden with waiter service in the courtyard of the former Schottenkloster/Scots Monastery)

★Hawelka, 1, Dorotheergasse 6; tel. 5 12 82 30 (rich in tradition and a favourite meeting-place for writers and artists)

Imperial, 1, Kärnter Ring 16; tel. 5 01 10–0 (piano music in the afternoons; delicious home-made gâteaux)

Kleines Cafe , 1, Franziskanerplatz 3 (with view of the Franziscanerkirche)

Korb, 1, Tuchlauben 10; tel. 5 33 72 15 (secluded garden with waiter service)

★Landtmann, 1, Dr Karl-Lueger-Ring 4; tel. 5 32 06 21 (popular with thespians and prominent politicians; beautiful terrace)

Monopol, 8, Floriangasse 2; tel. 43 44 66 (beautiful gardens)

Mozart, 1, Albertinaplatz 2; tel. 5 13 30 07 (exceptional pastries/desserts)

★Museum, 1, Friedrichstr. 6; tel. 56 52 02 (gallery café designed by Adolf Loos)

★Prückel, 1, Stubenring 24; tel. 5 12 61 15 (suppliers to the Imperial and Royal courts since 1903, famous for its pastries/desserts)

Rathaus, 8, Landgerichtsstrasse 5; tel. 43 12 82 (old Viennese ambience)

★Ritter, 6, Ottakringer Str. 117; tel. 46 12 53 (suburban coffee house rich in tradition; facilities for chess and billiards)

Sacher
See A to Z, Hotel Sacher

Schlosscafé Schönbrunn, 13, Schönbrunn Palace; tel. 8 77 56 42

★Sperl, 6, Gumpendorfer Str. 11; tel. 56 41 58 (protected building, very cosy; also billiards)

★Schmid-Hansl, 18, Schulgasse 31; tel. 43 36 58 (home of the "Wienerlied")

★Schwarzenberg, 1, Kärnterring 17; tel. 5 12 73 93 (smart summer terrace; excellent pastries/desserts)

Volksgartencafé, 1, Burgring 1; tel. 5 33 21 05 (open-air dancing)

★Walzerkonzert-Café DDS "Johann Strauss", 1, Schwedenplatz, boat on the Danube channel; tel. 5 33 93 67

Weimar, 9, Währinger Str. 68; tel. 34 12 06 (stylish café dating from the turn of the century; the "Apfelstrudel" is legendary

★Wortner, 3, Wiedner Hauptstr. 55; tel. 5 05 32 91 (highly-regarded gâteaux and secluded garden)

Zartl, 3, Rasumowskygasse 7; tel. 7 12 55 60 (café with concerts and literary readings)

Aida, Stock-im-Eisen-Platz 2; tel. 52 79 25 (beautiful view of Stephan-splatz/St Stephen's Square from the first floor)

Pâtisseries
(a selection)

★Demel (former Imperial and Royal confectioner)
See A to Z, Demel

Gerstner, 1, Kärnter Str. 15 (former Imperial and Royal confectioner)

Heiner, 1, Kärnter Str. 21–23; tel. 52 68 63, and Wollzeile 9; tel. 52 48 38
(former Imperial and Royal confectioner)

★Kurcafé-Konditorei Oberlaa, 1, Neuer Markt 16; tel. 5 13 29 36 (delicious
cakes and pastries and boxes of chocolates)

Currency

The unit of currency is the Austrian schilling (öS) which is divided into 100
groschen. There are banknotes in values of 20, 50, 100, 500, 1000 and 5000
schillings, and coins of 10 and 50 groschen and 1, 5, 10 and 20 schillings.

Unit of currency

The exchange rates fluctuate; they can be obtained from banks, exchange
offices and travel agents and are published in the national papers.

Exchange rates

There are no restrictions on the import or export of foreign currency.
Although there is no limit on the amount of Austrian currency which can be
imported into Austria, no more than 50,000 schillings may be taken out.

Currency
regulations

Eurocheques can be used up to a value of 2500 schillings and up to a similar
sum can be withdrawn from some bank machines by using a Eurocheque
Card (many machines also accept normal credit cards).

Eurocheques

Most international credit cards are accepted by banks, the larger hotels and
restaurants, car-rental companies and many shops but not generally at
petrol stations.

Credit cards

Customs Regulations

In theory there is now no limit to the amount of goods that can be taken
from one EU country to another provided they have been purchased tax
paid in an EU country, are for personal use and not intended for resale.
However, customs authorities have issued guide lines to the maximum
amounts considered reasonable for persons over 17 years of age. These
are: 10 litres of spirits or strong liqueurs, 20 litres fortified wine (port,
sherry, etc.) 90 litres of table wine (of which not more than 60 litres may be
sparkling wine), 110 litres of beer, 800 cigarettes or 400 cigarillos or
200 cigars). There is no limit on perfume or toilet water.

Allowances
between EU
countries

For those coming from a country outside the EU or who have arrived from
an EU country without having passed through custom control with all their
baggage, the allowances for goods obtained anywhere outside the EU for
persons over the age of 17 are: 1 litre spirits or 2 litres of fortified wine or
3 litres table wine, plus a further 2 litres table wine; 60cc perfume, 250cc
toilet water; 200 cigarettes or 100 cigarillos or 50 cigars

Entry from
Non-EU countries

The allowances for goods purchased "duty-free" from airports, on aircraft
and ferries are the same as for entry from non-EU countries above.

Duty-free
goods

Diplomatic representation

Great Britain	Embassy: 3 Jauresgasse 12; tel. (02 22) 7 13 15 75 Consular section: tel. (02 22) 7 14 61 17
United States	Embassy: 9, Boltzmanngasse 16; tel. (02 22) 3 13 39 Consular section: 1, Gartenbaupromenade 2, tel. (02 22) 31 55 11
Canada	Embassy: 1, Dr Karl-Lueger-Ring 10; tel. (02 22) 5 33 36 91

Emergencies

Doctor on call	Doctors' radio-telephone service (24 hours a day); tel. 141
Mobile emergency doctor	Tel. 144 (in case of accident). See also Medical Assistance.
Fire brigade	Tel. 122
Police	Tel. 133
Motoring breakdown	Tel. 120 (ÖAMTC); tel. 123 (ARBÖ)

Events

January	Jan. 1st: New Year concerts by the Vienna Philharmonic, the Vienna Symphony and the Vienna Hofburg orchestras
February	Thursday before "Fasching": Opera Ball international Dance Festival (until March) Alternate "Dance" and "Sounds of the World" Festivals (until March)
March	Spring International Trade Fair Haydn Festival
April	Spring Marathon (Schönbrunn Palace – Ringstrasse – Prater – Rathausplatz) Waltz and operetta concerts (until October) Spring Kite Festival on Danube Island Vienna Spring Festival (until May; see Festivals) Mozart Concerts (until October)
May/June	Vienna Festival (until June; see Festivals) Danube Festival with rock, jazz and folk music (end of June)
June	Art auction in the Dorotheum Summer Concerts ("Musical Summer" until September; see Festivals) Theatre in the Park (Stadtpark; until end of July) Flower parade in the Prater Concordia Ball in the Rathaus
July	Summer productions in Schönbrunn Palace Theatre (until August) Vienna Jazz Festival (see Festivals) Opera Film Festival on Rathausplatz (until August) International Dance Festival (until end of August)
August	Various events on Danube Island and on the "Old Danube" Folk Festival in the Prater
September	Vienna Autumn Trade Fairs Opening of the opera season Regattas on the Danube

Theatre premières Festival de Jeunesse (see Festivals) Viennale Film Festival (see Festivals)	October
Art and Antiques Fair Schubertiade (see Festivals) Modern Vienna Festival (see Festivals; until December)	November
Christmas market on the Rathausplatz Mozart Festival Nativity cribs in St Peter's Church Art auction in the Dorotheum Christmas Exhibition in the Künstlerhaus Dec. 31st: Imperial Ball in the Hofburg	December

See also Festivals and Programme of Events

Excursions

Regional tickets, available on rail and bus and covering popular areas such as the Semmering, the Vienna Woods, etc. can be obtained from Austrian Railways (ÖBB): see Railways.

Note

The Wienerwald (Vienna Woods), extending over 80sq.km/31 sq. miles, is the most popular local recreational district of Vienna. It lies in the extreme north-eastern part of the Eastern Alps, and, to the west of Vienna, falls in several terraces down to the Danube. In the north the scenery is charming, with broad hillocks and beech-woods; in the east it is sunny with stands of black pines; in the south-east rugged with gorge-like valleys. In the A–Z section some of the most beautiful and interesting places are described: in the south the Cistercian Monastery (see Heiligenkreuz), which was the impetus for settlement in this area; Gumpoldskirchen (see entry), where vines grow on the slopes of the Wienerwald; Laxenburg and Baden (see entries) where the Court used to pass the summer; in the north-west the vintners' village of Grinzing (see entry) and the vantage-point of Kahlenberg (see entry); in the north Klosterneuburg (see entry).

Wienerwald

Below, as an example, the route (38km/23½ miles) over the Hohenstrasse to Klosterneuburg is described. Although it is some 25km/15 miles longer than the direct route via Kahlenbergerdorf, with which it can be combined in a very pleasant round trip (50km/31 miles), it is nevertheless full of delightful scenery.

By taking the roads from Vienna leading to Neuwaldegg, Neustift am Walde, Sievering or Grinzing many other round trips can be put together.

Leave Vienna on the road to the west, passing near Schönbrunn and follow the Wien valley upstream. At Wien-Hacking (11km/7 miles) turn right and cross the River Wien. In 500m we reach Wien-Hütteldorf. Now follow the winding and scenically beautiful Wiener Höhenstrasse above the Wienerwald to the Kahlenberg (large car park). 1km beyond the car park the road to Klosterneuburg bears off to the left, but it is better to continue to the end of the Höhenstrasse at the Leopoldsberg (423m/1388ft), the most easterly promontory of the Wienerwald, high above the Danube. Here there is an inn and a Baroque church on the site of the former Babenburg castle, and from here the view is as fine if not finer than that from the Kahlenberg. We return to the Klosterneuburg turning and descend the winding road on the northern slope of the Kahlenberg to the monastery, some 5km/3 miles distant. Visitors who would like to walk in the Wienerwald are recommended to use routes 1 and 4 of the brochure published by the Stadtinformationsamt (see details at the end of this entry).

Excursions

March-Donauland

Fields and meadows, vines and woodland are the distinctive features of the March-Donauland to the east of Vienna. In the A–Z section of this guide two of the places in this area most deserving of a visit are described: these are Carnuntum (see entry), worth seeing for its Roman excavations, and Rohrau (see entry), Hadyn's birthplace.

The visitor who follows the 110km/68 mile-long route through the March-feld described here will be on historic ground. It was here that the Quadi fought against the Romans (1st–4th c.); it was here that battles were fought against the Hungarians in the Middle Ages, against the Turks in the 17th c. and against Napoleon at Aspern and Deutsch-Wagram in the 19th c.

We leave Vienna across the Praterstern and the Reichsbrücke, passing the impressive "UNO City". In 6km/4 miles the Kagran Bridge crosses the Old Danube, the former main course of the river. In Aspern (5km/3 miles) a stone lion outside the parish church is a memorial of the Battle of Aspern (1809), when Archduke Charles inflicted a defeat on Napoleon; the latter, however, succeeded a little later in crossing the Danube at Wagram. South of Aspern extends the Lobau Nature Reserve, a delightful scenic area of grassland, watered by the Old Danube. The route continues through Gross-Enzersdorf (5.5km/3 miles), Orth (14km/9 miles), which has a castle with four towers, and Eckartsau (9km/5½ miles), with a former imperial hunting lodge, to Stopfenreuth (7km/4 miles) where we turn north to the River March which here flows into the Danube. The route now passes through Engelhartstetten (4km/2½ miles) to Schlosshof Castle, built in 1725–29 by Johann Lukas von Hildebrandt for Prince Eugene and later enlarged for Maria Theresa, and finally reaches Marchegg (8.5km/5 miles) on the March which forms the boundary with Czechoslovakia and where the meadows are a nature reserve. The former hunting lodge houses the Hunting Museum of Lower Austria. From here we turn west and return to Vienna via Obersiedenbrunn (15km/9 miles) with a Baroque church and a castle, which was rebuilt for Prince Eugene in 1730, and through Markgrafneusiedl (6km/4 miles) on the Russbach.

Wine producing region

The largest wine-producing area of Austria is bounded in the north and east by the Czech and Slovak Republics and in the south by the Marchfeld. Mistelbach is the chief town in the eastern part, and Retz, on the slopes of the Manhartsgebirge, in the western quarter. The principal varieties of wine produced in this region are Grüner Veltliner, Blauer Portugieser, Neuburger, Rheinriesling, Müller-Thurgau and Blaufränkische. In the charming little villages many inns and Heurige cater for the refreshment needs of visitors.

The Österreich Werbung (see Information) has brochures of popular excursions in the area.

Semmering

Situated at an altitude of 1000m/3280ft, Semmering, on the boundary between Lower Austria and Styria, 90km/56 miles south of Vienna, is a mountain resort with a long tradition. A track over the pass existed as long ago as the 12th c. The present pass (modernised 1956–58) was developed from a road which Charles VI had laid out in 1728 and which was extended and enlarged in 1839–42. A trip on the Semmering railway is also very agreeable; this the first large-scale mountain railway in Europe, was constructed in 1848–54 by Karl von Ghega. It passes through fifteen tunnels and crosses deep gorges on sixteen arched viaducts, some of them consisting of several storeys. The maximum gradient is 1 in 40.

Chairlifts go up from the top of the pass to the Hirschenkogel (1324m/4345ft) and from Maria Schutz to the Sonnwendstein (1523m/4998ft). A toll-road leads from the pass to the Sonnwendstein from which there is a wonderful view of Rax and Schneeberg, the Alpine foreland and the Semmering railway far below.

Boat trips on the Danube

A trip on the Danube on one of the ships of the Erste Donau-Dampf-schiffsfahrts-Gesellschaft (DDSG) is another excellent excursion; for example to Budapest or to Bratislava (Pressburg). A nostalgic trip can be made on the MS "Stadt Passau", the last paddle-wheel steamer, which operates to and from Passau, or on a modern hovercraft or a traditional Danube ship. The trips last from two to four days. In the other direction, upstream, there are trips from Vienna to the Wachau or to Melk (taking in the abbey) and thence to Passau, returning to Vienna through the Wachau (tour of the old streets of Dürnstein, with wine-tasting) and the southern part of the Wienerwald (four days one-way). It is also possible to book for part of the route Vienna–Passau or to return from Passau to Vienna by rail (in this case three days).

These trips are operated from May to September (information from the Vienna Tourist Board (Wiener Tourismusverband; see Information) and from Wurm & Koch (94032 Passau, Höllgasse 26; tel. 0851/2056, fax 3 55 18).

There are also excellent walks to be enjoyed from Vienna. The Stadt-informationsamt (see Information) has put together ten walks in the brochure "Stadtwanderwege", in which not only are the individual walks indicated on corresponding small maps, but also included are the starting points (with details of suitable public transport), duration and length of walk, and places of refreshment on the route. The walks lead to the following venues:

Walks from Vienna

Walk 1: Kahlenberg 11km/7 miles
Walk 2: Hermannskogel 10km/6 miles
Walk 3: Hameau 11km/7 miles
Walk 4: Jubiläumswarte 7·5km/4½miles
Walk 5: Bisamberg 10·5km/6½ miles
Walk 6: Zugberg – Maurer Wald 12·5km/7¾ miles; this route also includes the Wotruba church (see A to Z, Wotruba Kirche)
Walk 7: Laaer Berg 15km/9 miles
Walk 8: Sophienalpe 11km/7 miles
Walk 9: Prater13km/8 miles

Festivals

The Vienna Festival Weeks are in May and June. Information and tickets can be obtained from: Direktion der Wiener Festwochen, Lehárgasse 11, A-1060 Wien; tel. 5 86 16 76–0.

Vienna Festival Weeks

In July, August and September musical events include arcade concerts (Arcade-courtyard of the New Town Hall), concerts in Schönbrunn Palace, in the Town Hall Square, in churches and town houses (with special emphasis on the music of Schubert and Haydn), as well as promenade and park concerts.

Music in summer in Vienna ("Klangbogen Wien")

Tickets are obtainable from: Klangbogen, Laudongasse 29, A-1082 Wien; tel. 40 00–84 00, fax 40 00 99 84 10. Box office: Friedrich-Schmidt-Platz (daily 10am–6pm). Wien-Ticket, Kärnter Str., near the Opera House (daily 10am–7pm). Since 1994 a ticket for the "Klangbogen Wien" events has also served as a ticket on public transport within Central Zone 100, during the period 2 hours before and 6 hours after the start of the performance.

The Danube Festival at the end of June and the popular Folk Festival in late August/early September in Prater are open-air festivals providing rock, jazz, folk and popular music, theatre and cabaret.

Open Air Festivals

In July international exponents of jazz and similar music perform in the State Opera House, in the Volkstheater and at open-air concerts.

Jazz festival

Information: Jazz-Fest Wien, A-1030 Wien, Esteplatz 3/13;
tel. 7 12 42 24, fax 7 12 34 34.
Tickets: Ticket Line, tel. 54 54 54–0.

In July and August the programme includes famous opera films and legendary concert recordings.

Opera film festival

International Dance Weeks	In February and March and in July and August visitors can watch performances by top dancers in ballet, ballroom and ultra-modern dance forms.
Special musical events	Every year Vienna remembers its great composers with a number of special festivals. These include the following: February and March: Haydn Days April/May: Spring Festival October: Festival der Jeunesse (Youth Festival) November: the Schubertiade November: "Wien modern" (contemporary composers) December: the Mozart Festival 　The above festivals are performed in either the Musikverein or the Konzerthaus. 　Information: Wiener Konzerthaus, A-1030 Wien, Lothringerstr. 20; tel. 7 12 12 11, fax 71 21 21 14; box-office open daily 9am–6pm, Sat. to 1pm; tel. 7 12 12 11; Wiener Musikverein, A-1010 Wien, Bösendorfer Str. 12; tel. 5 05 81 09, fax 5 05 94 09.
Viennale Film Festival	Details from: Viennale A-1070 Wien, Stiftgasse 6; tel. 5 26 59 47–0, fax 93 41 72.

Fiaker

Ranks	There are about three dozen horse-drawn "fiaker" plying for hire in Vienna. They can be found at Stephansplatz, in Augustinerstrasse in front of the Albertina art gallery and at the Heldenplatz.
Fiaker Museum	See A to Z

Food and drink

Meal times	The main meal of the day, generally of three substantial courses – soup, a meat dish and a sweet – is normally eaten between noon and 2pm In the evening the Viennese tend to have their meal between 6 and 9pm; many restaurants do not serve hot meals after 10pm.
Cuisine	The key to the success of the Viennese cuisine lies in its variety. The recipes owe a great deal to Bohemian, Hungarian, Croatian, Slovene and Italian influences. Neither light in texture nor low in calories, it nevertheless makes use of many natural ingredients. It includes an astonishing range of freshwater fish, and during the October/November season game dishes are exceedingly good. The "New Viennese Cuisine" is modelled on the French *nouvelle cuisine* but is only to be found in a small number of restaurants.
Soup	Beef broth (Rindsuppe) garnished with various types of pastry (Frittaten, Schörbell, Backerbsen); dumplings and noodles (Markknödel, Griessnockerl, Lungenstrudel, Milzschnitten) and pea or vegetable soup with fish roe (Fischbeutschelsuppe).
Fish	Carp in garlic butter (Wurzelkarpfen); fillet of pike-perch (Zander) fried in bacon fat or grilled, with paprika sauce; steamed catfish (Wels) and fish pie (Zwiebelfisch).

Schnitzel-style chicken (Backhendel); chicken with paprika (Paprikahen-del); stuffed breast of goose (Ganselbrust); capon (Kapaun) in anchovy sauce; pheasant (Faisan) roasted "in a bacon shirt"; woodcock (Schnepfen).

Poultry, game-birds

Wild boar (Wildschwein) in cream sauce with dumplings; ragout of veni-son (Hirschragout) with bacon; saddle of venison (Rehrücken) in a herb sauce; jugged hare (Hasenrücken) in a wine sauce.

Game

Wiener Schnitzel (i.e. veal cutlet coated with breadcrumbs and fried); cuts of beef: (Tafelspitz) with horseradish, (Beinfleisch) with chive sauce, roasted (Esterhazy-Rostbraten); larded veal (Kalbsvogerln); Viennese roast pork (Wiener Schweinebraten); stewed pork with horseradish (Kren-fleisch); salted meat (Selchfleisch); roasted sucking pig (Spanferkel); braised kidneys (Nierenbraten) and goulash (Gulasch).

Meat

Dishes made from kidneys, liver, sweetbreads, etc. (Salonbeuschel, Kavaliersbries).

Offal

Pancakes (Palatschinken); stuffed pancakes (Topfenpalatschinken, Kai-serschmarren); yeast dumplings with plums (Topfenknödel mit Zwetsch-kenröster), with poppyseed (Germknöderl), with apricots (Marillenknödel), with jam (Buchteln); mille-feuille (Millrahmstrudel) with vanilla sauce, plum purée (Powideltascherln/tatschkerln), and apple strudel (Apfelstrudel).

Hot sweets

Sachertorte, Dobostorte

Cakes

Apart from good beer (1 seidel = 0.6 pint, 1 krugel = 0.9 pint) the most popular beverage is wine. This comes mostly from Lower Austria and Burgenland and is often drunk "g'spritzt", that is mixed with soda water.

Drinks

The wines on offer include green Veltliner, Rhine Riesling, White Burgundy, Traminer, Welschriesling, Neuburger, Müller Thurgau, Zierfandler, Rotgip-fler, Gumpoldskirchner, Blaufränkischer, Blue Portuguese and Blue Bur-gundy.

An evening of wine-drinking is best spent at the "Heurige" or cellar bars (see Baedeker Special "The Bush", Practical Information, Heurige and Restaurants).

See entry

Restaurants

The legendary Viennese "Sachertorte"

Culinary terms

Frittaten	strips of pancake
Schöberl	sponge fingers
Nockerl	small elongated flour dumplings
Backerbsen	small balls of choux pastry fried in fat
Fleischlaberl	rissoles,
Fogosch, Schill	pike-perch
Gabelroller	rollmop herrings
Beuschel	braised calf's lung, spleen or heart
Beinfleisch	loin of beef
Tafelspitz	boiled loin of beef
Gulyás	goulash
Faschiertes	mince, meat loaf
Selchfleisch	smoked pork
Lungenbraten	loin of beef in a thick sauce
Lüngerl	strips of calf's lungs (and often also heart) boiled in vinegar
Kaiserfleisch	lightly cured pork spare rib
Kalbsvogel	small beef olives
Backhendl	roast chicken portions
Fisolen	green beans
Karfiol	cauliflower
Sprossenkohl	brussels sprouts
Stelze	knuckle of pork
Paradeiser	tomatoes
Häuptelsalat	lettuce
Kukuruz	maize
Kren	horseradish
Schwammerl	mushrooms
Topfen	curd cheese
Schlagobers/Schlag	whipped cream
Palatschinken	sweet filled pancakes
Strudel	thin pastry cases with all kinds of filling
Kaiserschmarrn	strips of pancake with raisins, fried in butter and sugar
Dobostorte	flan filled with chocolate cream
Sachertorte	chocolate cake filled with apricot jam
Buchteln	baked or steamed yeast-dough noodles (sometimes filled)
Powidl	thick plum purée without sugar
Germknödel	yeast dumplings filled with Powidl (see above)
Marillen	apricots
Ribisel	blackcurrants
Zwetschkenröster	stewed plums

Getting to Vienna

By air
: Vienna's Schwechat Airport (see Air travel) is served by flights from most major European cities. There are direct daily services between London and Vienna (British Airways, Austrian Airlines and Lauda Air), also from Birmingham and Edinburgh to Vienna (Austrian Airlines). During the winter months flights can be delayed by fog, so it is advisable during that period to book on late morning or early afternoon services.

By rail
: There are two main routes available from London; the most direct is from Victoria via Dover–Ostend which takes about 24 hours, the other from Liverpool Street via the Hook of Holland involves changes at Cologne and Wurzburg or Munich and takes longer.

The privately run Orient Express runs from London to Vienna on certain dates, but tickets are very expensive.

Vienna is about 1290km/800 miles from the channel coast. Most visitors taking their own car travel on the motorways via Cologne, Frankfurt, Nuremberg, Passau and Linz. In view of the long distance it is advisable to make one – or possibly two – overnight stops. There are motorail services from 's-Hertogenbosch in Holland to Salzburg and from Düsseldorf to Munich.

By road

There are numerous package tours by coach, either going direct to Vienna or including the Austrian capital in a longer circuit. For information apply to any travel agent.

From May to September the Donau-Dampfschiffahrts-Gesellschaft (DDSG – Danube Shipping Company) operates a fast service between Passau and Vienna. Details obtainable from the Vienna Tourist Board (see Information) and from Wurm & Köck, Höllgasse 26, D-94032 Passau; tel. (0851) 92 92 92, fax (0851) 3 55 18.

By boat

Rail passengers with international tickets can opt to travel by DDSG vessels if their rail ticket covers the stretches to Vienna from Passau, Linz and Melk. Vouchers, on which a supplement is payable, for the transfer from rail to river can only be obtained from the DDSG offices at points of embarkation.

Help for the disabled

Details from Vienna Tourist Board (see Information)

Hotel list/city plan

Heuriger

A brochure entitled "Heurige in Wien", obtainable from the Vienna Tourist Board (see Information) gives times of opening and facilities offered (garden, music, etc.).

Alte Weinpresse, 19, Paradiesgasse 12; tel. 36 12 71 (G)
Altes Bürgermeisterhaus, 19, Cobenzlgasse 49; tel. 32 72 33 (G)
Altes Presshaus, 19, Cobenzlgasse 15; tel. 32 23 93 (G)
Das "Alte Haus", 19, Himmelstr. 35; tel. 3 20 97 93 (G)
Bach-Hengl, 19, Sandgasse 7–9; tel. 32 24 39 (G)
Buschenschank Stary, 17, Czartonitzkygasse 141; tel. 4 70 15 51 (G)
Cobenzl Stübert, 19, Himmelstr. 2; tel. 32 39 46 (G)
Figlmüller, 19, Grinzinger Str. 55; tel. 32 44 57 (G)
Figlmüller, 1, Wollzeile 5; tel. 5 12 61 77 (G)
Fuhrgassl-Huber, 19, Neustift am Walde 68; tel. 44 14 05 (G)
Grinzinger Hauermandl, 19, Cobenzlgasse 20; tel. 3 22 04 44 (G)
Grinzinger Hof, 19, Grinziger Allee 86 20; tel. 32 63 13 (G)
Grinzinger Weinbottich, 19, Cobenzlgasse 28; tel. 32 42 37 (G)
Haslinger, 19, Agnesgasse 3; tel. 44 13 47 (G)
Hubers Buschenschank, 18, Pötzleinsdorfer Str. 97; tel. 47 53 32 (G)
Kalke's Gwölb, 23, Ketzergasse 465; tel. 88 75 08 (G)
Kierlinger, 20, Kahlenberger Str. 2; tel. 37 22 64 (G)
Landstrasse Heurigenkeller in the Hotel Biedermeier, 3, Landstrasser Hauptstr. 28; tel. 71 67 10–513
Mayer am Pfarrplatz, 19, Heiligenstädter Pfarrplatz 2; tel. 37 12 87 (G)
Presshaus Huber, 19, Neustift in Walde 77; tel. 44 12 38 (G)
Reinprecht "Wine Museum", 19, Cobenzlgasse 22; tel. 32 14 71 (G)
Schübel-Auer, 19, Kahlenberger Str. 22; tel. 37 22 22 (G)
Sirbu, 19, Kahlenberger Str. 210; tel. 37 13 19 (G)
Urban, 21, Stammerdorfer Str. 123; tel. 39 61 54 (G)

Heurige and Wine Cellars
(selection: G = Garden)

At the "Sign of the Bush"

Who can imagine Vienna without its "Heuriger"? For many people, an evening spent drinking this crisp wine in one of the unspoilt inns is what Vienna is all about. The term "Heuriger" in fact has two meanings; on the one hand it describes the young wine, and on the other the place where it is sold. Heuriger must not be confused with "Federweisser" (feather-white) or "Suser" wines. These are also sold in the year in which they are produced, but under the designation "Sturm". Heurige is the newest wine which is drawn from the barrel in spring and is on sale until the following year. From St Martin's Day (11th November) the current Heuriger is sold under the name "alter Wein" (old wine).

In 1784 the Emperor Joseph II granted to vintners the privilege of selling their own wine for 300 days in the year in their privately-run "Buschenschänken" (bush inns). The term refers to the bunch of spruce twigs which is hung out over the entrance to the establishment to indicate to the thirsty traveller that here he can obtain wine produced in Vienna or nearby.

A Heuriger inn in Grinzing

In no other European city are so many grapes grown and pressed within the city itself as in Vienna, which has some 720ha/1760acres of vineyards. The most famous Buschenschänken are to be found west of the city, in the former villages of Grinzing, Sievering, Nussdorf, Neustift and Heiligenstadt in the hills of the Viennese Forest, as well as on the northern bank of the Danube, in Stammersdorf and Strebersdorf at the foot of the flat Bisamerberg. Other classical Heuriger regions include Mauer and Oberlaa on the southern outskirts of the city as well as Gumpoldskirchen, Baden and Vöslau. There are signs erected in these places giving details of the inns which have opened up.

Where do the Viennese go when they feel happy? To the Heuriger!
Where do the Viennese go when they feel sad? To the Heuriger!

As Hugo Wiener said, you do not have to have a reason for going to the Heuriger. You can meet friends there, enjoy a concert evening at the Viertel Grünen Veltliner, experience the rapture of a first meeting in a romantic garden or taste of the young, tangy wine in one of the little bars. The atmosphere in the Buschenschänken is simple but extremely friendly and cosy, the wine is served in a glass with a handle, the food – mainly traditional plain fare – is generally self-service. Even though nowadays the traditional zither or "Schrammel" (guitar, accordion, violin) music is becoming less common, when music is heard it is usually quiet and sad. Those seeking this "heaven on earth", be it chic or more basic, can either choose from more than 200 Heuriger in Vienna or seek expert advice from the locals.

Zum Alten Stadl, 10, Leisingbachstr. 79; tel. 68 55 48 (G)
Zum Herrgott am Stoa, 16, Speckbachergasse 14; tel. 46 02 30 (G)
Zum Krottenbachl, 19, Krottenbachstr. 148; tel. 44 12 40 (G)
Zum Weihrauch, 19, Kaasgrabengasse 77; tel. 32 58 18 (G)
Zwölf-Apostel-Keller, 1, Sonnenfelsgasse 3; tel. 5 12 67 77

Hotels

Visitors are recommended to make and confirm reservations before departure. The Vienna Tourist Offices (see Information) and travel bureaux can
assist in finding accommodation.

Reservation

Visitors wishing to stay outside the city should apply to Nieder-
österreich-Information, Heidenschuss 2, A-1010 Wien; tel. 5 33 31 14–28;
open: Mon.–Fri. 8.30am–5.30pm.

Accommodation
Outside the city

For hotels suitable for the disabled see Help for the disabled.

Hotel guide for
the disabled

Hotels are officially classified in five categories: 5 star = Luxury, 4 star =
first-class, 3 star = good middle-class, 2 star = simple, 1 star = modest. The
list below follows this classification. b. = number of beds.

Categories

The prices given below in Austrian schillings are for accommodation (including breakfast, service and taxes). They are average prices, intended as
a guide to price levels.

Category	Double room	Single room
★★★★★	1650–5100	800–3900
★★★	800–2500	520–2450
★★★	660–1400	280–1150
★★	400–1380	210– 660
★	400– 850	200– 440

Ambassador, 1010, Neuer Markt 5, 176 b.; tel. 5 14 66
Ana Grand Hotel Wien, 1010, Kärnter Ring 9, 194 b.; tel. 5 15 80–0
Bristol, 1010, Kärnter Ring 1, 270 b.; tel. 51 51 60
Clima Villenhotel, 1190, Nussberggasse 2c, 60 b.; tel. 37 15 16
De France, 1010, Schottenring 3, 411 b.; tel. 34 35 40–0
Im Palais Schwarzenberg, 1030, Schwarzenbergplatz 9, 75 b.;
   tel. 78 45 15–0
Imperial, 1015, Kärnter Ring 16, 275 b.; tel. 5 01 10–0
Inter-Continental Wien, 1030, Johannesgasse 28, 996 b.; tel. 7 11 22–0
Renaissance, 1150, Ullmannstr. 71, 520 b.; tel. 85 04–0
Sacher, 1015, Philharmonikerstr. 4, 213 b.; tel. 5 14 56–0
SAS Palais, 1010, Weihburggasse 32, 310 b.; tel. 51 51 70
Vienna Hilton, 1030, Am Stadtpark, 1200 b.; tel. 7 17 00–0
Vienna Marriott, 1010, Parkring 12a, 608 b.; tel. 51 51 80
Vienna Plaza, 1010, Schottenring 11, 440 b.; tel. 3 13 90–0

★★★★★

Alba Hotel Accadia Wien, 1050, Margaretenstr. 53, 93 b.; tel. 5 88 50–0,
   (child-minding from 3 years of age)
Alba Hotel Palace, 1050, Margaretenstr. 92, 228 b.; tel. 55 46 86–0
Albatros, 1090 Liechtensteinstr. 89, 140 b.; tel. 34 35 08–0
Amadeus, 1010, Wildpretmarkt 5, 48 b.; tel. 5 33 87 38
Am Parkring, 1010, Parkring 12, 106 b.; tel. 5 14 80–0
Am Schubertring, 1010 Schubertring 11, 73 b.; tel. 7 17 02–0
Am Stephansplatz, 1010, Stephansplatz 9, 75 b.; tel. 7 17 02–0
Astoria, 1010, Fürichgasse 1, 180 b.; tel. 5 15 77–0
Bellevue, 1091, Althanstr. 5, 320 b.; tel. 3 13 48–0
Biedermeier, 1030, Landstrasser Hauptstr. 28, 420 b.; tel. 7 16 71–0
Capricorno, 1010, Schwedenplatz 3–4, 81 b.; tel. 5 33 31 04–0

★★★★

Hotels

City-Central, 1020, Taborstr. 8a, 114 b.; tel. 2 11 05–0
Clima Hotel Johann Strauss, 1040, Favoritenstr. 12, 118 b.; tel. 5 05 76 28
Europa, 1015, Neuer Markt 3, 152 b.; tel. 5 15 94–0
K & K Hotel Maria Theresia, 1070, Kirchberggasse 6–8, 246 b.;
   tel. 5 21 23–0
K & K Palais Hotel, 1010, Rudolfsplatz 11, 126 b.; tel. 5 33 13 53–0
Kaiserin Elisabeth, 1010, Weihburggasse 3, 119 b.; tel. 5 15 26–0
Kaiserpark-Schönbrunn, 1120, Grünbergstrasse 11, 90 b.; tel. 83 86 10
König von Ungarn, 1010, Schulerstr. 10, 70 b.; tel. 5 15 84–0
Kummer, 1060, Mariahilfer Str. 71a, 182 b.; tel. 5 88 95–0
Mailbergerhof, 1010, Annagasse 7, 70 b.; tel. 5 12 06 41–0
Maté, 1170, Ottakringer Str. 34–36, 230 b.; tel. 4 04 55–0
Modul, 1190, Peter-Jordan-Str. 78, 82 b.; tel. 4 76 60–0
Nestroy, 1020, Rotensterngasse 12, 120 b.; tel. 2 11 40–0
Parkhotel Schönbrunn, 1130 Hietzinger Hauptstr. 10–14, 798 b.;
   tel. 8 78 04–0
President Wallhotel, 1060, Wallgasse 23, 160 b.; tel. 5 99 90–0
Prinz Eugen, 1040, Wiedner Gürtel 14, 165 b.; tel. 5 05 17 41–0
Pullmann Belvedere, 1030, Am Heumarkt 35–37, 300 b.; tel. 75 25 35–0
Regina, 1090, Rooseveltplatz 15, 232 b.; tel. 42 76 81–0
Römischer Kaiser, 1010, Annagasse 16, 48 b.; tel. 5 12 77 51–0
Royal, 1010, Singerstr. 3, 161 b.; tel. 5 15 68–0
Scandic Crown, 1020, Handelskai 269, 800 b.; tel. 2 17 77–0
Schneider, 1060, Getreidemarkt 5, 101 b.; tel. 5 88 38–0
Stefanie, 1020, Taborstr. 12, 230 b.; tel. 2 11 50–0
Strudhof, 1090, Pasteurgasse 1, 101 b.; tel. 3 19 14 77–0
Tyrol, 1060, Mariahilfer Str. 15, 68 b.; tel. 5 87 54 15–0
Vienna Penta Renaissance, 1030, Ungarngasse 60, 684 b.; tel. 7 11 75–0

★★★   Alexander, 1090, Augasse 15, 114 b.; tel. 34 15 08–0
Arabella Jagdschloss, 1130, Jagdschlossgasse 79, 89 b.; tel. 8 04 35 08
Capri, 1020, Praterstr. 44–46, 80 b.; tel. 24 84 04
Clima Cityhotel, 1040, Theresianumgasse 21a, 78 b.; tel. 5 05 16 96
Ekazent, 1130, Hietzinger Hauptstr. 22, 64 b.; tel. 8 77 74 01–0
Fürst Metternich, 1060, Esterházygasse 33, 112 b.; tel. 5 88 70–0
Mozart, 1090, Nordbergstr. 4, 106 b.; tel. 34 15 37
Nordbahn, 1020, Praterstr. 72, 136 b.; tel. 2 11 30–0
Post, 1010, Fleischmarkt 24, 176 b.; tel. 5 15 83–0
Stieglbräu, 1150, Mariahilfer Str. 156, 86 b.; tel. 8 92 33 35
Wandl, 1010, Petersplatz 9, 232 b.; tel. 5 34 55–0
Zur Wiener Staatsoper, 1010, Krugerstr. 11, 40 b.; tel. 5 13 12 74–0

★★   Auhof, 1130, Auhofstr. 205, 62 b.; tel. 8 77 52 89
Cyrus, 1100, Laxenburger Str. 14, 50 b.; tel. 6 04 42 88
Gabriel, 1030, Landstrasser Haupstr. 165, 82 b.; tel. 7 12 32 05
Goldes Horn, 1050, Am Hundsturm 5, 25 b.; tel. 55 47 55
Kagraner Hof, 1222, Wagramer Str. 141, 42 b.; tel. 23 11 87
Rathaus, 1080, Lange Gasse 13, 77 b.; tel. 43 43 02
Stadt Bamberg, 1150, Mariahilfer Str. 167, 50 b.; tel. 8 93 42 87

★   Hospiz CVJM, 1070, Kenyongasse 15, 41 b.; tel. 93 13 04
Orient, 1010, Tiefer Graben 30–32, 51 b.; tel. 5 33 73 07
Praterstern, 1020 Mayergasse 6, 74 b.; tel. 24 01 23

Hotel with
child-minding

See ★★★★Alba Hotel Accadia
Children are looked after in the hotel's own nursery, including food, drawing, model-making, etc., and short excursions; baby-sitting in the evenings

Pensions

Pensions are generally fairly small establishments, often without restaurants, situated in residential or office buildings. Because of their family-like
atmosphere they are popular for fairly long stays.

Alla Lenz, 1070, Halbgasse 3–5, 26 b.; tel. 5 23 69 89   ★★★★
Arenberg, 1010, Stubenring 2, 42 b.; tel. 5 12 52 91–0
Barich, 1030, Barichgasse 3, 25 b.; tel. 7 12 22 75–0
Mariahilf, 1060, Mariahilfer Str. 49, 24 b.; tel. 5 86 17 81–0
Museum, 1070, Museumstr. 3, 28 b.; tel. 93 44 26
Neuer Markt, 1010, Seilergasse 9, 97 b.; tel. 5 12 23 16

Adria, 1080, Wickenburggasse 23, 23 b.; tel. 4 02 02 38   ★★★
Am Operneck, 1010 Kärnter Str. 47, 14 b.; tel. 5 12 93 10
Bosch, 1030, Keilgasse 13, 20 b.; tel. 78 61 79–0
Christina, 1010, Hafnersteig 7, 60 b.; tel. 5 33 29 61–0
Franz, 1090 Währinger Str. 12, 51 b.; tel. 34 36 37–0
Geissler, 1010, Postgasse 14, 58 b.; tel. 5 33 28 03
Kirschbichler, 1030, Landstrasser Haupstr. 33, 27 b.; tel. 7 12 10 68
Kurpension Oberlaa, 1107, Kurbadstr. 6, 62 b.; tel. 68 36 11
Lerner, 1010, Wipplingerstr. 23, 16 b.; tel. 5 33 52 19
Nossek, 1010, Graben 17, 46 b.; tel. 5 33 70 41–0
Residenz, 1010, Ebendorferstr. 10, 23 b.; tel. 43 47 86–0
Sankt Stephan, 1010, Spiegelgasse 1, 12 b.; tel. 5 12 29 90–0
Schweizer Pension Solderer, 1010, Heinrichsgasse 2, 20 b.; tel. 5 33 81 56
Stadtpark, 1030, Landstrasser Hauptstr. 7, 34 b.; tel. 7 13 31 23–0
Suzanne, 1010, Walfischgasse 4, 34 b.; tel. 5 13 25 07–0

Acion, 1010 Dorotheergasse 6–8, 43 b.; tel. 5 12 54 73–0   ★★
Amon, 1090, Daungasse 1, 19 b.; tel. 42 01 94
Columbia, 1080, Kochgasse 9, 23 b.; tel. 42 67 57

Seasonal hotels are student accommodation run as hotels from early July   Seasonal hotels
to the end of September. Service is generally provided by students.

Atlas, 1070, Lerchenfelder Str. 1–3, 304 b.; tel. 93 45 48–0   ★★★
Margareten, 1040, Margaretenstr. 30, 88 b.; tel. 58 81 50
Rosen-Hotel Burgenland 3, 1060, Bürgerspitalgasse 19, 240 b.;
   tel. 5 97 93 47–0
Rosen-Hotel Wieden, 1040, Schelleingasse 36, 208 b.; tel. 5 01 52–0

Academia, 1080, Pfeilgasse 3a, 672 b.; tel. 43 16 61–0   ★★
Alsergrund, 1080, Alser Str. 33, 118 b.; tel. 5 12 74 68
Aquila, 1080, Pfeilgasse 1a, 130 b.; tel. 42 52 35–0
Auersperg, 1080, Auespergstr. 9, 132 b.; tel. 43 25 49–0
Avis, 1080, Pfeilgasse 4, 117 b.; tel. 42 63 74–0
Haus Döbling, 1190, Gymnasiumstr. 85, 550 b.; tel. 34 76 31
Josefstadt, 1080, Buchfeldgasse 16, 70 b.; tel. 43 52 11–0
Rosen-Hotel Burgenland 1, 1090, Wilhelm-Exner-Gasse 4, 145 b.;
   tel. 4 03 91 22
Rosen-Hotel Burgenland 2, 1060, Mittelgasse 18, 275 b.; tel. 5 96 12 47–0
Rosen-Hotel Niederösterreich, 1020, Unter Augartenstr. 31, 204 b.;
   tel. 3 31 14

Auge Gottes, 1090, Nussdorfer Str. 75, 157 b.; tel. 34 25 85–0   ★
Rosen-Hotel Europahaus, 1140, Linzer Str. 429, 74 b.; tel. 97 35 36–0

1080, Laudongasse 7; tel. 4 02 60 61   Central Letting
The Central Letting Office (Mitwohnzentrale) acts as agent for the letting of   Office
private rooms and flats for short stays of three days or more; the amount of
commission payable depends on the length of the let.

Information

Great Britain	Austrian National Tourist Office 30 St George Street London W1R 0AL Tel. (0171) 629 0461
United States	500 Fifth Avenue Suite 2009–2022 New York NY 10110 Tel. (212) 944 6880
	11601 Wilshire Boulevard Suite 2480, Los Angeles CA 90025 Tel. (310) 477 3332
	1350 Connecticut Avenue N.W. Suite 501, Washington D.C. 20036 Tel. (202) 835 8962
	500 North Michigan Avenue Suite 1950, Chicago, IL 60611 Tel. (312) 644 8029
	1300 Post Oak Boulevard Suite 1700, Houston, Texas 77056 Tel. (713) 850 8888 9999
Canada	2 Bloor Street East Suite 3330, Toronto, Ontario M4W 1A8 Tel. (416) 967 3381
	1010 ouest, rue Sherbrooke, Suite 1410 Montreal Que H3A 2R7 Tel. (514) 849 37089
	Suite 1380, Granville Square 200 Granville Street Vancouver B.C. V6C 1S4 Tel. (604) 683 8695/5808
Vienna	Austrian National Tourist Office (Österreich Werbung) Margaretenstrasse 1 (corner Wiedner Hauptstrasse) A-1040 Wien. Tel. 5 87 20 00 (Open: Mon.–Fri. 10am–5pm, Thur. until 6pm)

Wien
Vienna·Vienne·Viena·ウィーン

Vienna Tourist Office (Wiener Fremdenverkehrsamt)
Kärntner Strasse 38, A-1010 Wien
Tel. 5 13 88 92 and 5 13 40 15
(Open: daily 9am–7pm)

Advance written information for Vienna:
Vienna Tourist Board (Wiener Tourismusverband)
Obere Augartenstr. 40
A-1025 Wien
Tel. 2 11 14, fax 2 16 84 92
Open: Mon.–Fri. 8am–4pm

Stadtinformation (in Town Hall)
Friedrich-Schmidt Platz 1, A-1010 Wien
Tel. 4 03 89 89
(Open: Mon.–Fri. 8am–6pm)

Official Tourist Information (also room reservations) at the west motorway access road (A.1), motorway station Wien–Auhof (Open: in Nov. daily 9am–7pm; Dec.–Mar. daily 10am–6pm; Apr.–Oct. daily 8am–10pm)

For motorists

Official Tourist Information (also room reservations) at the south motorway access road (A.2); turn off to centre, Triester Strasse (Open: Apr., May, June and Oct. daily 9am–7pm; July–Sept. daily 8am–10pm)

Official Tourist Information (also room reservations) at the east motorway access road (A.4); turn off Simmeringer Haide/Landwehrstrasse. Tel. 76 56 61 (Open: Apr.–Sept. daily 9am–7pm)

Official Tourist Information (also room reservations); access from the north (Floridsdorfer Brücke/Donauinsel) (Open: Apr.–Sept. daily 9am–7pm)

There are travel agencies in both West and South stations, where rooms can also be booked.
West Station: tel. 58 00–3 10 60 (open: daily 6. 15am–11pm)
South Station: tel. 58 00–3 10 50 (open: daily 6.15am–9pm)
Rail information: tel. 1700 (Mon.–Fri. 7am–8pm, Sat. 7.30am–1.30pm).
Time-table information: tel. 17 17.

For rail travellers

Official Tourist Information (also room reservations):
Arrival hall of airport; tel. 7 11 10
(Open: daily 8.30am–10pm, to 11pm June–Sept.)

For air travellers

Information desk of the DDSG (also room reservations):
Reichsbrücke landing-stage; also Handelskai 265, A-1024 Wien;
tel. 72 75 00, fax 2 18 92 38.
Time-table information: tel. 15 37, fax 2 18 92 38.
(Open: May–Sept. daily 7am–8pm, also Apr. and Oct. daily 7am–6pm)

For boat passengers

Dr-Karl-Renner-Ring, Bellaria-Passage, A-1010 Wien
Tel. 5 26 46 37
(Open: Mon.–Fri. noon–7pm, Sat. 10am–7pm)
Reduced price tickets for many events for young people aged between 14 and 26 can be obtained here.

Jugend-Info-Wien

Heidenschuss 2, A-1010 Wien; tel. 5 33 31 14–28
(Open; Mon.–Fri. 8.30am–5.30pm)
Visitors wishing to stay outside the city should apply to this office for details of accommodation.

Niederösterreich Information

Insurance

Visitors are strongly advised to ensure that they have adequate holiday insurance, especially medical cover, and including loss or damage to luggage, loss of currency and jewellery.
   For nationals of the United Kingdom in-patient treatment in public hospitals in Vienna is usually free (with a small charge for dependants) but prescribed medicines and other medical services must be paid for.
   You will need to produce your UK passport.

General

Visitors travelling by car should ensure that their insurance is comprehensive and covers use of the vehicle in Europe. A "Green Card" is strongly recommended.

Vehicles

See also Travel Documents.

Language

General

German, like English, is a Germanic language, and the pronunciation usually comes more easily to English-speakers than does a Romance language such as French. Much of the basic vocabulary, too, will be familiar to English speakers.

Standard German ("Hochdeutsch") is spoken in business and commercial circles throughout the country but many people in Vienna speak a strong local dialect.

Pronunciation

The consonants are for the most part pronounced broadly as in English, but the following points should be noted: *b, d* and *g* at the end of a syllable are pronounced like *p, t* and *k; c* (rare) and *z* are pronounced *ts; j* is pronounced like consonantal *y; qu* is somewhere between the English *qu* and *kv; s* at the beginning of a syllable is pronounced *z; v* is pronounced *f,* and *w* is pronounced *v.* The double letter *ch* is pronounced like the Scottish *ch* in "loch" after *a, o* and *u;* after *ä, e, i* and *ü* it is pronounced somewhere between that sound and *sh. Sch* is pronounced *sh,* and *th* (rare) *t.*

The vowels are pronounced without the diphthongisation normal in standard English; before a single consonant they are normally long, before a double consonant short. Note the following: short *a* is like the flat *a* of northern English; *e* may be either closed (roughly as in "pay"), open (roughly as in "pen") or a short unaccented sound like the *e* in "begin" or in "the"; *ä* is like an open *e; u* is like *oo* in "good" (short) or "food" (long); *ö* is like the French *eu,* a little like the vowel in "fur"; *ü,* like the French *u,* can be approximated by pronouncing *ee* with rounded lips.

Diphthongs: *ai* and *ei* similar to *i* in "high"; *au* as in "how"; *eu* and *äu* like *oy; ie* like *ee.*

Numbers

0	null
1	eins
2	zwei
3	drei
4	vier
5	fünf
6	sechs
7	sieben
8	acht
9	neun
10	zehn
11	elf
12	zwölf
13	dreizehn
14	vierzehn
15	fünfzehn
16	sechzehn
17	siebzehn
18	achtzehn
19	neunzehn
20	zwanzig
21	einundzwanzig
22	zweiundzwanzig
30	dreissig
40	vierzig
50	fünfzig
60	sechzig
70	siebzig
80	achtzig
90	neunzig
100	hundert
101	hundert eins

153	hundertdreiundfünfzig
200	zweihundert
300	dreihundert
1000	tausend
1001	tausend und eins
1021	tausand einundzwanzig
2000	zweitausend
1,000,000	eine Million

1st	erste
2nd	zweite
3rd	dritte
4th	vierte
5th	fünfte
6th	sechste
7th	siebte
8th	achte
9th	neunte
10th	zehnte
11th	elfte
20th	zwanzigste
100th	hundertste

Sunday	Sonntag
Monday	Montag
Tuesday	Dienstag
Wednesday	Mittwoch
Thursday	Donnerstag
Friday	Freitag
Saturday	Samstag, Sonnabend
Day	Tag
Public holiday	Feiertag

Good morning	Guten Morgen
Good day	Guten Tag
Good evening	Guten Abend
Good night	Gute Nacht
Goodbye	Auf Wiedersehen
Do you speak English?	Sprechen Sie English?
I do not understand	Ich verstehe nicht
Yes	Ja
No	Nein
Pardon	Entschuldigen
May I?	Darf ich?
Please	Bitte
Thank you (very much)	Danke (sehr)
How much?	Wieviel?
What is that?	Was ist das?
When?	Wann?
Where is?	Wo ist?
I need a doctor	Ich brauche einen Arzt
Arrival	Ankunft
Baggage/Luggage	Gepäck
Bill/Check	Rechnung
Departure	Abfahrt, Abflug (aircraft)
Hospital	Krankenhaus
Letter	Brief
Main post office	Hauptpost
Non-smoking	Nichtraucher

Railway station	Bahnhof
Room	Zimmer
Smoking	Raucher
Stamp	Briefmarke
Ticket	Fahrkarte
Today	Heute
Tomorrow	Morgen
Yesterday	Gestern

Glossary

Abfahrt, Abflug (aircraft)	departure
Ankunft	arrival
Bad	bath, spa
Bibliothek	library
Brücke	bridge
Brunnen	fountain
Burg	castle
Denkmal	monument, memorial
Dom	cathedral
Fremdenverkehrs- verband	tourist information office
Gasse	street, lane
Hof	court, courtyard
Kirche	church
Kloster	convent, monastery
Platz	square
Rathaus	town hall
Schloss (pl. Schlösser)	castle, palace, country house
Stadt	town, city
Strasse	street, road
Strassenbahn	tram
Vorsicht!	look out
Weinstube	wine-house, wine-bar

Libraries, archives

Archives of the Vienna Philharmonic
1, Bösendorferstrasse 12
Visits only by prior appointment; tel. 5 05 65 25–0

Library of the Academy of Fine Art
See A to Z, Akademie der Bildenden Künste

Library of the Albertina
See A to Z

Library of the Geologische Bundesanstalt (Federal Geological Institute)
3, Rasumofskygasse 23
Visits only by prior arrangement; tel. 7 12 56 74–0

Library of the Austrian Federal Railways (Österreichische
   Bundesbahnen)
2, Praterstern 3
Open: Mon.–Thur. 9am–3pm, Fri. 9am–noon

Library of the Armenian Monastery
7, Mechitaristengasse 4
Visits only by prior appointment; tel. 93 64 17

Library of the Literaturhaus
7, Seidengasse 13
Open: Mon.–Wed. and Fri. 9am–6pm
Having been converted by Gerhard Huber, this building serves as an information and communication centre with a department for documents relating to Austrian literature, a library, a literature data bank and a newspaper department.

Library of the Austrian Museum of Applied Art
See A to Z, Österreichisches Museum für Angewandte Kunst

Library of Parliament
See A to Z

Austrian National Library
See A to Z, Österreichische Nationalbibliothek

Austrian State Archives (Haus- Hof- und Staatsarchiv)
1, Minoritenplatz 1. Open: Mon.–Fri. 9am–4pm
War archives (Kriegsarchiv): 7, Stiftgasse 2; Central and Transport archives (Verkehrsarchiv): 3, Nottendorfergasse 2; open: Mon. Tues., Thur. 9am–5pm, Wed. 9am–7pm, Fri. 9am–3pm

University Library (Universitätsbibliothek), 1, Dr Karl-Lueger-Ring 1
Open: Mon.–Sat. 9am–1pm, Tues. and Thur. also 4–6.45pm.

Vienna City and State Archives and Library
(Wiener Stadt- und Landesarchiv bzw. Bibliothek)
1, Lichtenfelsgasse 2 (staircase 6 or 4)
Archives and Library (including the Hans Moser bequest)
Open: Mon.–Thur. 8am–6pm, Fri. 8am–4pm; closed public holidays

Lost property

9, Wasagasse 22; tel. 31 34 40
Underground station (U-Bahn) Schottentor (U2)
Open: Mon.–Fri. 8am–1pm

Central Lost Property Office

Property found on the railway is sent to the central collection point at Vienna West Station of Austrian Railways at Langauerstr. 2; (tel. 58 00–0) S-Bahn Station. Articles left in trams or buses are collected by the Vienna Department of Works (tel. 5 01 30–0) and after three days are transferred to the Central Lost Property Office.

Lost property office of the railway and the City Department of Works

Markets

Markets are open Mon.–Fri. 6am–6.30pm and Sat. 6am–1pm. Morning is the liveliest time in the Vienna markets with the greatest choice of goods.

Opening times

Augustinermarkt
3, Landstrasser Hauptstr./Erdbergstrasse

Provision markets

Brunnenmarkt
16, Brunnengasse

Meidlinger Markt
12, Niederhofergasse, Rosaliagasse

Meislmarkt
15, Meislstrasse/Wurmsergasse

Naschmarkt
See A to Z

Schwendermarkt
15, Schwendergasse/Reichsapfelgasse

Flea market

Naschmarkt
See A to Z

Antiques

See A to Z, Dorotheum and Practical Information, Antiques

Seasonal markets

Seasonal markets are also a special attraction. These include the Lent Market (Fastenmarkt) before Easter in Kalvarienberggasse, the Easter Market (Ostermarkt) on the Freyung (see A to Z), the Advent Magic (Adventszauber) and Christmas Markets (Christkindlmärkte) on Rathausplatz, Spittelburg and the Freyung, and the pre-Christmas Crib Display (Krippenschau) in the Peterskirche.

Medical assistance

Before arrival

Visitors should enquire of the DSS as to the most recent regulations concerning medical assistance in Austria. (See also Insurance.)

Doctor on call

Radio-telephone service (24 hours a day); tel. 141

Ambulance

Rescue service; tel.144
Cases of poisoning; tel. 43 43 43

Emergency dental treatment

Tel. 52 20 78 for addresses of dentists on duty

Motoring

Automobile clubs

ÖAMTC (Österreichischer Automobil-, Motorrad- und Touring-Club)
Schubertring 1–3, A-1010 Wien
Tel. 7 11 99–0; Breakdown: tel. 120

ARBÖ (Auto-, Motor- und Radfahrerbund Österreichs)
Mariahilferstr. 180, A-1150 Wien
Tel. 85 35 35–0; Breakdown: tel. 123

Road conditions report

ÖAMT traffic news service (daily): tel. 15 90
Austrian radio (Ö3) broadcasts brief information (in German) after the news on the hour. Blue Danube Radio (103.8 MHz in Vienna) transmits traffic news in English between 7 and 9am, noon and 2pm, and if there are serious delays, between 6 and 7.30pm.

Traffic Regulations

Generally traffic regulations in Austria are similar to those in other countries in western Europe where vehicles travel on the right. Information about toll-roads and additional tolls for caravans and trailers can be obtained from the motoring organisations (see above).

Speed limits

On motorways the speed limit for cars and motorcycles is 130km.p.h./80m.p.h., but 100km.p.h./62m.p.h. if towing a caravan or trailer. On all other main roads the maximum permitted speed is 100km.p.h./62m.p.h. for cars and motorcycles, but only 80km.p.h./49m.p.h. if towing a weight above 750kg/0·75 tonnes. In built-up areas the speed limit for all vehicles is 50km.p.h./31m.p.h. and the use of the horn is not permitted at night, and at all times in Vienna. Vehicles must give way to children crossing the road.

Lead-free normal (91 octane), lead-free super (Eurosuper 95 octane), leaded super (98 octane) and diesel are also available.	Petrol (gasoline) and diesel oil
The maximum permitted blood alcohol level is 0.8 pro mille.	Drinking and driving
Seat-belts must be worn by drivers and front-seat passengers, and, when fitted in the vehicle, also by passengers in the rear seats. Failure to observe this regulation may lead to a fine. Children under twelve years of age may not travel in the front seat.	Seat-belts
A red triangle must be carried in the vehicle in case of breakdown.	Warning triangle
Motorcyclists and moped riders must wear helmets and use dipped head-lights in daylight.	Motorcyclists
All vehicles (including motorcycles) must at all times carry a first-aid kit.	First-aid kit
Studded tyres and sometimes snow-chains are required for journeys in winter.	Winter equipment
From 15th December until 31st March parking in Vienna is prohibited from 8pm to 5am on all streets where there are tram-lines, in order to facilitate clearing when there has been a heavy snowfall. Parking in designated short-stay zones (city centre, Mariahilfer Strasse, squares outside the Town Hall (Rathaus), stations and airport) is limited to 1½ hours from 8am until 6pm; vehicles parked in these places must bear a parking disc. Parking tickets for 30, 60 and 90 minutes can be purchased from the ticket offices of the Vienna transport authority, from filling stations, tobacconists and from some branches of banks. Cancellation of parking tickets is effected by an indication of date and hour when the vehicles is parked (control is strict). Parking spaces are hard to find and multi-storey car parks are often full; public transport is a cheap alternative. It is best to walk in the city centre.	Parking
Parked vehicles causing serious obstruction to traffic are liable to be towed away. A visitor who discovers that the vehicle is no longer in the place where it has been parked will probably find it in the 10th district at Elbes-brunnengasse 9, where it can be recovered Mon.–Fri. 7am–3pm. Outside these times application should be made to the Magistratsabteilung (magis-trates' department) 48, 5, Einsiedlergasse 2.	Vehicles towed away

Museums and Memorial Locations

Admission to the municipal museums is free on Friday mornings, except for special exhibitions.	**Note**
By purchasing a museum pass (14 coupons valid at any time and transfer-able; obtainable in the museums) the admission fee is reduced by almost 30% for all these museums.	Museum pass

Academy of Fine Arts
See A to Z, Akademie der Bildenden Künste

Albertina Print Collection
See A to Z, Albertina (probably closed until 1998 for rebuilding work)

Armenian Monastic Museum
See A to Z, Mechitharist Congregation

Art Forum of the Bank of Austria
1, Freyung 8
Open: daily 10am–6pm, Wed to 9pm

Art Forum of the Bank of Austria on the Freyung

Arts and Crafts Museum (Kunstgewerbemuseum)
See A to Z, Österreichisches Museum für Angewandte Kunst

Art Hall (Kunsthalle)
See A to Z, Karlsplatz

Austrian Film Museum
See A to Z, Albertina

Austrian Folk Museum
See A to Z, Österreichisches Museum für Volkskunde

Austrian Horticultural Museum
10, Kurpark Laaer Berg (west entrance), Museumswiese; tel. 68 11 70
Open: May–Oct. Wed.–Fri. 10am–2.30pm, on the 1st and 3rd Sat. in each
month 1pm–5pm, on the 1st and 3rd Sun. in each month and public
holidays 10am–5pm

Austrian Resistance Movement Archives
See A to Z, Altes Rathaus

Austrian Museum of Applied Art
See A to Z, Österreichisches Museum für Angewandte Kunst

Austrian Theatrical Museum
See A to Z, Österreichisches Theatermuseum

Hermann Bahr Memorial Room
See A to Z, Österreichisches Theatermuseum

Baroque Museum
See A to Z, Belvedere-Schlösser, Österreichisches Barockmuseum

Eduard von Bauernfeld Memorial Room
(Döbling local museum), in the Villa Wertheimstein, 19, Döblinger
Hauptstr. 96; tel. 37 69 39
Open: Sat. 3.30–6pm, Sun. 10am–noon (closed July, Aug.)
Mementoes of the comic playwright Eduard von Bauernfeld (1802–90)

Beethoven Memorials
See A to Z, Pasqualatihaus, Heiligenstadt, Beethoven Denkmal
    (Monument)
Other memorial locations:
"Eroica House", 19, Döblinger Hauptstr. 92; tel. 3 69 14 24
Open: Tue.–Sun. 9am–12.15pm, 1–4.30pm
Beethoven worked here in 1803–04, especially on his third symphony, the
    "Eroica". Among the exhibits is the first impression of this work.
6, Laimgrubengasse 22; visits by arrangement, tel. 3 71 40 85. Beethoven
    resided in this house in Laimgrubengasse from 1822–23.

Beethoven Museum
See A to Z, Pasqualatihaus

Bell Museum (Ing. Plundner Bell Collection)
10, Troststr. 38; tel. 6 04 34 50 (closed at present for rebuilding work)

Johannes Brahms Memorial Room
See A to Z, Haydn Museum

Carnuntum
See A to Z, Petronell (Carnuntum)

Cathedral and Diocesan Museum
See A to Z, Dom- and Diözesanmuseum

Clock Museum
See A to Z, Uhrenmuseum der Stadt Wien

Collection of Old Musical Instruments
See A to Z, Sammlung alter Musikinstrumente

Collection of Popular Religious Art
See A to Z, Sammlung religiöser Volkskunst

Collection of Wagons (Carriage Museum)
See A to Z, Schönbrunn

Collection of Weapons
See A to Z, Waffensammlung

Court Tableware and Silver Collection
See A to Z, Hofburg

Criminal Museum
See A to Z, Leopoldstadt

Döblinger Regional Museum (Döblinger Bezirksmuseum)
98 Döblinger Hauptstr. 96
Open: Sat. 3.30–6pm, Sun. 10am–noon
Biedermeier villa with rooms commemorating Bauernfeld, the comic poet,
and Ferdinand von Saar, the lyric writer. Also wine museum.

Museums and Memorial Locations

Heimito von Doderer Memorial Room
(in the Alsergrund local museum)
9, Währinger Str. 43; tel. 4 02 35 75–229
Open: Wed. 9–11am (except July., Aug.), Sun. 10am–noon
Life and work of the author Heimito von Doderer (1896–1966). The "Strudl-
hofstiege" (a flight of steps), from which he took the name of his novel
which appeared in 1951, is to be found in Strudlhofgasse near
Liechtensteinstrasse.

Doll and Toy Museum
Puppen- und Spielzeugmuseum
(Vaclav Sladky/D. B. Polzer), 1, Schulhof 4/1st floor; tel. 5 35 68 60
Open: Tue.–Sun. 10am–6pm
Private collection of dolls-houses and over 600 dolls from 1830–1930

Ephesus Museum
See A to Z, Ephesus Museum

Esperanto Museum
See A to Z, Österreichische Nationalbibliothek

Fashion Collection of the Vienna Historical Museum
(Historisches Museum der Stadt Wien)
12, Hetzendorfer Str. 79, left side; tel. 8 02 16 57
Open: Tue.–Sun. 9am–12.15pm, 1–4.30pm

Federal Collection of Period Furniture
7, Mariahilfer Str. 88; tel. 5 23 42 40–0
(closed until 1997 for rebuilding work)

Federal Pathological/Anatomical Museum
9, Spitalgasse 2 (in the "Fools' Tower" of the General Hospital)
Tel. 43 86 72
Open: Wed. 3–6pm, Thur. 8–11am, first Sat. in every month 10am–1pm
(closed on public holidays and in Aug.)

Fiaker Museum
See A to Z, Fiakermuseum

Figaro House
See A to Z, Figarohaus

Film Museum
See A to Z, Albertina

Fire Brigade Museum
See A to Z, Am Hof

Football Museum
Fussballstadion im Praterstadion, 2, Meiereistrasse; tel. 7 27 18–0

(Sigmund) Freud Museum
See A to Z, Freud Museum

Fuchs Private Museum
14, Hüttelbergstr. 26
Open: Mon.–Fri. 10am–4pm, by prior arrangement only; tel. 94 85 75
In 1972 the doyen of the Viennese Realists, Ernst Fuchs (b. 1930), bought
and subsequently restored in its original form the first Art Nouveau villa
built by Otto Wagner in 1886–88. It is furnished with carpets, marble tiles
and beautiful furniture in accordance with the artist's designs, and is now a
museum with some 30 pictures by Fuchs.

Funeral Museum
Bestattungsmuseum, 4, Goldegasse 19
Open: Mon.–Fri. noon–3pm, by prior appointment only; tel. 5 01 95–227
800 exhibits document the history of funerals and cemeteries in Wien, as well as burial customs and forms of remembrance. Visitors can see expensive and luxurious tombstones, palls and smart livery worn by the "Pompfünebrerer", as Viennese undertakers are still called (from the French "pompes funèbres"), an alarm to awaken those in a state of suspended animation, the tram used at night to transport the victims of bombing raids in both World Wars, as well as the "re-usable" coffin introduced by Emperor Joseph II: as soon as the wooden coffin was suspended over the open grave a bolt was released, the coffin opened and the corpse fell into the grave; under pressure from public opinion, however, the relevant imperial decree was revoked in 1784.

Gallery of Austrian Art of the 19th and 20th c.
See A to Z, Belvedere Palaces

Geymüller-Schlössl/Sobek Clock Collection
See A to Z, Geymüller-Schlössl

Glass Museum
See Viennese Glass Museum (below)

Globe Museum
See A to Z, Österreichische Nationalbibliothek

Franz Grillparzer Memorial Room
See A to Z, Historisches Museum der Stadt Wien; also in the Hofkammer archives, 1, Johannesgasse 6
Open: Tue.–Sun. 9am–4.30pm
The furniture in Grillparzer's study is original

Haydn Museum
See A to Z

Heating Museum (Heizungsmuseum)
12, Längenfeldgasse 13–15, Stiege 2; tel. 8 52 95 03
Open: Tue. 1–6pm (except during the Viennese school holidays) and by appointment

Hermes Villa
See A to Z, Lainzer Tiergarten (zoo)

Horticultural Museum
See Austrian Horticultural Museum (above)

House of the Sea (Haus des Meeres/Vivarium Wien)
6, Esterházypark; tel. 5 87 14 17
Open: daily 9am–6pm
Here visitors can observe some 3000 live animals; the tropical and Mediterranean aquaria are particularly impressive.

Jewish Museum
See A to Z, Jüdisches Museum

Josefstadt Regional Museum
See A to Z, Alte Backstube (Old Bakery)

Josephinum (Medical History Museum)
See A to Z, Josephinum

Museums and Memorial Locations

Franz Kafka Memorial
See A to Z, Klosterneuberg

Josef Kainz Memorial Room
See A to Z, Österreichisches Theatermuseum

Emmerich Kálmán Memorial Room
See A to Z, Österreichisches Theaterumuseum

Kunsthalle
See A to Z, Karlsplatz

KunstHausWien
See A to Z

Franz Léhar Museum
See A to Z, Lehár Schlössl

Adolf Loss Room
See A to Z, Historisches Museum der Stadt Wien

Memorial to Austrian Freedom Fighters
See A to Z, Belvedere Palaces

Mozart Memorial Rooms
See A to Z, Figarohaus

Museum of Applied Art
See A to Z, Österreichisches Museum für Angewandte Kunst

Museum of Art History
See A to Z, Kunsthistorisches Museum

Museum of Clowns and Circuses (Zirkus- und Clownmuseum)
2, Karmalitergasse 9; tel. 2 11 06–127
Open: Wed. 5.30–7pm, Sat. 2.30–5pm, Sun. 10am–noon

Museum of Ethnology
See A to Z, Museum für Völkerkunde

Museum of Farriery and Saddlery
Museum für Hufbeschlag, Beschirrung und Sattelung
3, Linke Bahngasse 11; tel. 7 11 55–372
Open: Mon.–Thur. 1.30–3.30pm by prior arrangement only

Museum of Folklore
See A to Z, Österreichisches Museum für Volkskunde

Museum of Gold and Silversmith Work
7, Zieglergasse 22; tel. 93 33 88
Open: Tue. 3–6pm and by arrangement
(Tue., Thur. 9am–noon; tel. 5 23 40 96; closed July and Aug.)

Museum of the Institute of Medical History
See A to Z, Josephinum

Museum of Medieval Art
See A to Z, Belvedere Palaces

Museum of Military History
See A to Z, Heeresgeschichtliches Museum

Museum of Modern Art (Ludwig Wien Foundation)
See A to Z, Museum moderner Kunst Stiftung Ludwig Wien

Museum of the State of Lower Austria
See A to Z, Niederösterreichisches Landesmuseum

Museum of the 20th century
See A to Z, Museum moderner Kunst Stiftung Ludwig Wien

Natural History Museum
See A to Z, Naturhistorisches Museum

Caspar Neher Memorial Room
See A to Z, Österreichisches Theatermuseum

Neidhart Frescoes
See A to Z, Graben

North Bohemian Living Room (Nordböhmen Heimatstube)
8, Kochgasse 34
Open: Sun. 9am–noon

Old Bakehouse
See A to Z, Alte Backstube

Old Smithy
See A to Z, Schönlaterngasse

Period Furniture Collection
See Federal Collection of Period Furniture
(closed until 1997 for rebuilding work)

Pfunder Bell Collection
10, Troststr. 38; tel. 6 04 34 50 (closed at present for rebuilding work)

Planetarium
See A to Z, Prater

Post and Telegraphic Museum
See A to Z, Technisches Museum für Industrie und Gewerbe (closed until
1996 for rebuilding work)

Prater Museum
See A to Z, Prater

Railway Museum
See A to Z, Technisches Museum für Industrie und Gewerbe (closed until
1996)

Max Reinhardt Memorial Room
See A to Z, Österreichisches Theatermuseum

Roman Ruins
See A to Z, Am Hof, Petronell-Carnuntum and Hoher Markt

Ferdinand von Saar Memorial Room
In the Villa Wertheimstein
(Döbling local museum)
19, Döblinger Hauptstr. 96; tel. 37 69 39
Open: Sat. 3.30–6pm, Sun. 10am–noon
Mementoes of the writer Ferdinand von Saar (1833–1906)

Schottenstift (Scots Foundation) Picture Gallery
See A to Z, Schottenstift

Schubert Museum (house where he was born)
See A to Z

Schubert's Death Chamber
4, Kettenbrückengasse 6; tel. 5 73 90 72
Open: Tue.–Sun. 9am–12.15pm and 1–4.30pm
The Vienna History Museum has furnished the rooms in which Franz
Schubert spent his last days as a memorial to him and his brother Ferdi-
nand, who was also a composer.

Secession Art Gallery
See A to Z

Sobek Collection of Old Viennese Clocks
See A to Z, Geymüller Schlössl

Stifter Museum
See A to Z, Pasqualatihaus

Strauss Museum
See A to Z, Praterstrasse

Technical Museum of Industry and Trade
See A to Z, Technisches Museum für Industrie und Gewerbe
(closed until 1996 for rebuilding work)

Theatrical Museum
See A to Z, Österreichisches Theatermuseum

Hugo Thimmig Memorial Room
See A to Z, Österreichisches Theatermuseum

Tobacco Museum
See A to Z, Maria-Theresien-Platz

Tram Museum (Strassenbahnmuseum)
See A to Z, Strassenbahnmuseum

Treasuries in the Hofburg
See A to Z, Hofburg

Treasury of the German Order
See A to Z, Deutschordenshaus and Deutschordenskirche

Urania Observatory
1, Urania Str. 1; tel. 24 94 32
Conducted tours on clear nights; visitors can observe the skies through a
telescope and use computer graphics: Wed., Fri., Sat. 8pm, April–Sept.
9pm; Sun. 11am (closed in Aug.)

Vienna City Historical Museum
See A to Z, Historisches Museum der Stadt Wien

Viennese Glass Museum (Wiener Glasmuseum)
1, Kärnter Str. 26; tel. 5 12 05 08
Open: Mon.–Fri. 9am–6pm, Sat. 9am–1pm

Viennese Tram Museum
See Tram Museum (above)

Virgilian Chapel
See A to Z, Stephansplatz

Vivarium Wien
See House of the Sea (above)

Otto Wagner House
7, Döblergasse 4
Open: Mon.–Fri. 9am–noon (July–Sept. by arrangement only; tel. 93 22 33)
On display are numerous mementos of Otto Wagner (1841–1918), one of
the most celebrated Austrian architects.

Wine Museum
See Döblinger Regional Museum (above)

Music

The Vienna Tourist Board (Wiener Tourismusverband; see Information) publishes monthly a free list of events.

Forthcoming programme

See Advance Booking, except where otherwise stated.

Tickets

In the interests of the environment, the Raimundtheater, the Wiener Konzerthaus and the Theater an der Wien have arranged for their entrance tickets to be valid also for travel on public transport within Central Zone 100 for the period two hours before the start of the performance and up to six hours after.

Bus/tram tickets

State Opera
See A to Z, Staatsoper

Opera/Ballet

Theater im Künstlerhaus
1, Karlsplatz 5; tel. 5 87 05 04

Volksoper
9, Währinger Str. 78

Wiener Kammeroper
1, Fleischmarkt 24
Tickets direct from the theatre; tel. 5 12 01 00, fax 5 12 44 48–26

Theater an der Wien
See A to Z, Naschmarkt
Raimundtheater
6, Wallgasse 18; tel. 5 88 30–0, fax 5 88 30–33
Advance bookings from:
Vienna Ticket Services
Postfach 160
A-1043 Wien; tel. 5 87 98 43, fax 5 87 98 44

Operetta/Musicals

Ronacher
See A to Z

Altes Rathaus, 1, Schönlaterngasse 9; tel. 5 12 83 29

Concert Halls

Deutschordenhaus
Sala Terrana, 1, Sinngerstrs. 7; tel. 3 10 57 10

Funkhaus des Österreichischen Rundfunks (studios of Austrian Radio)
(Concerts, broadcasts with an audience)
Grosser Sendesaal
Argentinierstr. 30a
A-1040 Wien
Tickets: in advance from the above address or by telephone 5 01 01–88 81
(Mon.–Fri. 4–7pm)

Konzerthaus, 3, Lothringer Str. 20
Great Hall, Mozart Hall, Schubert Hall; orchestral music, soloists and chamber music.
Tickets: in advance by telephone 7 12 12 11 (Mon.–Fri. 9am–6pm, Sat. 9am–1pm)

Musikverein
See A to Z, Musikvereinsgebäude

Palais Schwarzenberg
3, Schwarzenbergplatz 9
Tickets from Neues Künstlerforum; tel./fax 7 13 11 07

Bösendorfer Saal
4, Graf-Starhemberg-Gasse 14; tel. 5 04 66 51
(box office: see Musikverein)

Schloss Schönbrunn, Elisabeth Saal
See A to Z, Schönbrunn

Urania
1, Uraniastrasse; tel. 7 12 61 91–0

Church Music
Augustinerkirche
See A to Z

Burgkapelle
See A to Z, Hofburg

Karlskirche
See A to Z

Michaelerkirche (St Michael's Church)
See A to Z, Michaelerplatz

Minoritenkirche
See A to Z

Stephansdom (St Stephen's Cathedral)
See A to Z

St Barbara (Ukrainian-Greek Orthodox Parish Church)
1, Postgasse 8

Collegiate Church of Heiligenkreuz
See A to Z, Heiligenkreuz

Collegiate Church of Klosterneuburg
See A to Z, Klosterneuburg

University Church 1, Dr-Ignaz-Seipel-Platz 1

Votivkirche
See A to Z

Jazz/Live music
See Nightlife

Festivals
See Festivals, see Events

Nightlife

Bermuda Triangle
This is the name which the Viennese have given to the nightlife district between the Cathedral and the Danube, in the area of Schönlaterngasse

and Bäckerstrasse (see A to Z) and extending to St Ruprecht's Church. Anyone who "dives" into a nightclub here will disappear and not remember anything of his experiences when he finally emerges into the daylight!

Alt Wien, 1, Bäckertsr. 9; tel. 5 12 52 22 (daily 10am–2am)

Apropos, 1, Rudolfsplatz 12; tel. 5 33 41 89 (Mon.–Fri. 10am–2am, Sat. Sun. 6pm–2am)

Bora-Bora, 1, Johannesgasse 12; tel. 5 12 27 84 (daily 8pm–4am)

Café Bar in the Wiener Secession, 1, Friedrichstr. 12; tel. 56 93 86 (daily 10am–2am)

Düsenberg, 1, Stubenring 4; tel. 5 13 84 96 (Mon.–Sat. 8pm–4am)

For Two, 1, Dorotheergasse 2–4; tel. 5 13 12 49 (10am–2am)

Griechenbeisl (daily 11am–1am), See A to Z

Hawelka, 1, Dorotheergasse 6; tel. 5 12 82 30 (Mon.–Sat. 8am–2am, Sun. and public holidays 4pm–2am)

Kleines Café, 1, Franziskanerplatz 3, (Mon.–Sat. 10am–2am, Sun. 1pm–2am)

Krah Krah, 1, Rabensteig 8; tel. 5 33 81 93 (daily 11am–2am)

Landtmann, 1, Dr-Karl-Lueger-Ring 4; tel. 5 32 06 21 (daily 8am–midnight)

MAK, 1, Stubenring 5; tel. 7 14 01 21 (Thur.–Sun. 10am–2am)

Oswald & Kalb, 1, Bäckerstr. 14; tel. 5 12 13 71 (daily 6pm–1am)

Wiener Stamperl, 1, Sterngasse 1; tel. 5 33 62 30 (Mon.–Thur. noon–2am, Fri. 11am–4am, Sat. 6pm–4am, Sun. 6pm–2am)

Popular night-spots

Casablance Inn, 1, Rabensteig 8; tel. 5 33 34 63 (Tue.–Fri. 6pm–4am, Sun., Mon. 6pm–2am)

George and the Dragon, 1, Rotenturmstr. 24; tel. 5 33 19 98 (Mon.–Sat. 10am–1pm)

Jazz Club 6th, Gumpendorfer Str. 9; tel. 56 87 10 (Sun.–Thur. 9pm–2am, Fri., Sat. 9pm–4am)

Jazzland, 1, Franz-Josefs-Kai 29; tel. 5 33 13 81 (Mon.–Sat. 7pm–2am, live music from 9pm)

La Colombie, 8, Laudongasse 57; tel. 4 08 30 45 (daily 5pm–2am)

On Broadway, 1, Bauernmarkt 21; tel. 5 33 28 49 (Mon.–Sat. 9pm–4am)

papas tapas, 4, Schwarzenbergplatz 10; tel. 5 05 03 11 (daily 8pm–2am)

Tenne, 1, Annagasse 3; tel. 5 12 57 08 (Mon., Tue. 8pm–2.30am, Wed. 8.30pm–2.30am, Thur. 8.30pm–3am, Fri. 8pm–2am)

Jazz and Live Music

Rincon Andino, 6, Münzwardeingasse 2; tel. 5 87 61 25 (Wed.–Sun. 10am–2am)

Latin-American Music

African Club, 1, Riemergasse 13; tel. 5 12 94 85 (Wed.–Sat. 9pm–4am)

Reggae

Atoll (summer disco), Copa Cagrana (Danube Island)

Beverly Hills, 1, Seilerstätte 1; tel. 5 12 53 87 (daily 9pm–4am)

Atrium, 4, Schwindgasse 1; tel. 5 05 35 94 (Thur.–Sun. 10am–2pm)

Can-Can, 9, Währinger Gürtel 96; tel. 42 26 28 (Tue.–Sun. 9pm–4am)

Chattanooga, 1, Graben 29a; tel. 42 26 68 (Fri., Sat. 8am–2am)

Jack Daniels, 1, Krugerstr. 6; tel. 5 12 43 96 (daily 10pm–4am)

Kisl, 8, Langegasse 61; tel. 42 03 70 (Mon.–Thur. 8am–2am, Fri. 8am–4am, Sat. 7pm–4am)

Lord's Club, 1, Karlsplatz 1; tel. 5 05 09 30 (Wed., Thur. 9pm–2am, Fri., Sat. 9pm–4am)

Move, 8, Daungasse 1; tel. 43 32 78 (daily 9pm–4am)

My Way, 22, Schlosshofer Str. 52; tel. 30 70 61 (Sun.–Tue. 8am–2am, Wed.–Sat. 8am–4am)

Pallas, 2, Taborstr. 36; tel. 2 14 24 01 (Thur. 8pm–2am, Fri., Sat. 8pm–4am)

P1, 1, Rotgasse 3; tel. 5 35 99 95 (Sun.–Thur. 9pm–4am, Fri., Sat. 9pm–6am)

Queen Anne, 1, Johannesgasse 12; tel. 5 12 02 03 (daily 10pm–5.30am)

Take Five, 1, Annagasse 3a; tel. 5 12 92 77 (Tue., Thur.–Sat. 10pm–5am)

Tanzcafé Volksgarten, 1, Volksgarten; tel. 5 33 05 18–0 (daily 8am–2am; May–Sept. in the open air)

Discos and Dancing

Opening times

Terrassencafé, 19, Cobenzlgasse 11; tel. 32 12 03 (Tue.–Sat. 9pm–4am)
U4, 12, Schönbrunner Str. 222; tel. 85 83 18 (daily 11pm–5am)
Wake Up, 1, Seilerstrasse 5; tel. 5 12 21 12 (daily 9pm–4am)

Bars

Alcazar, 1, Bösendorferstr. 2; tel. 5 04 35 45 (Mon.–Sat. 7pm–4am, Sun. 7pm–2am)
Bora-Bora, 1, Johannesgasse 12; tel. 5 12 27 84 (daily 8am–4am)
Chamäleon Cocktail-Bar, 1, Blutgasse 3; tel. 5 13 17 03 (Mon.–Thur. 5pm–2am, Fri., Sat. 5pm–4am)
Eden Club, 1, Plankengasse 2; tel. 5 12 49 69 (Mon.–Sat. 10am–2am, Sun. 5pm–2am)
Fledermaus, 1, Spiegelgasse 2; tel. 5 12 84 38 (theatrical performances from 8pm until the end)
Himmelpforte, 1, Himmelpfortgasse 24; tel. 5 13 19 67 (daily 11am–midnight)
New York, New York, 1, Annagasse 8; tel. 5 13 86 51 (Mon.–Wed. 5pm–2am, Thur.–Sat. 5pm–3am)
Porta, 1, Schulerstr. 6; tel. 5 13 14 93 (daily noon–4am)
Reiss-Chanpagne-Treff, 1, Marco-d'Aviano-Gasse 1; tel. 5 12 71 98 (Sun.–Fri. 11am–3am, Sat. 10am–3am)

Night spots

Blue Velvet, 1, Kramergasse 5; tel. 5 33 93 25
  (daily 2pm–5am)
Cabaret Renz, 2, Zirkusgasse 50; tel. 2 14 31 35
  (daily 2.30pm–6am)
Eve-Bar, 1, Führichgasse 3; tel. 5 12 54 52 (daily 4pm–4am)
Flamingo Bar, 16, Lerchenfelder Gürtel 31; tel. 4 92 09 20 (Mon.–Sat. 9pm–4am, Sun. 9pm–2am)
Maxim, 1, Opernring 11; tel. 56 33 40 (daily noon–5pm)
Moulin Rouge, 1, Walfischgasse 11; tel. 5 12 21 30
  (daily 10pm–6am)

Casino

In 1991 the Cercle Wien Casino moved back into the newly renovated Palais Esterhàzy in Kärnterstr. 41, one of the oldest palaces in the city. Those wishing to try their luck can choose between roulette, baccarat, blackjack (vingt-et-un) and poker (open: daily from 3pm; tel. 5 12 48 36–0)

Opening times

Banks

Mon.–Fri. 8am–12.30pm and 1.30–3pm (Thur. until 5.30pm)

Chemists

See entry

Museums, etc.

See entry

Post

Post-office counters are open Mon.–Fri. 8am–noon and 2–6pm. The main post office (Hauptpostamt) at 1, Postgasse 6/Barbaragasse and all post offices at railway stations are open daily day and night.

Shops

Mon.–Fri. 9am–6pm, Sat. 9am–noon
(Outside the inner city shops are closed between noon and 2 or 3pm)

Food shops often open at 7/8am and close at 6/7pm, but close for lunch from 12.30–3pm.

On 1st Sat. in month until 5pm and on Thur. until 8pm.

See Shopping

Police

Federal Police Headquarters of Vienna
(Bundespolizeidirektion Wien)
1, Schottenring 7–9
Tel. 3 13 10–0

District Police Headquarters
(Bezirkspolizeikommissariat)
Inner City
1, Deutschmeisterplatz 3
Tel. 31 76 01

Tel. 133 (24 hours a day)

Emergencies

Postal services

See Opening times

Post offices

As well as from post offices stamps are obtainable
from machines outside most post offices and from
tobacconists.

Stamps

Letters up to 20 grammes within Austria: 4 öS
To the United Kingdom: 7 öS
To the United States and Canada: 10 öS (plus
1.50 öS per 5 grammes for airmail)
Postcards within Austria: 2.50 öS
To the United Kingdom: 6 öS
To the United States and Canada: 7 öS

Postal rates

On Saturdays only newspapers are delivered, so that delays in receiving mail at weekends must be expected.

Deliveries

Telegrams can be sent by telephone (190) or from the central telegram office at 1, Börseplatz 1.

Telegrams

Programme of events

The Vienna Tourist Board issues a comprehensive programme every month of events at the theatres, galleries, museums, etc. The monthly programme is also printed in the "Hallo Wien Guide Book". The cultural magazine "Falter" which each week contains a prospectus of exhibitions, festivals, etc. The English-language magazines, "Rendezvous Vienna" and twice-yearly "Vienna Scene", both published by the Vienna Tourist Board also give advance information.

Blue Danube Radio (103.8 MHz) broadcasts in English, "What's on in Vienna?" daily at 1pm

Public holidays

1st January (New Year), 6th January (Epiphany), Easter Monday, 1st May (Labour Day), Ascension Day, Whit Monday, Corpus Christi, 15th August (Assumption), 26th October (National Holiday), 1st November (All Saints'), 8th December (Annunciation), 25th and 26th December (Christmas).

Public transport

U-Bahn (Underground) and S-Bahn (Express Railway) (Plan on pp 224–25) Tickets

Most of the city centre is designated as a pedestrian zone or is restricted to short-term parking. As a result, the best modes of transport are the U-Bahn, S-Bahn, trams or buses. Almost everywhere in Vienna can be reached quickly and easily by public transport.

"24-Stunden Netzkarte" (24-hour network tickets); must be personally cancelled by the passenger at the machine in the vehicle before commencing the journey.

"72-Stunden Netzkarte" (72-hour network tickets); must be cancelled in the same manner.

"Wochennetzkarte" (weekly season ticket); will be stamped; passport-size photograph required.

"4- and 8-Tage-Streifenkarte" (4- or 8-day strip ticket); permits the holder to travel anywhere within the Central Zone on 4 or 8 choosen days respectively; more than one person travelling together can use the card, but for fewer days.

All tickets allow as many journeys as you like over the period, changing to other routes or forms of transport as desired. Single tickets are cheaper if bought in blocks of five. Tickets can be purchased in advance at the ticket offices of the Vienna Transport Authority and at tobacconists (known as "Trafik"). the 72-hour network ticket can also be purchased at the Vienna Tourist Office in Kärnter Strasse (see Information). Single tickets are available on the trams and buses and in the U-Bahn and S-Bahn stations – have loose change available for the slot-machines!

Children's fares

Children under 7 are carried free. Foreign school-children under 16 and Austrian school-children under 20 travel free during the Vienna school holidays (be prepared to provide proof of age).

Night buses

In the nights of Fri–Sat., Sat.–Sun. and the nights preceding public holidays, night buses operate between 12.30 and 4am. The central departure point is Schwedenplatz.

Badener Bahn

Route: Oper–Vösendorf–Siebenhirten–Josefsplatz in Baden bei Wien.

"Vorortelinie" Hütteldorf– Döbling

The "Vorortelinie" (suburban line) between the districts of Hütteldorf and Döbling, which was reopened only in 1987 for passenger traffic, can almost be called a "tourist sight". Its bridges and tunnels and, especially, its stations were designed by Otto Wagner as an architectural unity in pure Art Nouveau style.

Theatre tickets used on public transport

See Music

Radio and television

ORF (Austrian radio/television) currently broadcast on two television and four radio stations.

Ö1: 514 m, 92 MHz
Radio
Ö2: 89.9 MHz
Ö3: 99.9 and 103.8 MHz
   The fourth programme is "Radio Österreich International" broadcasting
on short-wave (44 m, 6155 MHz) throughout the 24 hours.
   Vienna City Radio broadcasts information about the town daily from
2.05–4pm
   Blue Danube Radio (103.8 MHz in Vienna) broadcasts in English: news,
regional information and music from 6am to 1am

Information on BBC overseas radio transmissions in English may be
obtained from BBC World Service Publicity, PO Box 76, Bush House,
Strand, London WC2B 4PH.

The two television channels, FS1 and FS2, transmit the main news pro-
Television
gramme "Zeit im Bild" at 7.30pm
   There is also a satellite programme 3sat which is a common production
of all the major transmitting companies.

Railways

The Westbahnhof is the terminus of the lines serving the west of Austria,
West Station
Germany, Switzerland, France, Belgium and the Netherlands. The U6
Underground runs from the West Station to Meidling or Heiligenstadt,
from Längenfeldgasse to the Ring. An airport bus service runs to and from
the West Station.

The Südbahnhof is the terminus of lines serving the south of Austria, Italy,
South Station
Yugoslavia, Greece and Hungary. The U1 runs close by from Südtiroler
Platz to Karlsplatz and Stephansplatz; the Express line (Schnellbahn) runs
to Meidling and Wien-Mitte; tram 18 goes to Stadionbrücke and Wien-
Mitte. There is an express bus service from the station to the airport.

This station is the terminus for trains to and from northern Austria, the
Franz-Josefs
Czech and Slovak Republics and Berlin. U4 runs from the station (Friedens-
Station
brücke) to Schottenring and Heiligenstadt; tram D serves the inner city and
the Ring.

Central Information Office (open throughout the 24 hours); tel. 17 17
Train information
Services using the West Station; tel. 15 52
Services using the South Station; tel. 15 53

The Intercity Express Service (Austrotakt), implemented in 1991, provides
Rail services
an excellent service between the principal towns. For example, trains leave
within Austria
every hour from Vienna for Salzburg and Graz and every 2 hours to Villach
and Innsbruck.

Nostalgia trips: tel. 5800–3 80 80

The "Bundesnetzkarte" (Federal network Ticket), valid for a month or a year
Reduced-fare
(photograph required) allows the holder to use all trains and buses belong-
tickets
ing to the Austrian Federal Railways (ÖBB) and private railways whenever
he wishes, often at favourable rates (50% reduction on DDSG ships).
   Young people up to 25 years of age inclusive can travel in Austria for a
month at half-fare with an Inter-Rail Ticket (at present there are also reductions on shipping lines); senior citizens can obtain up to 50% reductions
with a Senior European Rail Card. Families can obtain reductions of between 50% and 75% with a Family European Rail Card. Children under 6
travel free accompanied by an adult, and at half-fare up to 15 years of age.
There are other reduced fares including the "Nahverkehrs-Rückfahrkarte"
(Short Trip Return ticket; 20% reduction, valid for 4 days, distance up to

Plan of the Vienna Underground (U-Bahn) and Express Railway (S-Bahn)

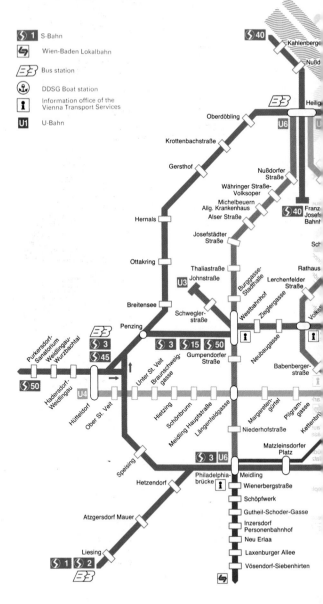

Legend:

- **S 1** S-Bahn
- Wien-Baden Lokalbahn
- **B** Bus station
- DDSG Boat station
- **i** Information office of the Vienna Transport Services
- **U1** U-Bahn

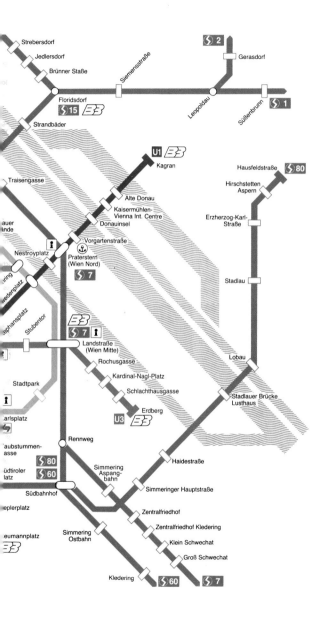

ZUM FIGLMÜLLER

★Villa Hans Moser, 13, Auhofstr. 76–78; tel. 8 77 47 47–0
   (high-class restaurant in the 19th c. villa of the popular actor Hans Moser,
   of whom there are many mementoes; pleasant terrace)
★Zu den drei Husaren, 1, Weihburggasse 4; tel. 5 12 10 92
   (perfect Viennese cuisine; relaxed atmosphere with piano music)
★Zum Kuckuck, 1, Himmelpfortgasse 15; tel. 5 12 84 70
   (a temple of gastronomical culture)
Zur Pfeffermühle, 14, Linzer Str. 18; tel. 92 35 16
   (superb steaks and game)

**Restaurants and
Beisln (inns)**

★Alte Backstube; tel. 4 06 11 01; see A to Z
Alter Rathauskeller, 1, Wipplingerstr. 8; tel. 5 35 33 36
   (stylish vaulted cellar with good plain fare)
★Altes Fassl, 5, Ziegelofengasse 37; tel. 55 42 98
   (picture-book inn with pretty garden)
★Alt Nussdorf, 19, Nussdorfer Platz 4; tel. 37 12 77
   (traditional inn serving giant portions)
Artiste, 1, Himmelpfortgasse 25; tel. 5 14 11 20
   (delicious nibbles in the Ronacher)
Barbanek, 11, Fuchsröhrenstr. 13; tel. 74 21 18
   (nostalgic "Gaststube" with hearty, plain fare)
Bei Max, 1, Landhausgasse 2; tel. 63 73 59
   (substantial Kärnter dishes and Neue Wiener Küche)
Biertufl, 3, Ungarngasse 5; tel. 7 12 65 03
   (more than 100 different beers)
Blausteiner, 6, Wallgasse 32; tel. 56 41 88
   (good address, named after a musical in the Raimundtheater)
Bockkeller, 19, Nussberggasse 2c; tel. 37 15 16
   (Tyrolean specialitity dishes)
★D'Landsknecht, 9, Porzellangasse 13; tel. 34 43 48
   (finest home-made strudels and pastries)
D'Rauchkuchl, 15, Schweglerstr. 37; tel. 92 13 81
   (Viennese speciality dishes; tasteful ambience)
★Eckel, 19, Sieveringer Str. 46; tel. 32 32 18
   (V.I.P. rendezvous, excellent cellar; bar with wooden tables, shady
   garden)
★Figlmüller, 1, Wollzeile 5; tel. 5 12 61 77
   (legendary Wiener Schnitzel)
Fischer Bräu, 19, Billrothstr. 17; tel. 3 19 62 64
   (inn/brewery with a happy clientele)
Florianhof, 8, Florianigasse 45; tel. 43 25 82
   (substantial home-cooked meals as well as "nouvelle cuisine")
Fuchsloch, 16, Baumeistergasse 46–50; tel. 46 23 54
   (old Viennese inn with idyllic garden)
Gösser Bierklinik, 1, Steindlgasse 4; tel. 5 35 68 97
   (16th c. inn; all brands of Gösser beer)
Göttweiger Stiftskeller, 1, Spiegelgasse 9; tel. 5 12 78 17
   (at one time Franz Schubert's "local"; old Austrian cuisine)

★Griechenbeisl; tel. 5 33 19 77; see A to Z

★Gulaschmuseum, 1, Schulerstr. 20; tel. 5 12 10 17
(the substantial goulash is second to none)

★Hauswirth, 6, Otto-Bauer-Gasse 20; tel. 5 87 12 61
(delicious "Topfenpalatschinken" = pancakes stuffed with curd cheese
and "Kaiserschmarrn" = strips of pancakes and raisins, fried in butter
and sugar)

★Hedrich, 1, Stubenring 2; tel. 5 12 95 88
(tiny but first-class)

Hietzinger Bräu, Auhofstr. 1; tel. 8 77 70 87
(traditional Viennese roast-beef dishes)

Hopferl, 1, Naglergasse 13; tel. 5 33 26 41
(public house with Münchner beer and giant sandwiches)

Kahlenberg, 19, Josefsdorf 1; tel. 32 12 51
(crispy pigs' trotters and roast chicken; terrace with fine views and an
adjoining "Heurige"; see entry)

Kleiner Rathauskeller, 1, Rathausstr. 11; tel. 42 61 49
(large selection of Austrian specialities; favourite meeting-place for
students)

Kulisse, 17, Rosensteingasse 39; tel. 45 38 70
(simple "Beisl" with interesting cabaret and theatrical programme)

★Leopoldsberg, 19, Am Leopoldsberg 1; tel. 37 16 80
(idyllic strudel with curd cheese; large terrace with magnificent
view)

Ludwig van, 6, Laimsgrubengasse 22; tel. 5 87 13 20
(where Beethoven lived for a while in 1822; now offers classical Viennese
cuisine; naturally cloudy "Hefeweizen" – a beer made from wheat, malt
and top-fermentation yeast – from the cask)

Meisl, 15, Hütteldorfer Str. 66; tel. 92 02 29
(small garden)

Metropol, 17, Hernalser Hauptstr. 55; tel. 43 35 43
(good value for money; Beisl culture scene, ranging from rock music to
Viennese songsters)

★Motto, 5, Schönbrunner Str. 30; tel. 5 87 06 72
(black interior with lavish floral ornamentation; cosy garden arbour)

★Oswald und Kalb, 1, Bäckerstr. 14; tel. 5 12 69 91
(excellent home-cooking)

Pastaron, 1, Jasomirgottgasse. 3; tel. 5 35 55 44
(creative Neue Wiener Cuisine)

★Peters Beisl, 16, Arnethgasse 48; tel. 46 53 75
(suburban Beisl for gourmets)

★Pfudl, 1, Bäckerstr. 22; tel. 5 12 67 05
(traditional Beisl with style)

★Pötsch, 10, Favoritenstr. 61; tel. 62 01 91
(extensive menu and giant portions)

★Pürstner, 1, Riemengasse 10; tel. 52 63 57
(excellent Viennese home-cooking)

★Rosa Elefant, 1, Fleischmarkt 4; tel. 63 75 30
(delicious stuffed pancakes; romantic atmosphere)

Schnattl, 8, Lange Gasse 40; tel. 42 34 00
(a favourite with thespians from the Burgtheater and the theatre in
Josefsstadt; good food at moderate prices)

Schweizerhaus, 2, Prater 116; tel. 2 18 01 52
(crispy, giant pigs' trotters; shady garden)

Silberwirt, 5, Schlossgasse 21; tel. 55 49 07
(its stuffed pancakes know no equal)

Servitenstüberl, 9, Servitengasse 7; tel. 34 53 36
(secluded garden)

Spatzennest, 7, Ulrichsplatz 1; tel. 5 26 16 59
(extremely cosy and "old Viennese")

★Waldviertlerhof, 5, Schönbrunner Str. 20; tel. 5 62 03 82
(beautiful garden and good choice of wines)

Shopping

Jeweller's shop front by Hans Hollein   *Quality chocolates at Demel's Vis-à-Vis*

Antiquarians	★Franz Deuticke, 1, Helferstorferstr. 4
	★Georg Fritsch, 1, Schönlaterngasse 7
	Wolfdietrich Hassfurther, 1, Hohenstaufengasse 7

Confectionery
★Altmann & Kühne, 1, Graben 30
★Demels Vis-à-Vis, Kohlmarkt 14
Gerstner, 1, Kärntner Str. 15
Heiner, 1, Kärnter Str. 21
★Oberlaaer Stadthaus, 1, Neuer Markt 16
★★Sacherstube, 1, Kärnter Str. 38

China and
porcelain
Albin Denk, 1, Graben 13
★Augarten-Porzellan, 1, Stock-im-Eisen-Platz 3–4 and Mariahilfer Str. 17
Gmunder Keramik, 1, Kärnter Durchgang
★Pawlata, 1, Kärnter Str. 14 (Gmunder china)
Rasper & Söhne, 1, Graben 15
★Wahliss, 1, Kärnter Str. 17

Delicatessen
Böhle, 1, Wollzeile 30
Da Conte Alimentari, 1, Kurrentgasse 12 (Italian specialities)
★Do & Co., 1, Akademiestr. 3 (with snack-bar)
★Gebrüder Wild, 1, Neuer Markt 10–11
Kaufhaus Hermansky (basement), Mariahilfer Str. 26–30
★Meinl am Graben, 1, Graben 19

Glass
Albin Denk, 1, Graben 13
Bakalowits Söhne, 1, Spiegelgasse 3
Lackinger Glas, 1, Weihburggasse 21
Lobmeyr, 1, Kärnter Str. 26

232

★Claudio Pascalini, 1, Freisingergasse 1 (exclusive models)
Don Gil, 1, Kärnter Str. 14 (good but expensive; 6 branches)
Hans Grandits, 9, Alserstr. 9 and 18 (mainly Armani, Boss and Burberry)
★Knize, 1, Graben 1 (elegant fashions)
Martin Mascherl Manufaktur, 5, Rechte Wienzeile 93–95 (bow-ties and silk scarves)
Wilhelm F. Silbernagel, 1, Kärnter Str. 15 (styles ranging from Cardin to Dior)
Sir Anthony, 1, Kärnter Str. 21–23 (elegant gents' outfitter with bar)

★Sven Boltenstern, 13, Schliessmanngasse 17
Caesar Juwelen, 1, Graben 26 (façade designed by Hans Hollein)
Heldwein, 1, Graben 13
★A. E. Köchert, 1, Neuer Markt 15
Haban, 1, Kärnter Str. 2
Schulin & Söhne, 1, Kohlmarkt 7 (façade by Hans Hollein)

★W. F. Adlmüller, 1, Kärnter Str. 41 (haute couture)
Brieftaube, 9, Nussdorfer Str. 20 (elegant knitware)
Brühl/Lady Ascot, 1, Kohlmarkt 2 (exclusively British)
Elite, 7, Neustiftgasse (evening wardrobe and bridal gowns)
Florucci, 1, Walfischgasse 6 (Italian casuals)
Foggensteiner, 1, Graben 26 (everything in fur and leather)
★W. & A. Jonak, Trattnerhof 2 (haute couture, including Chanel)
Laghani, 1, Kärnter Str. 8 (Versace fashions)
★Helmut Lang, 1, Esslingstrasse 5 (elegant young fashions)
Maldone, 1, Graben 29 (fashion clothes for young people; 14 branches)
Nikis Laden, 6, Mariahilfer Str. 53–55 (underwear)
★Resi Hammerer, 1, Kärnter Str. 113 (latest trends)
Rositta, 1, Kärnter Str. 17 (Viennese blouses and bodices)
Silhouette, 1, Kärnter Str. 35 (exclusive models)
Top Shop, 1, Weihburggasse 7 (mad fashions)
Vanessa, 19, Billrothstr. 24 (elegant swimwear and underwear)

Belinda, 6, Amerlingstr. 9

See entry

★Berta Smejkal, 1, Opernpassage, Ladenstr.
★Maria Stransky, 1, Hofburg-Passage 2

Boutique Flo, 4, Schleifmühlgasse 15 (1920–70) fashions)

Belleza, 1, Kärnter Str. 45
Da Giovanni, 1, Lugeck 7
★Materna, 1, Mahlerstr. 5 (made-to-measure)
★Karl Scheer, 1, Bräunerstr. 4

ABZ-Scout-Shop, 7, Breite Gasse 13
Dux, 1, Schottengasse 9
Kober, 1, Graben 14–15
Modellbahnzentrum, 4, Wiedner Hauptstr. 23
Spielkistl, 3, Landstr. 2
Zauberklingl, 1, Fürichgasse

Birkenhütte, 9, Nussdorfer Str. 26–28
Hubertus, 3, Landstrasser Hauptstr. 67
Eduard Kettner, 1, Seilergasse 12
Lanz, 1, Kärntner Str. 10
★Loden-Plankl, 1, Michaelerplatz 6
Lower Austrian Home Industries, 1, Herrengasse 6

Gentlemen's
fashions

Jewellery

Ladies fashions

Hire of ball-gowns
and bridal wear

Markets

Petit-point
needlework

Second-hand
goods

Shoes

Toys

Traditional
fashions

Shopping

★Resi Hammerer, 1, Kärntner Str. 29–31
★Joh. Springer's Erben, 1, Graben 10
★Tostmann, 1, Schottengasse 3a
Trachten-Just, 1, Lugeck 7
Trachten-Schmidt, 1, Stubenring 16

Wine	Vinothek, Piaristengasse 54
	★Vinothek St. Stephan, 1, Stephansplat 6

Young people's boutique	★Monika Kaesser, 1, Krugerstr. 17
	Backhausen, 1, Kärnter Str. 33

Shops with longer opening hours (continuous, early morning, late evening and weekends)

In the rail stations:
Vienna North (Wien-Nord), Praterstern
Open: daily 5.30am–9pm (food)

Vienna Central (Wien-Mitte), 3, Landstrasser Hauptstr. 1c
Open: daily 5.30am–10pm (food)

Franz Josefs Station, 9, Julius-Tandler-Platz 2–4
Mini supermarket with chemist's
Open: Mon.–Sat. 8am–10.30pm, Sun. 9.30am–10.30pm
Tabak-Traffik
Open: daily 5.45am–8.15pm (tobacco goods and newspapers)

South Station (Südbahnhof), 10, Wiedner Gürtel 1
Open: daily 7am–11pm (food)

West Station (Westbahnhof), 15, Europlatz 1
Open: daily 7am–11pm (food)

Wien-Schwachat Airport
Supermarket
Open: Sat.–Thur. 7.30am–7pm, Fri. 7.30am–8pm, Sun.10am–6pm

Filling stations (with 24 hour service):
Shell-Center South, 10 Triester Str. 6a–8
Shell-Center West, 14 Hadikgasse 128–134

In the city:
AKH-Expresso, 9, Lazarettgasse 14
Open: Mon.–Sat. 6.30am–9pm, Sun. and public holidays 9am–9pm (food, chemist)

Bücher Hirtl, 3 Landstrasser Hauptstr. 2a (in AEZ)
Open: Mon.–Fri. 7am–7pm, Sat. 9am–6pm, Sun.11am–6pm (books)

Feinkost Patzak, 19, Nussdorfer Platz 3
Open: Tues.–Fri. 7.30am–1.30pm, Sat. 7.30am–8pm, Sun. and public holidays 2–8pm (delicatessen)

Hairdressers:
Hair Style W. Jost, 8, Josefstädter Str. 54
Open: Mon.–Thur. 9am–6pm, Fri. 9am–6.30pm, Sat. 9am–3pm

Janele in the Bärenmühle, 4, Operngasse 18
Open: daily 6.30am–7pm (food)

Mobilmarkt, 11, Grenzackerstr. 2
Open: 24 hours a day (food, mini-drugstore)

Schwarz, 13, Auhofstr. 133
Open: Mon.–Sat. 6.30am–8pm, Sun. 11am–8pm (food)

Zur Grüne Hütte, 2, Prater 196 (entrance Ausstellungsstr.)
Open: daily 7am–10pm (good selection of food and frozen food, chemist)

See entry

Markets

Visitors to Austria who purchase goods to take home with them can reclaim
the "Mehrwertsteuer" (Value Added Tax), representing a refund of about
20% on most goods, providing the purchase amounts to at least 1,000
Austrian schillings and is made from a shop displaying the "Tax Free for
Tourists" sign. In this case the sales assistant must make out a bill in the
name of the purchaser showing the amount of tax, and fill in form U34.
  Both documents and the goods themselves must be produced to the
Austrian customs officials when leaving the country. They will stamp form
U34 and on receiving this receipt the shop from which the purchase was
made will remit the VAT. Car drivers may be able to obtain the refund at the
border offices of the ÖAMTC, and air passengers can do so at the sub-post
office in the transit section of Schwechat airport.

Tax

Sightseeing Programme

The recommendations below are designed to help first-time visitors to
Vienna to make the most of their stay in the city.

Recommended
tours

Places of interest which are described in the A to Z section of this guide are
printed in **bold type**.

Note

To get a first flavour of Vienna and to find out where the most important
sights can be found, the visitor is recommended to make a tour on foot
through the inner city. The starting point is the **Staatsoper** (State Opera
House), on the corner of the Ring and Kärntner Strasse. Behind the Opera
turn left into Philharmoniker Strasse, where the famous **Hotel Sacher** is
situated. On the Albertinaplatz can be seen the equestrian statue of Archduke Albrecht on the top of the **Albrechtsrampe**, while in the street the
celebrated "Fiaker" (see Practical Information, Fiaker) wait for their clients.
Now continue through Tegetthofstrasse to the **Neuer Markt** (New Market)
with the Donnerbrunnen (or Providentia Fountain); here stands the **Kapuzinerkirche** (Capuchin church). Now follow the Plankengasse on the left, turn
left again into Dorotheergasse, where the **Dorotheum** and the **Jüdische
Museum** (Jewish Museum) have their premises and regain the Augustiner-
strasse. On the left stands the **Augustinerkirche** (church of the Augustines),
the exterior of which is quite plain. Nearby lies **Josefsplatz** with the monument to Joseph II; one of the finest squares in Vienna, it is bordered by the
Österreichische National Bibliothek (Austrian National Library), the **Spanish Riding School**, the **Palais Palffy** and the Palais Pallaivicini. A passage in
the far corner of the square leads to the **Hofburg** (for plan see page 79). In
the "Alter Hofburg" (Schweizerplatz) is the entrance to the Treasury and
the Hofburg Chapel, where the Vienna Boys' Choir can be heard on Sundays. The Schweizer Tor (Swiss gate) opens on to the square called "In der
Burg", where there is a monument to Francis II. On the right stretch the
buildings of the Reichkanzleramt (Imperial Chancellery), while the upper
end of the square is taken up by the Amalienburg – these two buildings
house the Emperor's Apartments – with the Leopoldinische Trakt (Leopold
range) on the left. A passage links the square with the area of the Neuer
Burg, where the **Ephesus Museum**, the **Museum für Völkerkunde** (Austrian
Folk Museum) and the **Sammlung Alter Musikinstrumente** (Collection of
Old Musical Instruments) and the **Waffensammlung** (Collection of Weapons) are to be found, and Heldenplatz (Heroes' Square) with equestrian
statues of Prince Eugene and Archduke Karl. Leave the Heldenplatz
through the Burgtor onto the **Ballhausplatz**, where now stands the Bundeskanzleramt in which Imperial foreign policy was once decided. A pleasant stroll northwards through the **Volksgarten**, where the memorials

One day

include one to the Empress Elisabeth (Cissy), brings the visitor into Bankgasse which should be followed for a short way, passing the **Palais Liechtenstein**, and then turn right into Abraham-a-Sancta-Clara-Gasse which leads into the Minoritenplatz. Dominating the square is the **Minoritenkirche**. Proceed through Landhausgasse and (on the right) Herrengasse past the **Niederösterreiches Landesmuseum** to arrive in **Michaelerplatz**, which is framed by the Michaeler range (with steps up to the Hoftafel, Silberkammer and apartments), the **Hofburg**, the Michaelerkirche, and the Art-Nouveau Loos House. In the Kohlmarkt street it would be pleasant to pause and pay a visit to the **Café Dehmel**, the former confectioner to the Royal and Imperial Court, before strolling on into the **Graben**, which leads into **Stock-im-Eisen Platz** and **Stephansplatz**, beneath which the medieval Virgil chapel was excavated; here rises the **Stephansdom**, the cathedral and symbol of Vienna. As a break from sightseeing a stroll through the best known shopping street in the city, **Kärntner Strasse** is suggested. If only one day is available for sightseeing the afternoon should be spent either at **Schönbrunn** or at the **Belvedere-Schlösser**, which house the Austrian Gallery, the Austrian Baroque Museum, the Museum of Medieval Austrian Art and the Gallery of 19th and 20th c. Art. The palaces are situated in a magnificent park, an ideal place for a brief rest. In the evening sightseeing can be continued. The DDSG (see Excursions, Boat Trips on the Danube) organises from mid-May until late September evening excursions with music on the Danube; however, the visitor who would like to see another side of Vienna and experience something of the traditional "Wiener Gemütlichkeit" – almost untranslatable but akin to the French "bonhomie" – might visit one of the numerous Heurige inns (see Practical Information, Heuriger) or a "Beisel", for example the **Griechen** (Greek) **Beisel** (see also Practical Information, Restaurants). Night-owls must take care not to disappear in the "Bermuda Triangle" (see Practical Information, Night-life).

Two days

A two-day stay will provide an opportunity of exploring more thoroughly some of the places mentioned in the one-day programme. In the morning it is very pleasant to see the Lippizaner horses being put through their paces (see **Spanish Riding School**) in the **Hofburg**. If the visitor has already seen this perhaps a visit to one of the larger museums (see Practical Information, Museums) would be rewarding. If the choice falls on the **Kunsthistorisches Museum** (Museum of Art History) or the **Natur Historisches Museum** (Natural History Museum) then it would be convenient to continue walking along the Ring in the direction of Dr-Karl-Renner-Ring and Dr-Karl-Lueger-Ring, passing the **Parlament** (Parliament Building), the **Rathaus** (Town Hall), the **Burgtheater** and the **Universität** to the **Votivkirche**. An alternative is to turn right at the Burgtheater into Löwelstrasse/Teinfalterstrasse and reach the open space called **Freyung**, with the Austria Fountain; here the **Schottenstift**, the **Schottenkirche** and the Café Central in the Palais Ferstel invite the visitor to pause for a while. From here continue along Heidenschluss Strasse to the square and church of **Am Hof**; the square is surrounded by old town houses and palaces. The Bognergasse leads back to the shopping centre around the Graben and Kärntner Strasse. Take the opposite direction from the Art and Natural History Museums along the Opernring and turn right at Robert-Stolz-Platz to reach the **Akademie der Bildenden Künste** (Academy of Fine Arts) and via Marktgasse come to the **Secession** (art gallery), where Klimt's "Beethoven Frieze" is now again on display. From here it is only a few steps to the lively and colourful **Naschmarkt** (also flea market on Saturdays) which is surrounded by cafés, theatres, nightspots and snackbars. On the opposite bank of the little River Wien Treitlstrasse leads to the **Karlskirche**; on the left near the church stands the **Historische Museum der Stadt Wien** (Vienna City Historical Museum). In Dumbastrasse which branches off Karlsplatz is the **Musikvereinsgebäude**, and in **Karlsplatz** itself the Art-Nouveau Pavilion of the City Railway (Stadtbahn). The Wiedner Hauptstrasse leads back to the **Staatsoper** (State Opera House). A drive in a Fiaker (see Practical Information, Fiaker) provides a different perspective of the sights of Vienna.

The evening can be spent at a theatre, a concert or at the opera. For theatre lovers the choice ranges from the **Burgtheater** to the politically critical avant-garde productions (see Practical Information, Theatres). The musical life of the city is equally comprehensive (see Practical Information, Music).

In addition to the sights mentioned above, there is also the oldest quarter of Vienna, behind the cathedral, waiting to be explored. Follow Rotenturmstrasse and come to the **Hoher Markt** on the left; here can be seen the impressive Anker Clock, while underground are Roman remains dating from the earliest period of the history of Vienna. The Neihardt Frescoes (see **Graben**) in the Tuchlauben are the oldest secular paintings in the city, and in the **Judenplatz**, reached along the Jordangasse, stands the house called "Zum grossen Jordan". If the sunnier side of Vienna is preferred a detour can be made to the **Danube Island** (see also Practical Information, Swimming Baths), with its many recreational and leisure facilities.

Three days

The afternoon could be taken up by a visit to **Kloster Neuburg** in the Vienna Woods. On the way there along the Wiener-Höhenstrasse beautiful views can be enjoyed (see Practical Information: Excursions, Wienerwald).

As the end of a third day in Vienna approaches, one of the best ways of taking leave is to visit the **Prater** in the evening and admire the views of the city from a cabin on the giant wheel.

Sport and Recreation

Fitness Center Donaupark, 22, Arbeiterstrandbadstr. 122; tel. 23 36 61
Fitness-Center John Harris, 1, Nibelungengasse 7; tel. 5 87 37 10
Fitnesscentre Stadtpark, 1, Johannesgasse 33; tel. 7 14 77 75
Fitness Zimmermann, 7 Kaiserstr. 43; tel. 5 26 20 00

Fitness centres

Praterstadion, 2, Prater, Meierstr.; tel. 26 21 10–0
  Venue for international games and rock concerts
Hannastadion, 14, Keisslergasse 6; tel. 94 76 70
  Home ground of SK Rapid football club
Horrstadion, 10, Fischofgasse; tel. 68 53 94
  Home ground of Austria Memphis footbal club

Football grounds

Golf-Club Wien, 2, Freudenau 65a; tel. 2 18 95 64–0
Golf-Club Schönfeld, 2, Obere Donaustr. 97; tel. 26 13 20
Golf-Club Am Wienerberg, 10, Gutheil-Schodergasse 9; tel 6 61 23–0

Golf

Trotting course, Trabrennbahn Krieau, 2, Pratergelände;
tel. 2 18 00 46–0
Information; tel. 15 56
Season: September to June

Horse racing

Racecourse, Galopp Rennbahn, 2, Freudenau 65, Pratergelände
Information: Wiener Rennverein, 1, Josefsplatz 5;
tel. 5 12 25 38–0
Season: Spring and autumn

Donaupark-Eishalle, 22, Wagramer Str. 1; tel. 23 61 23
Eislaufanlage Engelmann, 17, Syringgasse 6–8; tel. 42 14 25/6
Eisring-Süd, 10, Windenstr. 2; tel. 6 04 44 43
Stadthalle, 15, Vogelweidplatz 14; tel. 9 54 92 53
Wiener Eislaufverein, 3, Lothringer Str. 22; tel. 73 63 53

Ice skating

See Swimming Baths

Sauna/Swimming

Swimming Baths

Squash	Squash-Haus Penzing, 14, Linzer Str. 183; tel. 9 42 45 12 and 94 85 51 Squash Spotanlagen, 17, Hernalser Hauptstr. 13; tel. 4 03 60 50 Squash Club Top Fit, 10, Erlachplatz 2–4; tel. 6 02 24 45
Tennis	Tennislage Minarik, 10, Kledaringer Str. 62–64; tel. 68 13 07 Tennis Club Florisdorfer, 21, Lorettoplatz 5; tel. 38 12 83 Tennis Center Merkur, 17, Frauengasse 25–27; tel. 46 51 81 Tennis Point Vienna, 3, Baumgasse; tel. 7 99 99 97–0

Swimming Baths

Covered baths (most with saunas) **Information**: (opening times) tel. 15 35	Amalienbad 10, Reumannsplatz 9 (beautifully restored Art Nouveau baths) Dianabad, 2, Lilienbrunnengasse 7–9 (modern sports pool) Hallenbad Döbling 19, Geweygasse 6 (also open-air bath) Hallenbad Floridsdorf 21, Franklinstr. 22 Hallenbad Simmering 11, Florien-Hedorfer-Str. 5 (also open-air bath) Jörgerbad 17, Jörgerstr. 42–44 Rodauner Bad (no sauna) 23, An der Au 2 Theresienbad 12, Huferlandgasse 3 (Vienna's oldest baths) Thermalbad Oberlaa 10, Kurbadstr. 14 (See A to Z Oberlaa Health Centre)
Open-air baths	Bundesbad Schönbrunn 13, Schönbrunner Schlosspark Freibad Baumgarten 14, Hackinger Str. 26a Freibad Donuastadt 22, Portnergasse 38 (also covered bath) Freibad Grossfeldsiedlung 21, Oswald-Redlich-Str. 44 (also covered bath) Freibad Hadersdorf-Weidlingau 14, Hauptstr. 41 Freibad Hietzing 13, Atzgersdorfstr. 14 (also covered bath) Kongressbad 16, Julius-Meinl-Gasse 7a

Krapfenwaldbad
19, Krapfenwaldgasse 65–73

Laaer-Berg Bad
10, Ludwig von Höhnel-Gasse 2

Liesinger Bad
23, Perchtoldsdorfer Str. 14–16

Neuwaldegger Bad
17, Promenadegasse 58

Ottakringer Bad
16, Johann-Staud-Str. 11 (also covered bath)

Satzbergbad
14, Am Satzberg, Steinböckengasse 100

Schafbergbad
18, Josef-Redel-Gasse 2

Schwimmbad Pratersauna
2, Walsteingartenstr. 135

Stadionbad
2, Prater, Krieau

Strandbad Gansehaufel
22, Mossigasse 21 (artificial waves)

Strandbad Stadlau
22, Am Mühlwasser

Theresienbad
12, Hufelandgasse 3 (also covered bath)

City Club Vienna des Club Méditerranée | ★City Club Vienna
Parkallee 2 in Wien-Vösendorf; tel. 69 35 11–0
Fun and adventure pool with tropical-like wave-pool under a 40m/130ft high glass pyramid, pool-bar, sauna complex, fitness centre, restaurant, tennis courts and golf courses, and a luxury hotel with conference centre.

Only a few minutes from the city centre (e.g. by U1) lie Vienna's most popular bathing places on the Old Danube (12km/7½ miles of beach) and on Danube Island ("Copa Cagrana"; 42km/26 miles of beach, naturist areas, summer discos) with boating facilities, sailing schools, bicycle rental, restaurants, barbecue sites, etc. Many events take place in summer. Information from Verein ARGE Alte Donau, 1, Stubenring 8–10; tel. 5 14 50–257; also tel. 53 42 72 04. | Popular bathing places

Danube Island
Weideinger, 22, Raffineriestr./Lobgrundstr. (sun-terrace, restaurant and open-air disco)

Old Danube
Angelikabad, 21, on the Upper Old Danube (bathing beach, pool for small children, mini-golf, tennis)
Strandbad Alte Donau, 22, Arbeiterstrandbadstr., 91 (bathing beach, 3 swimming pools, table-tennis, mini-golf, restaurant)
Arbeiterstrandbad, 22, Arbeiterstrandbadstr., 87–89 (quiet bathing, ladies' sun-bathing area, table-tennis, restaurant)
★Gänsehäufel, 22, Moissigasse 21 (the oldest and largest bathing beach (1·2km/1300yd), nudist area, wave-pool, water-chute, play areas, tennis, mini-golf and café)

Taxis

Taxis ply for hire from official ranks or they can be ordered by telephone (radio taxis). Hailing a taxi in traffic, even if the "frei" sign is illuminated, is officially forbidden, but in practice this is possible in quiet streets.

Radio taxis
Tel. 3 13 00, 4 01 00, 6 01 60, 8 14 00, 17 16
For journeys to the airport and outside the city; tel. 3 19 25 11, 3 13 00

Taxi ranks
Corner of Opernring/Operngasse; tel. 56 52 05
Babenbergerstrasse/Burgring; tel. 93 23 55
Hoher Markt/Marc-Aurel-Strasse; tel. 63 04 98
Dr-Karl-Lueger-Ring, 14; tel. 5 33 12 60
Stubenring; tel. 5 12 32 36, etc.
   Other ranks (without telephones) include those at Petersplatz, Kärntner Strasse/corner of Mahlerstrasse (on the left, near the Opera).

Fares
In the city fares are calculated on the taximeter (basic price plus price per km).
   There is higher basic rate for journeys at night (11pm–6am) and on Sundays and public holidays, and a surcharge for radio taxis and journeys to and from the airport and outside Vienna city limits.

Telephone

Calls abroad can be made from all public coin boxes. For local calls 1 öS coins are required and for long-distance calls 10 or 20 öS coins. Many call-boxes now accept telephone-cards (see below)

Charges
A telephone call to the United Kingdom costs 14 öS per minute; to the United States and Canada 40.50 öS per minute. After 6pm and at weekends long-distance calls are cheaper.
   Telephone cards ("Telefonwertkarten) can be purchased from post offices or tobacconists in sums of 50 and 100 schillings.

Telephone codes
To Vienna from the United Kingdom: 00 43 1
To Vienna from the United States and Canada: 011 43 1
From Vienna to the United Kingdom: 00 44
From Vienna to the United States and Canada: 001
   In dialling an international call the zero prefix of the local code should be omitted.

Telephone service
See Useful Telephone Numbers

Telegrams
Tel. 190

Theatres

Advance programme details
A free survey of theatrical programmes is available from the Vienna Tourist Board (see Information); details also appear in the list of events (see Programme of Events) which is published every month.

Tickets
Tickets can be booked in advance (see Advance Booking) or direct at the theatres.

Federal Theatres
Akademietheater
3, Lisztstr. 1; tel. 5 14 44–29 59
Burgtheatre company

Burgtheater
See A to Z

Kammerspiele
1, Rotenturmstr. 20; tel. 5 33 28 33–0
Satire and comedy with the company from the Theater in der Josefstadt

Theater in der Josefstadt
8, Josefstädter Str. 26; tel. 4 02 51 27
Light contemporary productions

International Theatre (performances in English)
1, Porzellangasse 8/Müllnergasse; tel. 3 19 62 72

Kleine Komödie im Theater am Kärntnertor
1, Walfischgasse 4; tel. 5 12 42 80
Contemporary comedies and thrillers

Vienna's English Theatre
8, Josefsgasse 12; tel. 4 02 12 60
Plays in English

Volkstheater
7, Neustiftgasse 1; tel. 5 23 35 01–0
Contemporary drama; sometimes avant-garde productions

Ateliertheater am Naschmarkt
6 Linke Wienzeile 4; tel. 5 87 82 14

Auerspiel 15 Theater
8, Auerspergstr. 15; tel. 43 07 97

Drachengasse 2 Theater/Courage
1, Fleischmarkt 22; tel. 5 13 14 44

Ensemble Theater am Petersplatz
1, Petersplatz 1; tel. 5 33 20 39 and 5 35 32 00

Experiment am Lichtenwerd
9, Liechtensteinstr. 132; tel. 3 19 41 08

Freie Bühne Wieden
4, Wiedner Haupstr. 60b; tel. 5 86 21 22

Graumann Theater & Café
1, Wipplinger Str. 24; tel. 5 35 12 45

Komödie am Kai
1, Franz-Josefs-Kai 29; tel. 5 33 24 34

Kulisse
17, Rosensteingasse 39; tel. 45 38 70

Original Pradler Ritterspiele
1, Biberstr. 2; tel. 5 12 54 00
Romantic plays

Serapionstheater im Odeon
20, Taborstr. 10; tel. 2 14 55 62

Spitzbuben-Pawlatschen
19, Hackhofergasse 13; tel. 37 1 85

Small theatres
(selection)

Theater am Schwedenplatz
1, Franz-Josefs-Kai 21; tel. 5 35 79 14

Theater Brett
6 Münzwardeingasse 2; tel. 5 87 06 63

Theater des Augenblicks
18, Edelhofgasse 10; tel. 4 79 68 87

Theater "Die Tribüne" in the Café Lantmann
1, Dr-Karl-Leuger-Ring 4; tel. 63 84 85

Theater-center-Forum
9 Porzellangasse 50; tel. 3 10 46 46

Theater Gruppe 80
6, Gumpendorfer Str. 67; tel. 56 52 22

Theater Spielraum
3, Rechte Bahngasse 18; tel. 7 13 04 60

Cabaret

Hernalser Stadttheater (Metropol)
17, Geblergasse 50; tel. 43 35 43

Kabarett & Komödie am Naschmarkt
6, Linke Wienzeile 4; tel. 5 87 22 75

Kabarett Niedermair
8, Lenaugasse 1a; tel. 4 08 44 92

Metropolino
17, Hernalser Hauptstr. 55; tel. 43 35 43

Spektakel
5, Hamburgerstr. 14; tel. 5 87 06 53

Theater Kabarett Simpl
1, Wollzeile 36; tel. 5 12 47 42

Children's and young people's theatre (a selection)

Akzent
4, Theresianumgasse 16–18; tel. 5 01 64–33 06

Bühne WVK. 9, Währinger Str. 59; tel. 40 12 10

Märchenbühne "Der Apfelbaum"
7, Kirchengasse 41; tel. 93 17 29

Niedermair Kindertheater
8, Lenaugasse 1a; tel 4 08 44 92

Theater der Jugend
7, Neubaugasse 38; tel. 5 21 10

Variety

Ronacher (see A to Z)

For Opera, Operetta, Musicals, Ballet, Concerts, see Music

Time

Austria observes Central European Time (one hour ahead of Greenwich Mean Time; six hours ahead of New York Time). From late March to late

September Summer Time (two hours ahead of Greenwich Mean Time;
seven hours ahead of New York Time) is in force.

Tipping

It is customary to tip waiters, hotel room-maids, taxi-drivers, hairdressers,
etc. 10–15% of the bill. A tip is also expected even when (as in restaurants)
service is already included in the bill.

Do not, however, tip the self-styled "parking attendants" (called in
Vienna "Türlschnapper" = little door snappers) who hang around the
car-parks used by tourists.

Travel documents

Visitors to Austria who are citizens of the United Kingdom, the United
States or most Commonwealth countries require only a passport to enter
the country. No visa is required unless the visit exceeds three months (six
months for citizens of the United Kingdom) or the visitor proposes to work
in the country.

Personal
documents

National driving licences and car registration documents from the above
countries are recognised in Austria and should be carried. Foreign vehicles
must bear an oval nationality plate. It is advisable to carry an international
insurance certificate ("Green Card").

Vehicle
documents, etc.

See also Motoring

When to go

Vienna has much to offer at any time of year. In spring the temperature is
pleasant for strolling about the city and making visits to places of interest;
the café gardens are already open and the Vienna Spring Festival provides
the first cultural highlight of the year. The festival weeks are continued in
summer by the "Wiener Musik Sommer" (see Festivals; Events) and it is in
summer that there are numerous opportunites for swimming and bathing
(see Swimming Baths; and A to Z, Danube Island) and for interesting
excursions in the surrounding area (see Excursions). Autumn is the time for
tasting the new wine (see Heuriger) and sees the opening of the theatrical
and concert season (see Theatres, Music), while winter offers further musical events, especially the fashionable balls.

Youth Hostels

ÖJHV-Wien
Mariahilfer Str. 24, A-1070 Wien;
tel. 93 71 58–0 and 93 71 67–0, fax 93 71 58–22

Central
information office

Hostel Ruthensteiner
15, Robert Hamerlinggasse 24, A-1150 Wien;
tel. 8 93 42 02 and 8 93 27 96
Open: all year; 24 hours a day

Hostels

Jugendgästehaus der Stadt Wien–Hüttelsdorf–Hacking
13, Schlossberggasse 8, A-1130 Wien; tel. 8 77 02 63
Open: all year; 7am–11.45pm

Youth Hostels

Jugendgästehaus Wien–Brigittenau
20, Friedrich-Engels-Platz 24, A-1200 Wien; tel. 33 28 29 40
Open: all year; 24 hours a day

Jugendherberge Wien–Myrthengasse
7, Myrthengasse 7, A-1070 Wien,
tel. 5 23 63 16
Open: all year; 7.30am–1am

Turmherberge Don Bosco
3, Lechnerstrasse 12; tel. 7 13 14 94
Open: Mar.–Nov. daily 6am–noon, 5–11.45pm

Schlossherberge am Wilhelminenberg
16, Savoyenstr. 2, A-1160 Wien; tel. 45 85 03–700
Open: all year; daily 7am–11.45pm

Useful Telephone Numbers at a glance

Emergencies
    Ambulance   144
    Breakdown (24 hours a day)
        ARBÖ   123
        ÖAMTC   120
    Chemist on duty   15 50
    Doctor on call (24 hours a day)   141
    Fire brigade   122
    Police   133

Information
    Airline information   7 11 10
    Bus timetable (ÖBB)   7 11 01
    Cinema programmes   15 77
    City information (Vienna)   403 89 89
    Complaints (tourist office)   43 16 08–0
    Danube trips (DDSG)   72 75 00
    ÖAMTC traffic information   15 90
    Rail information (central)   17 00
        Long distance (south)   58 00–3 10 50
        Long distance (west)   58 00–3 10 60
    Tourist-Information (Austria)   5 87 20 00
    Tourist-Information (Vienna)   2 11 14, 5 13 88 92,
        5 13 40 15
    Vienna Sightseeing Tours   7 12 46 83–0
    Youth-Information   5 26 46 37
    Weather   15 66

Embassies
    United Kingdom   7 13 15 75
    United States   3 13 39
    Canada   5 33 36 91

Airline information (reservations)
    Austrian Airlines   7 17 99
    British Airways   5 05 76 91–0
    TWA   5 86 19 09

Lost property
    Central office   31 34 00
    Central office of the ÖBB (railways)   58 00–0

Taxis   3 13 00, 4 01 00, 6 01 60,
    8 14 00, 17 16

Telegrams   190

Telephone International Dialling Codes
    to United Kingdom   00 44
    to United States or Canada   001

Index

Imprint

130 colour photographs, 12 plans, 7 general maps, 3 special plans, 2 city plans, 1 coat of arms, 1 logo, 1 large city map (inside back cover)

Text: Dr Madeleine Reincke; additional text: Eva Marie Blattner, Helga Cabos, Rainer Eisenschmid, Dr Peter Jordan, Dr Gerda Rob and Bernhard Wolf

Editorial work, Revision: Badedeker-Redaktion

Cartography: Gert Oberländer, Munich; Hallweg AG, Berne (plan of city)

General direction: Dr Peter Baumgarten, Baedeker Stuttgart

English translation: Babel Translations, Norwich

Updating and additional text: Alec Court, David Cocking

Editorial work: Margaret Court

Source of illustrations: Bohnacker (1), Graf (1), Historia Bilderkunst (2), H. Lade Foto-agentur (1), Dr Reincke/Cabos (116), Schuster Bildagentur (2), Ullstein Bilderdienst (7)

3rd English edition 1995

© Baedeker Stuttgart
Original German edition 1994

© 1995 Jarrold and Sons Ltd
English language edition worldwide

© 1995 The Automobile Association: United Kingdom and Ireland

Published in the United States by:
Macmillan Travel
A Simon & Schuster Macmillan Company
1633 Broadway
New York, NY 10019–6785

Macmillan is a registered trademark of Macmillan, Inc.

Distributed in the United Kingdom by the Publishing Division of the Automobile Association, Fanum House, Basingstoke, Hampshire RG21 2EA

Licensed user: Mairs Geographischer Verlag GmbH & Co., Ostfildern-Kemnat bei Stuttgart

The name *Baedeker* is a registered trademark

A CIP catalogue record of this book is available from the British Library

Reproductions: Eder Repro GmbH, Ostfildern (Scharnhausen)

Printed in Italy by G. Canale & C.S.p.A – Borgaro T.se –Turin

ISBN 0–02–860492–X US and Canada